305.80097
R116

DETROIT PUBLIC LIBRARY

3 5674 01365531 2

W9-BLZ-241

RACISM

IN AMERICA
OPPOSING VIEWPOINTS®

CH MAR - - 1993

Other Books of Related Interest in the Opposing
Viewpoints Series:

From the Opposing Viewpoints ISMS Series:

RACISM
IN AMERICA
OPPOSING VIEWPOINTS®

David L. Bender & Bruno Leone, *Series Editors*

William Dudley, *Book Editor*
Charles Cozic, *Assistant Editor*

OPPOSING VIEWPOINTS SERIES ®

Greenhaven Press, Inc.   PO Box 289009   San Diego, CA 92198-9009

No part of this book may be reproduced or used in any form or by any means, electrical, mechanical, or otherwise, including, but not limited to, photocopy, recording, or any information storage and retrieval system, without prior written permission from the publisher.

Library of Congress Cataloging-in-Publication Data

Racism in America / William Dudley and Charles Cozic, book editors.
    p. cm. — (Opposing viewpoints series)
    Includes bibliographical references and index.
    Summary: Presents opposing viewpoints on racism in America and how serious this problem is.
    ISBN 0-89908-157-6 (pbk.) :— ISBN 0-89908-182-7 (lib. bdg.) :
    1. Racism—United States. 2. United States—Race relations. 3. Minorities—United States. [1. Racism. 2. Race relations.] I. Dudley, William, 1964- . II. Series.
E184.A1R328   1991
305.8'00973—dc20   91-14293

Copyright © 1991 by Greenhaven Press, Inc.
Every effort has been made to trace owners of copyright material.

"Congress shall make no law . . . abridging the freedom of speech, or of the press."

First Amendment to the U.S. Constitution

The basic foundation of our democracy is the first amendment guarantee of freedom of expression. The Opposing Viewpoints Series is dedicated to the concept of this basic freedom and the idea that it is more important to practice it than to enshrine it.

Contents

Why Consider Opposing Viewpoints?

"It is better to debate a question without settling it than to settle a question without debating it."

Joseph Joubert (1754-1824)

The Importance of Examining Opposing Viewpoints

The purpose of the Opposing Viewpoints Series, and this book in particular, is to present balanced, and often difficult to find, opposing points of view on complex and sensitive issues.

Probably the best way to become informed is to analyze the positions of those who are regarded as experts and well studied on issues. It is important to consider every variety of opinion in an attempt to determine the truth. Opinions from the mainstream of society should be examined. But also important are opinions that are considered radical, reactionary, or minority as well as those stigmatized by some other uncomplimentary label. An important lesson of history is the eventual acceptance of many unpopular and even despised opinions. The ideas of Socrates, Jesus, and Galileo are good examples of this.

Readers will approach this book with their own opinions on the issues debated within it. However, to have a good grasp of one's own viewpoint, it is necessary to understand the arguments of those with whom one disagrees. It can be said that those who do not completely understand their adversary's point of view do not fully understand their own.

A persuasive case for considering opposing viewpoints has been presented by John Stuart Mill in his work *On Liberty*. When examining controversial issues it may be helpful to reflect on this suggestion:

The only way in which a human being can make some approach to knowing the whole of a subject, is by hearing what can be said about it by persons of every variety of opinion, and studying all modes in which it can be looked at by every character of mind. No wise man ever acquired his wisdom in any mode but this.

Analyzing Sources of Information

The Opposing Viewpoints Series includes diverse materials taken from magazines, journals, books, and newspapers, as well as statements and position papers from a wide range of individuals, organizations, and governments. This broad spectrum of sources helps to develop patterns of thinking which are open to the consideration of a variety of opinions.

Pitfalls to Avoid

A pitfall to avoid in considering opposing points of view is that of regarding one's own opinion as being common sense and the most rational stance, and the point of view of others as being only opinion and naturally wrong. It may be that another's opinion is correct and one's own is in error.

Another pitfall to avoid is that of closing one's mind to the opinions of those with whom one disagrees. The best way to approach a dialogue is to make one's primary purpose that of understanding the mind and arguments of the other person and not that of enlightening him or her with one's own solutions. More can be learned by listening than speaking.

It is my hope that after reading this book the reader will have a deeper understanding of the issues debated and will appreciate the complexity of even seemingly simple issues on which good and honest people disagree. This awareness is particularly important in a democratic society such as ours where people enter into public debate to determine the common good. Those with whom one disagrees should not necessarily be regarded as enemies, but perhaps simply as people who suggest different paths to a common goal.

Developing Basic Reading and Thinking Skills

In this book, carefully edited opposing viewpoints are purposely placed back to back to create a running debate; each viewpoint is preceded by a short quotation that best expresses the author's main argument. This format instantly plunges the reader into the midst of a controversial issue and greatly aids that reader in mastering the basic skill of recognizing an author's point of view.

A number of basic skills for critical thinking are practiced in the activities that appear throughout the books in the series. Some of the skills are:

Evaluating Sources of Information. The ability to choose from among alternative sources the most reliable and accurate source in relation to a given subject.

Separating Fact from Opinion. The ability to make the basic distinction between factual statements (those that can be demonstrated or verified empirically) and statements of opinion (those that are beliefs or attitudes that cannot be proved).

Identifying Stereotypes. The ability to identify oversimplified, exaggerated descriptions (favorable or unfavorable) about people and insulting statements about racial, religious, or national groups, based upon misinformation or lack of information.

Recognizing Ethnocentrism. The ability to recognize attitudes or opinions that express the view that one's own race, culture, or group is inherently superior, or those attitudes that judge another culture or group in terms of one's own.

It is important to consider opposing viewpoints and equally important to be able to critically analyze those viewpoints. The activities in this book are designed to help the reader master these thinking skills. Statements are taken from the book's viewpoints and the reader is asked to analyze them. This technique aids the reader in developing skills that not only can be applied to the viewpoints in this book, but also to situations where opinionated spokespersons comment on controversial issues. Although the activities are helpful to the solitary reader, they are most useful when the reader can benefit from the interaction of group discussion.

Using this book and others in the series should help readers develop basic reading and thinking skills. These skills should improve the reader's ability to understand what is read. Readers should be better able to separate fact from opinion, substance from rhetoric, and become better consumers of information in our media-centered culture.

This volume of the Opposing Viewpoints Series does not advocate a particular point of view. Quite the contrary! The very nature of the book leaves it to the reader to formulate the opinions he or she finds most suitable. My purpose as publisher is to see that this is made possible by offering a wide range of viewpoints that are fairly presented.

David L. Bender
Publisher

Introduction

"The problem of the twentieth century is the problem of the color line."

W.E.B. DuBois, 1903.

"We hold these truths to be self-evident, that all men are created equal, that they are endowed by their Creator with certain unalienable rights, that among these are Life, Liberty and the pursuit of Happiness." With these unambiguous words, Thomas Jefferson not only justified America's break from Great Britain, but also set forth a vision of what kind of nation America was to be: a country of equality and liberty. Ironically, Jefferson and many other signers of the Declaration of Independence owned black slaves who were granted neither.

This paradox of America's ideals versus its treatment of minority groups has continued to haunt American society for over two hundred years. In the mid-nineteenth century, it led to a bloody Civil War that freed the slaves but did not end racism or create racial equality. A century later, the civil rights movement succeeded in its push for laws outlawing racial segregation and discrimination and ensuring blacks and other minorities the right to vote. Today laws exist to ensure equal treatment of all races, and the more blatant vestiges of racism are condemned by most Americans. But as historian Robert Weisbrot writes,

> The goal of racial equality remains an infinitely receding vision. Blacks endure a poverty rate of more than 30 percent (three times that for whites), an unemployment rate more than twice the national average, persistent housing discrimination and confinement in ghetto slums, low enrollment in colleges and graduate schools, near exclusion from top corporate posts, and pervasive racial stereotyping.

Despite the fact that fewer Americans today profess explicitly racist ideologies, inequality between racial and ethnic groups persists in the U.S. and relations between members of different groups are still fraught with tension and misunderstanding. *Racism in America: Opposing Viewpoints* examines how racism continues to affect our lives today and debates whether racism is truly the primary cause of such problems as poverty and economic inequality. The volume deals with the problems Hispanics,

Asian Americans, American Indians, and other minority groups face. The majority of the viewpoints, however, focus on the continuing troubled relationship between black and white America, a relationship sociologist Bob Blauner says is "getting better and worse at the same time." The questions debated are How Serious Is the Problem of Racism in America? Is Racism Responsible for Minority Poverty? Does Affirmative Action Alleviate Discrimination? Should Minorities Emphasize Their Ethnicity? How Can Racism Be Stopped?

Whether America can live up to the ideals so simply expressed in its Declaration of Independence remains to be seen. Author Nicholas Lemann sees reason for hope. "The United States has an undeniable strain of racial prejudice in its character," he writes, "but it also has a racial conscience that periodically comes to the fore." The viewpoints in this volume examine this struggle that taxes the American conscience.

How Serious Is the Problem of Racism in America?

Chapter Preface

"Racist faith, that belief system which invests ultimate meaning in the biology of white skin color, has permeated American history from the beginning," writes theology professor Calvin S. Morris. Racism in American history, he argues, can be seen in the treatment of American Indians, Asian immigrants, and above all, blacks, who were brought to America as slaves and after the abolition of slavery were subjected to racist laws and practices.

The question Americans face is whether now, a quarter century after the civil rights movement inspired the nation to end official racial segregation, racism remains a serious problem. Author David Horowitz is among those who argue that the civil rights movement succeeded in making race a less significant problem than before. "In a single generation," he writes, "discriminatory practices and segregationist laws in America have been declared unconstitutional and universally abolished."

But others argue that the gains of the civil rights movement have proved illusory and that racism remains a stain on America's conscience. "Racism has not declined in significance," writes political scientist Manning Marable. "Racial inequality continues despite the false rhetoric of equality." Marable and others argue that blacks, Hispanics, and other minorities have fewer opportunities to succeed in the U.S. than whites do because of continuing racism, and that many continue to face racial hostility from whites.

The following viewpoints examine the state of race relations in the U.S. today, and whether racism remains a critical problem.

"Strong negative beliefs about minorities continue to underlie the policy debate on many racial issues."

Race Relations Are Worsening

Lynne Duke

One way to measure racism in the U.S. is by using opinion polls. In the following viewpoint, Lynne Duke analyzes the results of a poll surveying racial attitudes and concludes that racism remains a serious problem in the U.S. Many Americans still hold negative racial attitudes, Duke writes, and these attitudes reduce support for policies promoting racial equality. Duke is a staff writer for the *Washington Post.*

As you read, consider the following questions:

1. How was the opinion survey structured, according to Duke?
2. What kinds of racial stereotypes does the author say many people still hold?
3. According to Duke, how might racism be reduced?

Lynne Duke, "But Some of My Best Friends Are . . . ," *The Washington Post National Weekly Edition,* January 14-20, 1991, © 1991, The Washington Post. Reprinted with permission.

A majority of whites questioned in a nationwide survey say they believe blacks and Hispanics are likely to prefer welfare to hard work and tend to be lazier than whites, more prone to violence, less intelligent and less patriotic.

Authors of the survey, conducted by the National Opinion Research Center at the University of Chicago, say the results show that despite progress in race relations since the 1950s, whites' negative images of blacks and other minorities continue to be pervasive.

Persistent Prejudice

"Since the beginning of the civil rights movement there was great emphasis on ending segregation and creating a series of laws that treated all racial, religious and ethnic groups equally," says Tom W. Smith of the research center, who wrote the report. The feeling was "we'll intermingle and we'll get to know one another and the stereotypes will drop away."

Instead, strong negative beliefs about minorities continue to underlie the policy debate on many racial issues, according to the survey.

The beliefs in part explain white resistance to government help such as affirmative action and quotas for minority groups, and the opposition of some whites to race-mingling and neighborhood integration—even though they may support equality in theory.

"All this says is that in part the reason why people are against affirmative action or quotas is that they have images of minorities that brand minorities as undeserving of help; that is they think they are less hard-working and they think they are more likely to want to live off welfare," Smith says.

The sources of these feelings are historically complex and rooted deeply in the culture, says Lawrence Bobo, professor of sociology at the University of California at Los Angeles and head of a committee that designed the survey questions.

"Once you have well ensconced some system of unequal relations between majority and minority groups, a set of ideas that sort of justifies that societal order is likely to take shape, and that will include a set of ideas about the traits of minority group members that putatively explain why it is they should occupy a lesser, subordinated status," Bobo says.

The Survey

The survey series, which is sponsored by the National Science Foundation, has focused on various social issues almost yearly for two decades, and its methodology is respected.

The latest survey was conducted between February and April of 1990. Individuals in randomly selected households in 300 communities were asked to rate the behavioral or personality characteristics of whites, Jews, black Americans, Hispanic Americans, Asian Americans and Southern whites.

Of the 1,372 survey respondents, about 170 were black, 50 were Hispanic, 30 were Jewish, fewer than 10 were Asian and the rest were white, including 330 Southern whites. Because the sample included so few minorities, their views on whites were considered statistically insignificant. Respondents were presented with a scale on which to rate each group.

In presenting their perceptions of black Americans, a majority of the white, Hispanic and other non-black respondents—78 percent—said blacks are more likely than whites to "prefer to live off welfare" and less likely to "prefer to be self-supporting."

Further, 62 percent said blacks are more likely to be lazy; 56 percent said they are violence-prone; 53 percent said they are less intelligent; 51 percent said they think blacks are less patriotic.

Hispanics were rated at equally negative levels. Among non-Hispanics, 74 percent said Hispanics are more likely to prefer to live off welfare; 56 percent thought them more lazy, 50 percent thought them more violence-prone, 55 percent thought them less intelligent and 61 percent thought them less patriotic.

Thirty-four percent of the respondents said Asians are likely to be lazy, 30 percent said they are violence-prone, 36 percent said they are less intelligent, 46 percent said they prefer to live off welfare, and 55 percent said they are less patriotic.

On many of the indicators in the survey, whites rated Jews higher than themselves, with the exception of patriotism. Overall, each group rated itself significantly more positively than whites rated it.

Minority Disadvantages

This persistence of negative racial images was a pervasive theme as the National Urban League presented its 16th annual State of Black America report.

It documented, as it has in previous years, the spectrum of economic, political, educational, social and cultural disadvantages still faced by blacks.

The report reiterated the league's call for an "urban Marshall plan" to bring jobs, economic development and anti-crime measures to inner cities. And Urban League President John Jacob says the civil rights measure that President George Bush called a "quota" bill and vetoed in the fall of 1990 is "a litmus test of America's resolve that it is unacceptable to deny job opportunities to people because they are black" or members of other minority groups.

Ironically, however, such calls for help from representatives of black communities, although they are based on real and legitimate needs, may serve to reinforce the negative perceptions held by whites, Bobo says.

It is a fact that a disproportionate number of blacks are incarcerated, that blacks are victims and perpetrators of a disproportionate number of homicides, are disproportionately on welfare, and that a disproportionate number of U.S. blacks live in poverty.

Toles. Copyright 1989 *The Buffalo News.* Reprinted with permission of Universal Press Syndicate. All rights reserved.

In these facts, those whites who are already prone to hold negative images of blacks can find a "kernel of truth" to support their views, Bobo says.

Bobo and Smith say possible solutions to this persisting racism include better education of whites about minority groups and more interaction. Smith suggests that whites need to see more minority role models whose success defies stereotypes.

In addition, Jacob and Derrick Bell, a Harvard University law professor who wrote an essay for the Urban League, say whites need to understand that their negative views of minorities and the resulting discrimination have a direct economic impact in terms of potentially lost productivity as the work force over time becomes populated by fewer whites and more minorities.

"Blacks are far more satisfied with the quality of their lives than they were a decade ago, and whites have grown far more tolerant."

Race Relations Are Improving

Burns W. Roper

Burns W. Roper is chairman of the Roper Organization, Inc., a public opinon research firm based in New York. In the following viewpoint, Roper says that despite much negative media publicity on racism, polls show that U.S. race relations are actually improving. He cites polls which show increasing racial tolerance and satisfaction with social conditions.

As you read, consider the following questions:

1. What is one of the most valuable contributions of public opinion polls, according to Roper?
2. What polls does Roper cite to support his contention that race relations are improving?
3. Why does the author believe that reports of racial violence do not necessarily indicate that racism is a widespread problem?

Burns W. Roper, "Race Relations in America." This article originally appeared in the July/August 1990 issue of *The Public Perspective*, a bimonthly magazine published by the Roper Center for Public Opinion Research at the University of Connecticut. It is reprinted with permission.

I have always believed that public opinion polls make one of their greatest contributions when used to assess the validity of "common knowledge." With respect to race relations in America, the polls reveal how wrong "common knowledge" is. From what is said in much of the news media today, we would think the state of race relations in America had deteriorated to a post-war low. But this is far from the truth.

Isolated Events

There's no question that the racial climate in New York City is tense. Howard Beach, Bensonhurst, the Central Park jogger, Tawana Brawley: These bring to mind serious examples of racial animus, deserving of wide attention and condemnation.

And New York City holds no monopoly on racial enmity. Black students battled white police officers in Virginia Beach, Va. And a former Ku Klux Klansman is making a credible run for the US Senate in Louisiana.

Although there may be reason to fear a rise in racial violence in cities and on campuses across the country, these remain isolated events that do not reflect the views or experiences of the vast majority of Americans—black or white. Blacks are far more satisfied with the quality of their lives than they were a decade ago, and whites have grown far more tolerant.

Polling Data

A Roper poll in 1978 sought to measure the conditions of the races, unaffected by any mention of race. To accomplish this, we asked people about conditions "here in this neighborhood."

Compared to whites, blacks that year reported far higher rates of unemployment, crime, drug abuse, and violence. In some cases, blacks were two, three, or even four times as likely as whites to criticize the living conditions in their respective neighborhoods.

In 1990 we again asked the same series of questions and found major improvements. Although the experiences of blacks are still worse than those of whites, the differences have narrowed remarkably.

Fewer than a third of blacks complain, for example, about juvenile delinquency in their neighborhoods, down from half in 1978. At the same time, juvenile delinquency was mentioned as a problem by a fifth of whites, down from a quarter. Housing conditions also appear to have improved for blacks. Only 28 percent now cite a lack of good local housing, down 11 percentage points over the past dozen years. And fewer than a fifth criticize treatment by police, down 10 points.

Other problems are mentioned much less frequently by blacks in 1990 than in 1978: auto thefts (down 18 points), drug dealing (down 22 points), attacks on older people (down 23), break-ins (down 25), and unemployment (down 28).

The topic of race was then raised in a later part of the survey. The most significant changes came in the area of employment opportunities. Asked to consider a situation in which a black and white person of equal intelligence and skill applied for the same job, a plurality of whites in 1978 feared reverse discrimination—they said the black would get the job; today the dominant answer is that both would have an equal chance.

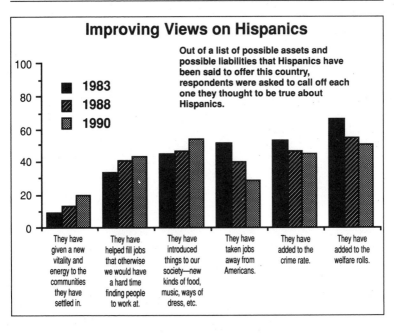

SOURCE: Roper Reports

The shift in outlook among blacks is even more dramatic: Only a third now think the white person would have the better chance of being hired, down from half. Four in 10 blacks—twice as many as 12 years ago—say both candidates would have an equal chance. Half of all blacks call conditions for black people excellent or good, up from only 39 percent 12 years ago.

Attitudes about race and ethnic differences are shifting in other areas, too. Our 1990 survey indicated a more positive view among Americans of the country's growing Hispanic population. Seven years ago, for instance, 66 percent of respondents in a similar poll felt that Hispanics added to the welfare rolls. That number is now down to 50 percent. Fifty-two percent then believed that Hispanics were taking jobs away from other Americans; in 1990 that had fallen to 29 percent.

Asked if Hispanics have given "a new vitality and energy to the communities they have settled in," 20 percent in 1990 said yes. In 1983, only 9 percent agreed with that assessment. The only category where perceptions of Hispanics became slightly more negative concerned their willingness to learn English.

Increased Sensitivity

How do we square these findings with the sense of racial violence? It may be that our equality-minded society has grown more sensitive to racial discord—that we've come to notice displays of racial animosity more than we used to.

The news media also bear some responsibility for overplaying stories of racial tension. Indeed, when a poll of New Yorkers asked them which of nine individuals and institutions were making race relations worse in the city, the top two answers were the Rev. Al Sharpton (a black activist who has seemingly sought racial confrontation, mentioned by 84 percent) and the news media (69 percent). On this question, blacks and whites were in complete agreement.

"Racism has to do with the power to dominate and enforce oppression, and that power in America is in white hands."

Whites' Racist Attitudes Are a Serious Problem

Jim Wallis

Jim Wallis is editor of *Sojourners*, a magazine published by the Washington, D.C.-based Christian community of the same name. In the following viewpoint, Wallis argues that American society is fundamentally marred by white racism toward blacks and other minorities. Wallis asserts that while blacks and other minorities may hold racial prejudices, they cannot be considered racist because they lack the power to harm whites. Wallis calls on whites to fight their own racism and to work to change society.

As you read, consider the following questions:

1. What was the original purpose of racism, according to the author?
2. What evidence does Wallis cite of racism's continuing existence in the U.S.?
3. Why does Wallis argue there is no such thing as black racism?

From "America's Original Sin," by Jim Wallis, *Sojourners*, November 1987. Reprinted with permission from *Sojourners*, PO Box 29272, Washington, DC 20017.

The United States of America was established as a white society, founded upon the genocide of another race and then the enslavement of yet another.

To make such a statement today is to be immediately accused of being rhetorical or, worse yet, of being "reminiscent of the '60s." The reaction is instructive and revealing. The historical record of how white Europeans conquered North America by destroying the native population and how they then built their new nation's economy on the backs of kidnapped Africans who had been turned into chattel are facts that can hardly be denied. Yet to speak honestly of such historical facts is to be charged with being polemical or out of date. Why?

Not a Hot Topic

One reason is that racism is no longer a hot topic. After the brief "racial crisis" of the '60s, white America, including many of those involved in the civil rights movement, has gone on to other concerns. Also, the legal victories of black Americans in that period, as far as most white Americans are concerned, have settled the issue and even left many asking, "What more do blacks want?"

Federal courts have recently interpreted civil rights legislation—originally designed to redress discrimination against black people—as applying to the grievances of whites who believe affirmative action programs have "gone too far." In addition, popular racial attitudes have changed, attested to by the opinion polls and the increased number of black faces appearing in the world of sports, entertainment, the mass media, and even politics. . . .

Indeed, in the two decades since the passage of momentous civil rights legislation, some things have changed and some things haven't. What have changed are the personal racial attitudes of many white Americans and the opportunities for some black Americans to enter the middle levels of society. (The word "middle" is key here, insofar as blacks have yet to be allowed into the upper echelons and decision-making positions of business, the professions, the media, or even the fields of sports and entertainment where black "progress" has so often been celebrated.) Legal segregation has been lifted off the backs of black people with the consequent expansion of social interchange and voting rights, and that itself has led to changes in white attitudes.

What has not changed is the systematic and pervasive character of racism in the United States and the condition of life for the majority of black people. In fact, those conditions have gotten worse.

Racism originates in domination and provides the social rational and philosophical justification for debasing, degrading, and doing violence to people on the basis of color. Many have pointed out how racism is sustained by both personal attitudes and structural forces. Racism can be brutally overt or invisibly institutional, or both. Its scope extends to every level and area of human psychology, society, and culture.

Racism and Prejudice

Prejudice may be a universal human sin, but racism is more than an inevitable consequence of human nature or social accident. Rather, racism is a system of oppression for a social purpose.

In the United States, the original purpose of racism was to justify slavery and its enormous economic benefit. The particular form of racism, inherited from the English to justify their own slave trade, was especially venal, for it defined the slave not merely as an unfortunate victim of bad circumstances, war, or social dislocation but rather as less than human, as a thing, an animal, a piece of property to be bought and sold, used and abused.

The slave did not have to be treated with any human consideration whatsoever. Even in the founding document of our nation, the famous constitutional compromise defined the slave as only three-fifths of a person. The professed high ideals of Anglo-Western society could exist side by side with the profitable institution of slavery only if the humanity of the slave was denied and disregarded.

The heart of racism was and is economic, though its roots and results are also deeply cultural, psychological, sexual, even religious, and, of course, political. Due to 200 years of brutal slavery and 100 more of legal segregation and discrimination, no area of the relationship between black and white people in the United States is free from the legacy of racism.

America's Sin

In spiritual and biblical terms, racism is a perverse sin that cuts to the core of the gospel message. Put simply, racism negates the reason for which Christ died—the reconciling work of the cross. It denies the purpose of the church: to bring together, in Christ, those who have been divided from one another, particularly in the early church's case, Jew and Gentile—a division based on race.

There is only one remedy for such a sin and that is repentance, which, if genuine, will always bear fruit in concrete forms of conversion, changed behavior, and reparation. While the United States may have changed in regard to some of its racial attitudes and allowed some of its black citizens into the middle class, white America has yet to recognize the extent of its racism—that we are and have always been a racist society—much less repent of its racial sins.

And because of that lack of repentance and, indeed, because of the economic social, and political purposes still served by the oppression of black people, systematic racism continues to be pervasive in American life. While constantly denied by white social commentators and the media, evidence of the persistent and endemic character of American racism abounds.

RACISM'S FULL CIRCLE

Danziger for *The Christian Science Monitor* © 1990 TCSPS.

The most visible and painful sign of racism's continuation is the gross economic inequality between blacks and whites. All the major social indices and numerous statistics show the situation to be worsening, not improving. The gap between white and black median family income and employment actually widened in the decade between 1970 and 1980, even before Ronald Reagan took office. And the Reagan administration has been like an economic plague to the black community; black unemployment has skyrocketed, and the major brunt of slashed and gutted social services has been borne by black people, especially women and children.

All this has especially affected black youth, whose rate of unemployment has climbed above 50 percent. The last time I checked the unemployment rate for young black people in Washington, D.C., it was 61 percent. The very human meaning to such grim statistics can be seen in the faces of the kids in my inner-city neighborhood. They know they have no job, no place, no future, and therefore no real stake in this country. As one commentator has put it, society has ceased to be a society for them. Alcohol, drugs, poverty, family disintegration, crime, and jail have replaced aspirations for a decent life and a hopeful future.

It is the economy itself that now enforces the brutal oppression of racism, and it happens, of course, invisibly and impersonally. In the changing capitalist order, manufacturing jobs are lost to cheaper labor markets in the Third World or to automation while farm labor becomes extinct; both historically have been important to black survival. In the new "high-tech" world and "service economy," almost the only jobs available are at places like McDonalds.

Increasingly, we see a two-tiered economy emerging: one a highly lucrative level of technicians and professionals who operate the system, and the other an impoverished sector of unemployed, underemployed, and unskilled labor from which the work of servicing the system can be done. That blacks are disproportionately consigned to the lower economic tier is an indisputable proof of racism. The existence of a vast black underclass, inhabiting the inner cities of our nation, is a testimony to the versatility of white racism 20 years after legal segregation was officially outlawed. . . .

The cold economic savagery of racism has led to further declines in every area of the quality of life in the black community—health, infant mortality, family breakdown, drug and alcohol abuse, and crime. The majority of black children are now born to single mothers; a primary cause of death for young black men today is homicide; and nearly half of all prison inmates in the United States now are black males.

Segregated and Inferior

Despite landmark court decisions and civil rights legislation, two-thirds of black Americans still suffer from education and housing that is both segregated and inferior. Such conditions, along with diminishing social services, lead to despair, massive substance abuse, and criminality, and the fact that this reality is still surprising or incomprehensible to many white Americans raises the question of how much racial attitudes have really changed.

In the face of such structural oppression, the deliberate rollback of civil rights programs during the Reagan administration becomes even more callous. The resurgence of more overt forms of white racism and violence, as exemplified by the incidents in Howard Beach, New York; Forsyth County, Georgia; and other places, is quite foreboding as yet another occasion when the discontented alienation of poor whites is displaced and expressed against blacks instead of at the system that oppresses them both and has always sought to turn them against each other. . . .

The strategies for how black people must confront and finally overcome the ever-changing face of white racism in America must always originate within the black community itself. White allies have and can continue to play a significant role in the struggle against racism when black autonomy and leadership are sufficiently present to make possible a genuine partnership. But an even more important task for white Americans is to examine ourselves, our relationships, our institutions, and our society for the ugly plague of racism.

White Racism

Whites in America must admit the reality and begin to operate on the assumption that theirs is a racist society. Positive individual attitudes are simply not enough, for, as we have seen, racism is more than just personal.

All white people in the United States have benefited from the structure of racism, whether or not they have ever committed a racist act, uttered a racist word, or had a racist thought (as unlikely as that is). Just as surely as blacks suffer in a white society because they are black, whites benefit because they are white. And if whites have profited from a racist structure, they must try to change it.

The Age of Lincoln

Today most white Americans would state that blacks are their equals. But if white Americans really were committed to their words, then this nation would be unwilling to tolerate the cruel conditions of life—in health, education, housing, employment and other areas—that increasing numbers of black Americans face. The Civil War ended 125 years ago, yet we are still in "the age of Lincoln," unable to overcome white resistance to the prospect of equality between the races.

William E. Cain, *In These Times*, May 9-15, 1990.

To benefit from domination is to be responsible for it. Merely to keep personally free of the taint of racist attitudes is both illusory and inadequate. Just to go along with a racist social structure, to accept the economic order as it is, just to do one's job within impersonal institutions is to participate in racism.

Racism has to do with the power to dominate and enforce oppression, and that power in America is in white hands. Therefore, while there are instances of black racial prejudice against whites in the United States today (often in reaction to white racism), there is no such thing as black racism. Black people in America do not have the power to enforce that prejudice.

White racism in white institutions must be eradicated by white people and not just black people. In fact, white racism is primarily a white responsibility.

We must not give in to the popular temptation to believe that racism existed mostly in the Old South or before the 1960s or, today, in South Africa. Neither can any of our other struggles against the arms race, war in Central America, hunger, homelessness, or sexism be separated from the reality of racism.

"Blacks in America justly condemn . . . white racism in this country, yet many turn a blind eye to the equally repugnant phenomenon of black bigotry."

Minorities' Racist Attitudes Are a Serious Problem

Mark Mathabane and Clarence Page

The following two-part viewpoint examines the phenomenon of racial prejudice within minority groups. In it, the two authors decry the spread of racism in minority communities and argue that minority prejudice worsens U.S. race relations. Part I of the viewpoint is by Mark Mathabane, a South African-born writer whose books include *Kaffir Boy* and *Kaffir Boy in America*. Part II is by Clarence Page, a nationally syndicated columnist.

As you read, consider the following questions:

1. What examples of minority racism toward other racial groups do the authors describe?
2. According to the authors, what is the origin of racial prejudice?
3. How does the prejudice of blacks worsen race relations, according to the authors?

Mark Mathabane, "The Blight of Black Racism," *The New York Times*, August 23, 1989. Copyright © 1989 by The New York Times Company. Reprinted by permission. Clarence Page, "Racism, Bias, and Wasted Power," *The Washington Times*, May 18, 1990. Reprinted by permission: Tribune Media Services.

I

Blacks in America justly condemn apartheid in South Africa and white racism in this country, yet many turn a blind eye to the equally repugnant phenomenon of black bigotry. Some even deny the existence of such a thing; others unwittingly condone it under the names of black power, black pride and black solidarity.

During appearances on several radio shows promoting my new book, I was asked by some angry black callers why I had sympathetically portrayed whites in my autobiography, given their responsibility for apartheid in South Africa and racism here.

Not All Whites Are Racist

I responded that not all the whites I had met were racist. In fact, several had played pivotal roles in helping me overcome the traumas of apartheid, in my quest for a decent education, and in my escape from the ghetto of Alexandra to freedom and success in America.

I explained that black policemen and soldiers, along with despotic leaders of several of South Africa's tribal homelands, routinely commit atrocities against fellow blacks.

And in America, black drug dealers daily poison the minds of fellow blacks with crack and other deadly drugs. These experiences, I pointed out, have taught me that there are good and bad people among both races—thus the importance of judging people according to the contents of their characters, rather than by the color of their skin.

But some of the callers insisted that, in the name of black solidarity, I had to regard all whites as enemies. "We're in a state of war against these people," one caller said. "You have to choose which side you're on."

"Any black man who does not hate whites is a traitor," said another.

Us Against Them

This us-against-them attitude is not confined to the angry black person in the street or to the likes of Al Sharpton and those who perpetrated the Tawana Brawley hoax. At colleges, I have found the same attitude among otherwise reasonable black students who, in their militant rage against white racism, advocate "fighting back in kind."

These students regard whites as racist by nature. Using the concept of collective guilt, they blame every white person for the suffering of African Americans during slavery and Jim Crow and for the pernicious effects of bigotry on the black community.

When I was in college, I and a few other black students were labeled Uncle Toms for sitting with whites in the cafeteria, sharing with them black culture, working with them on projects and

33

socializing with them. Our accusers failed to realize that only through communication could the two racial groups begin to understand each other better and respect and benefit from cultural differences.

A Nation of Minorities

We live in a nation of minorities, where nearly everyone belongs to some group or shares some heritage that has been victimized by discrimination. There is no such dominant group as "white males," as some would have us believe. That overinclusive category represents people of varying ethnic, religious, national origin and sexual preference backgrounds. The recent history of this country includes episodes of anti-Irish, anti-Italian, anti-French-Canadian, anti-Arab, anti-Jewish and anti-Scandinavian bigotry. Nor have racial minorities been entirely innocent of all such bigotry. Blacks, Hispanics, Asians and others have discriminated against each other. There is more than enough prejudice in every corner of American life to allow anyone to feel superior.

Alan Dershowitz, *The Washington Times*, January 29, 1991.

Another form of prejudice is based on shades of skin color within the black community. The film maker Spike Lee depicted this well in his controversial movie "School Daze." And in Georgia, a light-skinned black employee for the Internal Revenue Service is suing her darker-skinned supervisor for color discrimination.

Interracial Marriages

Finally, there's the prejudice that leads many blacks to oppose interracial relationships and marriages. If a black man dates or weds a white woman, the act is construed as hatred and disrespect for the black woman. If a black woman goes out with or marries a white man, she is regarded as having betrayed black manhood by uniting with her "slavemaster."

The irony in all this is that black opposition to interracial couples accomplishes precisely what white segregationists have long sought: no "miscegenation" because blacks are supposedly genetically inferior to whites. It is interesting that the same blacks who oppose interracial relationships and marriages in America condemned the now repealed Immorality and Prohibition of Mixed Marriages Acts in South Africa.

Black bigotry undermines the struggle against white racism. Failure to acknowledge that there are good and bad people among all races, and that friendship and love transcend color and creed, negates the crucial point blacks are trying to make: Judge us according to the contents of our characters and you will find many of us the equal of any man or woman.

It is necessary for more blacks to make it clear that black bigotry is as reprehensible and corroding to the soul as white racism and will not be tolerated under any guise.

II

Of all the bold and audacious statements uttered recently by Rep. Gus Savage, a politician well known for boldness and audacity, one of the most intriguing was his pronouncement that "there ain't no black racism."

The black Chicago Democrat's statement came to mind when I heard about the three Asian men who found themselves surrounded by a group of black youths who beat one of them almost to death in New York City. Accounts of the incident vary, but I imagine it is safe to bet the three Asian men disagree with Mr. Savage's view that blacks can't be racist.

As an African-American who has felt the sting of racism more than a few times, I deplore the way the three Asians felt the power of black numbers surrounding them in a very negative way, especially when we could be using the power of our numbers in a very positive way.

Abuse of Power

First we must recognize racism as an abuse of power. It is evil but, like power, not limited to any one race, contrary to what Mr. Savage said at a press conference he called to defend himself against charges that his criticism of America's foreign aid to Israel had begun to smack of anti-Semitism and anti-white racism.

"Racism is white," he snapped blamelessly. "There ain't no black racism."

The remark was dismissed by those who saw it as just another example of bold and audacious bulljive from "goofy Gus."

But Mr. Savage was describing in his own bold and audacious way how power defines relationships in our society. Anyone can be prejudiced, but to be "racist," according to dictionaries, you must believe that your race is naturally superior to others.

Since the racism of America's dominant culture and institutions is too pernicious to lead anyone, including blacks, to believe blacks are superior, Mr. Savage is saying, blacks cannot be racist.

It is a persuasive but unconvincing argument. White dominance may be a message with which blacks and other children of color grow up every day, but that message grows increasingly weak as blacks grow increasingly strong.

If racism is an infliction of the empowered at the expense of the powerless, as Mr. Savage suggests, his statement that blacks cannot be racist implies that blacks can never have power. If that were the case, he and everyone else who believes in black

35

empowerment might as well pack up and go home.

In fact, blacks have gained considerable hard-earned economic and political power. And with that power comes the responsibility to use it wisely.

The Essence of Bigotry

The essence of bigotry is stereotyping and overgeneralization based on race, national origin, gender or other factors beyond the control of the individual. Bigotry may be more understandable and less dangerous when it emanates from minorities who lack the power to impose institutional oppression. But it sends an equally pernicious message of hate and discrimination.

Alan Dershowitz, *The Washington Times*, January 29, 1991.

Prejudice against blacks persists, of course, but as long as we persist in thinking of ourselves as victims even as many of us gain unprecedented offices and opportunities, we will continue to behave like victims even as the moral authority and public sympathy our victimization brought us in the past dwindles away.

That dichotomy can only lead to further despair—or worse, as David Dinkins, New York's first black mayor, is discovering with the racial powder keg he now tries to govern.

Accounts sharply vary over what exactly led to the clash between African-Americans and three Vietnamese in Brooklyn's Flatbush neighborhood early [one] Sunday that left one Vietnamese man hospitalized with a fractured skull. Early reports indicated that Vietnamese were the victims of bitter feelings that have spilled over from demonstrations a few blocks away by blacks who charge two Korean-owned grocery stores with bad treatment.

Blacks and Immigrants

Long-standing bitterness wells up like a volcano around such incidents. It brings to mind a long-standing belief in black communities that the first thing immigrants learn when they arrive on these shores is a derogatory slang word for their race. The word immediately gives them someone else to whom they can feel superior, it is reasoned.

Prejudices often result from a misdirected yearning for self-esteem. Self-esteem is valuable, even when it is earned at someone else's expense.

The biggest irony of the black-Asian clash, one that is being repeated in cities across the country, is that the new wave of immigrants setting up shop in inner cities is predominantly nonwhite, another reminder of the continuing inability of black leadership to move beyond questions of racial justice to the more nettlesome questions of economic empowerment.

After all, the same energy that black demonstrators have expended in their daily demonstrations against two Korean grocers could be used by blacks to open our own groceries. With proper direction, entrepreneurship could restore a vibrant economy to economically devastated areas, fueled by the $220 billion black consumer market. Instead, it provides a pipeline to the American Dream for more waves of immigrants, only this time, in the bitterest of ironies, the immigrants are non-European.

Take Advantage of Opportunities

We need to do more than get angry. We need to take advantage of opportunities earlier civil rights reforms opened up. Now that the world has seen us at our worst, we need to show the world our best.

"Asian Americans are clearly discriminated against."

Racism Is a Serious Problem for Asian Americans

Thea Lee

Asian Americans are one of the fastest-growing minority groups in the U.S. They have a median family income higher than that of whites, and have often been called a "model minority" in light of their successes in education and business. However, Thea Lee in the following viewpoint argues that Asian Americans face significant racial discrimination and prejudice. Their status as a "model minority," she argues, obscures their problems and creates false stereotypes. Lee is a staff editor for *Dollars & Sense*, a monthly socialist magazine.

As you read, consider the following questions:

1. How can economic statistics distort the true situation facing Asian Americans, according to Lee?
2. According to the author, what stereotypes of Asian Americans prevent their promotion to high positions?
3. How have the racial barriers Asian Americans face changed over time, according to Lee?

From "Trapped on a Pedestal," by Thea Lee, *Dollars & Sense*, March 1990. *Dollars & Sense* is a progressive monthly economics magazine. First-year subscriptions are available for $14.95 from the office at One Summer St., Somerville, MA 02143.

"Visit 'Chinatown U.S.A.' and you find an important racial minority pulling itself up from hardship and discrimination to become a model of self-respect and achievement in today's America. At a time when it is being proposed that hundreds of billions be spent to uplift Negroes and other minorities, the nation's 300,000 Chinese-Americans are moving ahead on their own—with no help from anyone else."

—U.S. News & World Report,
December 26, 1966

"Asian Americans are our exemplar of hope and inspiration."

—Ronald Reagan
as quoted in the *New Republic*, 1985

In the mid-1960s, when relaxed restrictions dramatically increased Asian immigration to the United States, the popular press, politicians, and others assigned Asian Americans the role of "model minority." When the 1980 Census revealed that median family income for Asian Americans actually surpassed that of whites by almost 13%, the stories resurfaced with renewed intensity. *Fortune* ran an article entitled, "Super-minority," and the *New Republic* chimed in with "America's Greatest Success Story."

The Model Minority

The model-minority label, enviable though it might seem, has served Asian Americans badly. It obscures real differences among Asian Americans and exacerbates the resentment of other minority groups. The stories of spectacular achievement are presented as proof that Asian Americans either do not face or have overcome adverse racial discrimination. This not only denies Asian Americans legal and social protection against discrimination, but creates a backlash of its own—as majority or other minority groups lobby to offset their perceived advantage.

Although the nation's 6.5 million Asian Americans still make up less than 3% of the total U.S. population, they are the fastest-growing minority group in the country. According to current estimates, the ethnic Asian population in the United States doubled between 1980 and 1990, as it did between 1970 and 1980. The rapid growth brings with it equally dramatic changes in its composition, rendering the old stereotypes ever more obsolete.

Filipinos recently overtook the Chinese to become the largest single Asian group in the United States. The Japanese-American population remained relatively stable in the 1980s, while the number of Indochinese more than tripled. The number of Asian Indians and Koreans continued to grow at a steadily high rate, with each of those groups constituting a little over 10% of the Asian-American population.

Judged by standard measures of success, the achievements of Asian Americans—as a group—seem impressive. Their median family income in 1979 was $23,100, compared to the national median of $19,900. Moreover, a 1988 study by the Civil Rights Commission found that the hourly wages of most American-born Asian men exceed those of whites with comparable levels of education and experience. According to the 1980 Census, 34% of Asian Americans completed four or more years of college, compared to only 16% of the total U.S. population. And at elite universities, Asian Americans are even more disproportionately represented: in 1986, Asian Americans made up 12% of the freshman class at Harvard, 22% at MIT, and 27% at the University of California at Berkeley.

However, the economic and social reality of Asian immigrants is far more complex than these statistics indicate. Focusing on averages and success stories misses an equally striking case of Asian "over-representation": at the bottom of the barrel. Although Asian Americans are three to five times as likely as whites to be engineers and doctors, they are also two to four times as likely to work in food services or textiles. Many of the poorest Asian Americans are undocumented or paid under the table at sweatshops or restaurants; their incomes are likely to be under-represented by official figures. And offsetting their high educational attainment as a group is the fact that 6% of Asian Americans have not completed elementary school—three times the rate for whites.

To a large extent, deep differences among Asians from different countries, between recent immigrants and long-time residents, and between refugees and skilled professionals swamp the similarities, rendering generalizations misleading. For example, the median income of a Laotian family in 1979 was $5,000 compared to $27,400 for a Japanese family and $25,000 for an Indian family.

The stereotype of the successful minority hurts those Asian Americans who need the most help, because the success of some is used as an excuse to deny benefits to all. The most striking example is in college admissions. Most schools no longer consider Asians a "disadvantaged minority," excluding them from special consideration in the admissions process and in the awarding of financial aid. Some schools have gone a step further and rigged their admissions standards to handicap Asian students. Patrick Hayashi, now the vice-chancellor in charge of admissions at Berkeley, testified that in the mid-1980s, people "seemed to be deliberately searching for a standard which could be used to exclude Asian immigrant applications."

The American Dream?

Inappropriate and sometimes irrelevant comparisons contribute to racial tension between Asian Americans and other minorities. Black conservative Thomas Sowell, among others, has suggested that blacks would do well to follow the example of Asian Americans—work hard, get a good education, and achieve the American dream.

But American blacks face barriers quite different from those faced by Asian immigrants. Although both black Americans and early Asian immigrants endured legal and personal discrimination during their history in this country, Asian Americans at least came voluntarily. Furthermore, the 1965-75 wave of Asian immigrants consisted largely of highly educated, financially solvent professionals.

Race, a Barrier to Assimilation

While Asians are often thoroughly assimilated into American culture after a generation, many say that no matter how integrated they become, they will never be considered bona fide Americans because of an "otherness" factor based entirely on race. The claims of an American meritocracy also ring hollow to some skilled immigrants. Says Dr. Jagjit Sehdeva, a member of the Los Angeles human-relations commission: "It is almost impossible for medical graduates from India to find residency positions in hospitals here. Many wind up in lower-paying jobs as lab technicians or hospital orderlies." Says Dr. Stanley Sue, director of the National Research Center on Asian American Mental Health: "Some people want you to be American, but then they treat you differently. Why, then, would you want to assimilate?"

Howard G. Chua-Eoan, *Time*, April 9, 1990.

Another advantage of some Asian immigrant groups is that they have developed alternative ways to raise capital, ways that depend more on informal financial arrangements among families and acquaintances than on commercial banks. One such method is the rotating credit association.

Called *hui* in Chinese, *kye* in Korean, and *tanomoshi* in Japanese, these self-financing pools originated centuries ago to help families finance major expenses like weddings and funerals. The pools serve an important need once immigrants come to the United States, providing start-up capital to people who might be denied loans by conventional banks for lack of collateral or a poor credit rating. Up to 40 people participate, each contributing savings to a pool, which is loaned out to each participant in turn.

Should blacks, Latinos, and native Americans take a clue from Asian Americans, and set up similar institutions in their communities? That would be one way of dealing with the inadequate and racially discriminatory lending policies of U.S. financial institutions. But the path is a risky one, due to its very informality: If the leader is dishonest, or if one member cannot pay her or his share, the other members can lose their entire investment. As the *Wall Street Journal* points out, "There is no deposit insurance covering these free-wheeling banks, only the integrity of the leader, and stories about crooked operators and defaulted contributions abound in Asian communities."

Moreover, rather than urging other minorities to emulate the circuitous path Asian Americans have taken, policy-makers should work to lift the barriers in the U.S. economy—particularly in the financial system—facing all people of color and recent immigrants. Setting up one minority as the "good minority," and another as "bad" misses the point entirely. Both blacks and Asian Americans suffer from discrimination, albeit different kinds, and both have needs that are unmet by the U.S. economy and current policy.

At face value, the 1980 Census seemed to prove conclusively that Asian Americans no longer face discrimination in U.S. labor markets. If they earn more than whites, the argument went, then if anything they must enjoy a relatively advantageous position.

But upon closer scrutiny the Asian income figures reveal a more complex picture, even beyond the differences among nationalities. For one thing, the Asian income advantage evaporates when per capita incomes, rather than median family incomes, are compared. Since Asian-American families tend to be larger than average, with more workers per household, per capita Asian income in 1979 was actually slightly lower than the U.S. average. . . .

Trouble at the Top

Lumping Asian Americans together obscures the fact that within occupations and in some regions of the country, Asian Americans are clearly discriminated against. The most successful Asian Americans—those held up as examples of superachievement—are routinely paid less and promoted less often than comparable whites. This effect grows as they climb higher, both in academia and in corporations.

U.S.-born Asian men are less likely to hold managerial positions than whites with comparable skills and characteristics. While Asian Americans make up 4.3% of professionals, they are only 1.4% of officials and managers. The stereotype of Asians as passive and technically oriented may impede their promotion to top managerial positions.

Even though Asian Americans are famous—or infamous?—for their relatively high investment in higher education, both as families and as individuals, they tend to receive a lower return on their education than whites. A study by Jayjia Hsia using 1980 Census data found that Asian-American faculty with stronger than average academic credentials and more scholarly publications were paid less than average. In sum, the labor-market position of Asian Americans—even those at the top—is hardly enviable. They invest heavily in education, only to catch up to whites who have invested somewhat less. They work for corporations, only to find that their bosses have already decided how far they can advance.

The Plague of Racism

Racism in one form or another, subtle or blatantly obvious, plagues many Asian Americans. Sometimes strong biases brought over by the immigrants themselves—including racial prejudice, clannishness and a reluctance to make problems public—hamper their assimilation into the majority. More often, however, Asians are the victims of discrimination. The very visible success of some Asian immigrants and the power of Asian finance have triggered a backlash.

Howard G. Chua-Eoan, *Time*, April 9, 1990.

One way that Asian Americans have coped with limited upward mobility and relatively lower access to skilled union jobs has been to buy small businesses. Asian Americans have a high rate of business ownership compared to other minority groups—54.8 business owners for every 1,000 Asians or Pacific Islanders, compared to 12.5 for blacks and 17 for Latinos. The Koreans, Chinese, and Japanese business rates are higher than that for all Americans (64.0 per 1,000).

Although they have provided some opportunities for recent immigrants, small businesses are notoriously difficult to run. A Los Angeles-based study showed that Korean-American-owned enterprises in that city are heavily concentrated in two labor-intensive and highly competitive industries: retail and selected services. These businesses are small, both in terms of the number of employees and the value of sales. Four-fifths of these firms hire five or fewer employees, and nine-tenths hire ten or fewer. Virtually all had sales under one million dollars. Typical of Asian-owned businesses in the rest of the country, their geographic locations are usually outside mainstream markets, in mostly minority communities with high crime and poverty rates. Like all small businesses, they are particularly vulnerable to business cycles, with a higher than average failure rate.

The visibility and the "foreignness" of Asian merchants in the inner cities make them easy targets for resentment. Edna Bonacich, a sociologist at the University of California at Riverside, points out that merchants of any race, by definition, make their livings by making a profit from their customers. Since many of these merchants live elsewhere, she argues, they also tend to reinvest their profits elsewhere. And since many of these Asian-owned businesses employ family members, they offer relatively few jobs to the community.

Bonacich argues that the Asian merchants act as "minority middlemen," and are themselves exploited by the corporations whose goods they sell. It isn't profitable for large chain supermarkets or department stores to sell in inner-city neighborhoods, so Asian immigrants fill the void. Their willingness to face the personal and financial risks involved in operating a business in high-crime areas allows large corporations a bigger market for their goods.

In recent years, black leaders in Harlem, Bedford-Stuyvesant, and elsewhere have led boycotts and protests against Asian merchants in their communities. This anger is misdirected. Asian immigrants buy stores in poor neighborhoods not to take advantage of residents, but because they can't afford the higher rents in more affluent neighborhoods.

Who's the Enemy?

Many Asian Americans, especially those whose grandparents or great-grandparents came to this country in the late nineteenth or early twentieth century, regard the glowing praise heaped upon the new "model minority" with some skepticism and irony. They may be the new darlings of the media, but for most of the earlier part of this century, Asian Americans were despised, feared, and legally excluded from many rights other Americans—black and white—took for granted.

In 1870, foreign-born Asians were singled out as the only racial group not eligible for U.S. citizenship. In 1882, the Chinese Exclusion Act virtually barred Chinese from immigrating to the United States. Additional laws passed in the early 1900s extended the ban to Japanese, Koreans, and Filipinos. In many states, Asian Americans could not legally own land or marry whites until after World War II.

In 1965, the U.S. government removed the last vestiges of anti-Asian discrimination from its immigration laws. Today, Asian Americans struggle more with stereotypes and ignorance than with legal discrimination. Confusion between Asian countries and people of Asian ancestry living in this country can lead to anger and sometimes violence from people frustrated over the outcome of the Vietnam war, the loss of U.S. jobs to Japanese firms, the increasing Japanese ownership of U.S. assets, or even the U.S. trade deficit with Japan.

This confusion cost 110,000 Japanese-Americans their homes, jobs, and freedom during World War II, when the war against Japan spilled over into a war against Japanese-American citizens. In 1982, the same confusion cost Vincent Chin, a Chinese-American man from Detroit, his life when he was beaten to death with a baseball bat by two men reportedly angered by the Japanese success in automobile markets.

Such incidents share roots in economic frustration. Given the current structure of the U.S. and world economies, there really aren't enough jobs, housing, and resources for everyone, especially in poor neighborhoods. In the short run, it is easier for politicians to take sledgehammers to Japanese-built consumer goods than it is to improve the U.S. position in the world economy. It is easier for conservative economists or sociologists to compare blacks unfavorably to Asian Americans than it is to look at ways in which both face discrimination in U.S. labor markets. But it is important that progressives and organizers in minority and working-class communities resist these same quick-fix solutions.

A Realistic Assessment

Less Japan-bashing and more frequent acknowledgement of existing discrimination are a necessary first step to a more realistic assessment of the difficult and sometimes tenuous position of new immigrants and non-white Americans. The portrayal of Asian Americans as a super-minority not only dehumanizes Asian Americans, but creates unreasonable expectations (much as the super-mom image does). And setting up one minority group against others inevitably creates inter-racial tensions, and sometimes violence. To the extent that blacks and Asians are squabbling over who gets to own ghetto grocery stores, neither is asking why conventional banks aren't lending to either one of them.

"Those very people who would disavow their racism would . . . repudiate American Indian existence."

Racism Is a Serious Problem for American Indians

Carol Hampton

American Indians, also called native Americans, are descendants of the people who inhabited North America before the arrival of the Europeans. Approximately two million American Indians live in the U.S. today. Many face severe problems of poverty, unemployment, and alcoholism. In the following viewpoint, Carol Hampton argues the problems American Indians face are rooted in white racism. Whites have tried to systematically destroy the culture and identity of American Indians, she writes. Hampton works for the Native American Ministry of the Episcopal Church, and is a member of the Caddo Indian Nation.

As you read, consider the following questions:

1. What examples of racism toward American Indians does Hampton cite?
2. What significance does the author attach to Christopher Columbus's arrival in 1492?
3. Why does Hampton have hope for the future of American Indians?

From "A Heritage Denied," by Carol Hampton, *Sojourners*, January 1991. Reprinted with permission from *Sojourners*, PO Box 29272, Washington, DC 20017.

Almost 500 years ago Europeans came to our land, came to stay. Others had come before them to fish or for some other reason, incidentally bringing diseases to coastal peoples, wiping out whole communities along the Atlantic shore. But they had not stayed.

With the arrival of Columbus, history took another course. His appearance in our land set in motion a chain of events which led to destruction of native nations, usurpations of native land and its gifts, and slavery.

We helped those early explorers; we led them. We aided early conquerors, hoping they would rid us of our enemies. Always willing to learn, we listened to early missionaries . . . after they finally decided that we had souls.

We thought those early Europeans were like us. But we learned that similarities were shallow and often merely physical. We only dimly understood their purpose—and that understanding came too late. We thought they were like us. The newcomers' greed—their need to plunder the Earth and steal its riches; to grasp all the gifts of the Western Hemisphere and take them back to sustain their own world; and to take native land for their own purposes—made them very different from those who greeted and welcomed them to their homeland.

As we little understood Europeans 500 years ago, today we still little understand European descendants who rationalize and justify actions of their ancestors by denying our very existence. Almost every year more scholars of European heritage write learned books postulating a smaller and smaller population of the Western Hemisphere prior to European arrival. Those who live their lives outside of academe cherish their secular saint—Christopher Columbus—because he "discovered America." It seems both groups yearn for an America existing from time immemorial, pristine and unpeopled, awaiting European "discovery."

Defining Racism

Many of our closest "friends" ask us what harm such a yearning could cause. What hurt could come from innocent celebrations of Columbus Day? Indeed, what can such innocent thinking, feeling, and yearning mean to descendants of those hospitable people who shared their gifts from the Creator with newcomers? What does negation of our lives mean to us? Can this possibly be a form of racism? What is racism?

Some years ago, the National Council of Churches defined prejudice and racism this way:

> Prejudice is a personal attitude towards other people based on a categorical judgement about their physical characteristics, such as race or ethnic origin. . . . Racism is racial prejudice plus power. Racism is the intentional or unintentional use of power to

isolate, separate, and exploit others. This use of power is based on a belief in superior racial origin, identity, or supposed racial characteristics. Racism confers certain privileges on and defends the dominant group, which in turn sustains and perpetuates racism. . . . Institutional racism is one of the ways organizations and structures serve to preserve injustice.

"I am not a racist! There are no blacks in my community—and only a few in the whole state!" This is a common comment heard in places such as South Dakota that have a large American Indian population. Such comments reflect a part of the difficulty in achieving racial justice for American Indians: Is racism only directed against African Americans? Is racism only a white-over-black issue?

Those very people who would disavow their racism would obstruct American Indian access to sacred sites, trivialize tribal traditions and cultures, interfere with tribal and intertribal religious practices, denounce tribal governments, assault American Indians in their homes and walking down urban streets, and, at the same time, repudiate American Indian existence. Such actions "isolate, separate, and exploit" American Indians.

This is racism, although the form it takes against American Indians may often appear different from that against African Americans. What forms, then, does racism against American Indians take?

Personal Experience

I cannot speak for all Indians. That would be presumptuous. As D'Arcy McKnickle wrote, "No Indian individual, even within his own family, speaks for another individual. No tribe presumes to speak for another tribe. To act otherwise is to act discourteously if not indecently."

I am a Caddo—and I am a woman. Together they make me who I am, and I can only speak out of that identity and a matriarchal heritage. That heritage allows me to offer you glimpses of racism against Indians.

In addition, my job is one of "listening" to other American Indians and Alaska Natives. My work takes me to all the Episcopal Church's missions and ministries with American Indians and Alaska Natives to learn from them what concerns them. It allows me to draw on experiences of others.

First, a personal experience: When I was in the 7th grade at a public school in Oklahoma City, I took a class in Oklahoma history—a class mandated by the state legislature for every public school student to complete. I was a good student and enjoyed school, and I looked forward to learning more about Oklahoma history.

Now you must understand that I came to the study of Oklahoma history with some knowledge. Both of my grandmothers had told me many stories about the past. Sometimes I was privileged to sit with them and listen to them exchange stories—each from her own side of the frontier, for one of my grandmothers was Caddo and the other was Irish and German. So, I knew something of the history of that place now called Oklahoma.

The first day or so my Oklahoma history teacher told us that Indians were a part of the history of Oklahoma, and I really got interested then. Of course, I knew that Indians were a part of the history of Oklahoma. My Caddo grandmother had told me many stories and she and all the other elders were living proof.

The teacher then told the class that there were five tribes in Oklahoma's history. That puzzled me because, besides Caddos, I knew Wichitas, Delawares, Kiowas, Cheyennes, Comanches, Apaches, and Arapahoes. But I was a good child and eager to learn so I listened to her identify the five tribes. They were the "Five Civilized Tribes"—Cherokee, Choctaw, Chickasaw, Creek, and Seminole. Four "C"s and an "S" but not Caddo, not Comanche, not Cheyenne, nor any of the other tribes I knew. I learned something about educational institutions and the world that afternoon, but I did not learn historical truth.

Relearning History

Later I learned that my grandmother was more nearly right than my state-certified 7th grade teacher. There were indeed Indians in the history of what became the state of Oklahoma—but not just the so-called Five Civilized Tribes.

Sixty-seven tribes became a part of the history of Oklahoma when the government forced most of them to Indian Territory during the 19th-century period of history known as "Indian Removal." Caddos, Wichitas, Osages, and occasionally Kiowas and Comanches had lived or hunted in the area which became the state of Oklahoma long before the arrival of those walking the "trails of tears."

That long-ago afternoon a 12-year old Caddo girl learned that not only was she not civilized, but her tribe did not even exist. She began to learn the lesson that people in power view history only from their own perspective.

History is written by the conquerors, and they tell the story as they perceive it. I remember recognizing the truth spoken by a young woman serving with me on a committee for social justice in higher education—truth not for those of us sitting in the room, but for the world: "I know you. I know all about you because you have taught me all about you. I attended your schools from the time I was 6 years old. Your teachers taught me well."

I would carry her words further. I know your history, your values, your thoughts, and your beliefs. You taught me that my history mattered not at all unless it impinged on yours and then you taught my history only from your perspective. You taught me that

49

only your values were valid and that mine stood in the way of progress. You taught me that your beliefs were the only true way of believing and that mine were superstition. You taught me that only you think and I cannot.

You have sent your anthropologists to view my life and determine from my actions what my beliefs are. You taught me that your thoughts about the world and relationships between people and all of creation are classified as philosophy, but that I do not have a philosophy. You taught me that when you theorize about God that is theology, but that I do not have a theology. You taught me that I and my ancestors before me were savages, pagans, barriers to be removed from your path.

Racism and Genocide

The most virulent form of the disease of racism has been used against Native America. Like other oppressed people, we have known slavery, poverty, and political conquest. We have also known something else—genocide. The greatest mass extermination of any race, any culture, any people happened here. It happened to us.

Western colonialism may speak of an American history. Native People speak of an American holocaust. If racism is the mathematics of hate, then genocide is its ledger book. How many Native People died in the American holocaust? Thirty million? Forty million? Fifty million? How many were slaughtered? How many were sent to concentration camps? How many died of diseases they couldn't even name? The American holocaust is our experience. It is our testimony.

Steve Charleston, *Sojourner*, November 1987.

You continue to teach my children and grandchildren that they have inferior and inadequate minds. But you don't know me. You have never really wanted to know me. You never asked me what I thought, perhaps because you were too busy denying my existence as a human being. And that is another face of racism.

Recognizing Our Existence

One of the faces racism has presented to American Indians is a refusal to recognize our reality, and particularly our existence in the 20th century. Many people seem to think that American Indians disappeared at the end of the 19th century. Historians and government officials have told us that the frontier closed in 1890 and its symbol, the American Indian, vanished for all time. Certainly that was the stated goal both of the "pacification of the Plains," a euphemistic name for wars of extermination that followed the Civil War, and the "peace policy" that resulted from the failure of extermination policies.

Well-meaning people, many of them representing their churches, presented federal government agents with a policy of assimilation of American Indians. If they failed at annihilating us, they would obliterate us through making us in their image, albeit darker. As one of those good-hearted men said, "Kill the Indian and save the man."

If we were to survive, our tribal identities would cease to exist. These "friends" of ours looked at our reservations and saw what they referred to as poverty, filth, and pagan rituals. They failed to see the beauty, spirituality, generosity, and love of the land that marked our lives. Believing that they would "save" us, they took the land that sustained us.

That policy lasted for about 50 years before the federal government and our so-called "friends" abandoned it. In the meantime government policy had banned our political structures, forced our ceremonies to be held in hidden places, renamed us Christian names, and taken many of our reserved lands from us through a process of allotment. The stated purpose of the government was eradication of the Indian race.

Fighting for Racial Identity

A hundred years later in the 1980s, American Indians, surviving still, continue in their quest to protect their racial identity. Now that Indians have little land remaining to them, the focus of the battle has shifted to rights reserved through treaties which had ceded tribal land.

U.S. congressional representatives regularly introduce bills to abrogate treaties with American Indian tribes so that they can seize the remaining few acres and confiscate health and educational services and water, hunting, and fishing rights that Indians have retained in exchange for ceded land.

Tribes constantly battle against federal, state, and county governments and private associations to retain their tribal sovereignty, identity, and integrity. Historically, U.S. policy has vacillated between assimilation of American Indian people—with its consequent repudiation of tribal identity and authority—and extermination.

In the late 20th century, separation and recognition of tribal sovereignty has become the current government rhetoric, recognizing tribal identity and self-determination. Observers note, however, similarities between current policy and the policy of "termination," so-called because it terminated treaty rights and special government-to-government relationships between tribes and the federal government during the 1950s.

"Self-determination," "termination," or "assimilation" all would abrogate treaty rights by denying the existence of American Indian tribes or people. Whatever language federal policy makers use, all three policies result in cultural genocide. That, too, describes one of the faces of racism.

While Indians fight to retain tribal sovereignty and treaty rights, they also must confront attacks against their religions. Recently Indians have lost almost every religious freedom court case. Courts have denied Indians rights of access to sacred sites while protecting rights of hikers and skiers to trails, platforms, and lifts in areas of spiritual renewal rituals. The Northwest Indian Cemetery Protective Association lost the fight to prevent the construction of a logging road through Indian burial grounds, land obviously sacred to them.

The Anti-Indian Movement

The anti-Indian movement is rearing its head with an ugly vengeance: In Wisconsin and Minnesota, Indian resource rights are being challenged. In Arizona and New Mexico, Indian land rights are being challenged, with some people suggesting the relocation of tribes. Many white extremist groups are calling for a repeal of treaty obligations with Indian nations altogether.

Bob Hulteen, "Unsettled Scores of History," *Sojourners*, January 1991.

Indians, and perhaps all religious people, lost a significant case in a 1990 decision of the Supreme Court of the United States. Oregon state law had prohibited peyote use even in the religious ceremonies of members of the Native American Church, arguing that it had to protect its citizens from harmful drug use.

Ceremonial use of peyote by Indians predates the arrival of Columbus. A cactus growing primarily in the southwest and Mexico, it contains at least 15 interactive alkaloids, some of which may create visions when ingested. Native American Church members affirm that peyote enables believers to communicate with God through these visions and thus is essential to the practice of their religion.

Church members had hoped the courts would exempt them from Oregon state law as other states had done. The Supreme Court, however, held that Oregon state law in no way infringed upon constitutional rights of freedom of religion. Rather the interference with religious practices was considered simply an incidental effect of the law. Now, as for the past 500 years, American Indians await non-Indian respect for their customs, traditions, and religions. . . .

There is hope. A young man of American Indian heritage said to me: "Imagine growing up an American Indian halfbreed with the blood of Caddo, Choctaw, and Chickasaw tribes in you. . . .

"Imagine growing up . . . knowing that you belong to a culture long native to this land before the white man 'discovered' it. Imagine trying to assert your identity when the majority of society affirms that 'Indians are a dead race.' Imagine constantly dealing with people who try their hardest to convince you that you are not an Indian. Imagine."

Fighting for Identity

"America. 'Land of the free and the brave.' Land where all should be free. Land where American Indians have been and will be consistently assaulted by others, if not with guns, then with alcohol, money, technology, or simply words. With words of dismissal, the politicians wipe out the tribes' meaning and deface them of their honor. With words, they strip American Indians of race, culture, philosophy, reason. With words they cover the Indians with a gloss of alienation and meaninglessness, leaving them hollowed-out entities, repeating over and over the rules of a society that was never their own.

"This fight for identity is an enormous undertaking. To strive to keep one's heritage in the face of imminent annihilation nears impossibility, but it is not impossible."

Every time people in powerful positions tell us we no longer exist as a people, a race, we are reminded that we have far to go down the good road toward racial justice. When our "friends" regard us as curiosities; comment on our clothes instead of our words and thoughts; interpret our ceremonials instead of accepting our religious knowledge; realize something lacking in their own spirituality and take and trivialize ours; and when they try to assimilate us into their culture by destroying our identity, thereby depriving us of opportunities to offer our gifts to church and society, then we wonder if we will ever realize our dream of racial justice.

But as the young man indicated, we are survivors—500 years of attempted physical and cultural genocide has proven that.

"The upsurge in campus racism is the most disturbing development in university life across the nation during the past decade."

Racism in Higher Education Is a Serious Problem

Jon Wiener

Racist incidents in America's colleges and universities, such as hate mail, racist graffiti, and verbal abuse, have received growing public attention. In the following viewpoint, Jon Wiener argues that racism on college campuses is a growing national problem. Wiener describes several strategies and programs to counter racism, and argues that more colleges and universities should adopt such programs. Wiener is a contributing editor to *The Nation* and teaches history at the University of California at Irvine.

As you read, consider the following questions:

1. What role does Wiener assign Ronald Reagan and George Bush in connection with racism in colleges and universities?
2. What role do fraternities play in campus racism, according to the author?
3. What kinds of programs should colleges adopt to fight racism, according to Wiener?

Jon Wiener, "Racial Hatred on Campus," *The Nation*, February 27, 1989. Copyright © 1989, The Nation Company, Inc. Reprinted with permission.

The Boston Red Sox had just lost the World Series to the New York Mets. At the University of Massachusetts, Amherst, hundreds of students, many of them drunk, poured out of the dorms. White Red Sox fans began shoving Mets fans who were black; soon a white mob of 3,000 was chasing and beating anyone who was black. Ten students were injured. Joseph Andrade recalls thinking, "My God, my life is being threatened here—and it's because I'm black."

Campus Racism

The U-Mass explosion—on October 27, 1986—may be the most emblematic outbreak of student hatred of the 1980s. But it is by no means the only one. The upsurge in campus racism is the most disturbing development in university life across the nation during the past decade. More than anything, it reveals how white attitudes toward minorities have changed on campus during the Reagan years, even at institutions that historically have been bastions of liberalism.

At the University of Michigan, Ann Arbor, for example, the campus radio station broadcast a call from a student who "joked": "Why do blacks always have sex on their minds? Because all their pubic hair is on their head. . . ." At Dartmouth College, the *Dartmouth Review* attacked a black music professor, William Cole, describing him as "a cross between a welfare queen and a bathroom attendant." Then four *Review* staff members confronted Cole after a class and, in front of his students, apparently attempted to provoke him into a fight. Esi Eggleston, a black student who witnessed the confrontation, told PBS's *Frontline*: "That moment let me know that there are people in this world who hate you just because of your color. Not dislike you, or choose not to be friends with you, but hate you."

At the University of Wisconsin, Madison, a fraternity held a "slave auction" as part of a pledge party. At U.C.L.A. [University of California at Los Angeles] white and Chicano students fought on campus during a student election. At Purdue, a black academic counselor found "Death Nigger" scratched on her office door. A headline in [an] issue of *The Montclarion*, the student newspaper at Montclair State College in New Jersey, read, "Attention focused on racial tension at M.S.C."

Why is all this happening now? Shelby Steele, a black associate professor of English at San Jose State University, tends to blame the victim. In the February 1989 *Harper's*, he argues that the problem on campus is not white racism but rather black "feelings of inferiority," which give rise to "an unconscious need to exaggerate the level of racism on campus—to make it a matter of the system, not just a handful of students." Instead of "demonstrating for a black 'theme house,'" Steele writes, black students "might be better off spending their time reading and studying."

Duchesne Paul Drew, a Columbia University junior who is black, offers a different explanation: "Reagan was president during the formative years of today's students." When Reagan was elected in 1980, 1989's freshman class was 10 years old. Their political consciousness was formed while the White House used potent code words and attacked social programs to legitimize a subtle racism. Columbia students report that racist remarks are seldom made to blacks but frequently are heard in conversations among whites. The litany is that black people tend to be criminals, drug addicts and welfare cheats; that they don't work; and that black students aren't as smart as whites.

This, of course, is the image of blacks George Bush sought to project in his campaign to succeed Reagan. The Republicans' Willie Horton television spots suggesting that blacks are rapists and murderers played not just in living rooms but in dormitories and student centers for most of the fall semester. Undergraduate viewers may have been even more vulnerable to the Horton propaganda than was the rest of the TV audience, because most of them lacked the experience and knowledge required to challenge racist imagery—especially after eight years of Ronald Reagan.

The Legitimization of Racism

The Reagan administration gave its blessing to the *Dartmouth Review*, the best-known purveyor of campus racism and intolerance. The *Review* (which is not an official Dartmouth publication) boasts that several of its former staff members have gone on to prestigious jobs in Reagan's Washington: One became a speechwriter for President Reagan, another for Vice President Bush. *Review* columnist and president Keeney Jones penned a notorious racist parody, "Dis Sho Ain't No Jive Bro," that purported to quote a black student at Dartmouth: "Dese boys be sayin' that we be comin' here to Dartmut an' not takin' the classics. You know, Homa. . . ." Jones was subsequently hired as a speechwriter for Secretary of Education William Bennett. The editor who published that column, Dinesh D'Souza, went on to a career as a policy analyst in the Reagan White House.

This legitimization of racism has been accompanied by other developments. Admission to top colleges, including some public universities like the University of California, Berkeley, and U.C.L.A., has become fiercely competitive: Berkeley had 21,200 applications to its 1987 freshman class, and enrolled 3,700—14 percent. Many students with straight A averages in high school were denied admission. At the same time, some college campuses are beginning to reflect the diversity of the American population: Berkeley's incoming class in 1987 was 12 percent black, 17 percent Latino, 26 percent Asian and only 40 percent white.

This new alignment comes as a shock to many white students,

especially those who grew up in all-white, middle-class suburbs. Some of them respond to campus racial diversity by proclaiming that all blacks and Latinos have been admitted under affirmative action programs and thus are taking places away from "more qualified" whites. That argument is often turned around, however, as a justification for hostility toward Asians, who are criticized for being supercompetitive.

University administrators at many campuses prefer to ignore racial incidents or keep them out of the news, but antiracist student organizations have successfully focused attention on the problem. After the U-Mass incident following the World Series, campus officials at first denied that race had played any part in what the campus police termed a brawl among sports fans. That made it hard for black students to follow Shelby Steele's advice and spend their time "reading and studying." Not until students demonstrated did U-Mass Chancellor Joseph Duffey admit that his campus had a racial problem. At Penn State, eighty-nine students were arrested at a campus sit-in in April 1988. At U-Mass, 200 students held a five-day sit-in; at Wisconsin in November 1987, 100 protesters marched outside the Phi Gamma Delta ("Fiji") fraternity house, where a racist incident had occurred, chanting, "Hey, Fijis, you can't hide, drop the sheets and come outside!" As a result of dozens of scenes like these, the student campaign against racism has provided the focus for campus politics at many colleges and universities.

Antiracist Strategies

Campus antiracist activists have put forward a variety of strategies. One of these identifies the problem as ignorance among white kids, many of whom grew up in isolated lily-white suburbs and need to learn about the diversity of American culture. Advocates of this approach insist that all students should take a course in ethnic studies or cultural diversity, often taught by newly hired minority faculty members. The Universities of Indiana and Minnesota each require two courses in U.S. cultural pluralism; the University of Wisconsin, Madison, has just established a one-course ethnic studies requirement and the University of California, Berkeley, is currently debating a similar measure.

Minority student organizations across the country enthusiastically support an ethnic studies requirement for graduation. Charles Holley, co-president of the Black Student Union of the Madison campus, argues that the courses teach "what minorities are all about, where we came from, what we feel." The student government officers at Berkeley, in a joint statement, declared that "students commonly graduate without reading the work of a minority author, studying under a minority professor, or having learned the vital histories of people of color. In a state that will soon have a non-white majority, such an undergraduate experience dangerously perpetuates false stereotypes."

Another strategy focuses on the empowerment of targets of violence. Much racial harassment typically goes unreported, even though it makes life miserable for minority students. When these students have their own campus centers and organizations, they don't have to suffer in isolation; they can—and increasingly do—rally their forces against their antagonists. In the aftermath of racial flareups minority students have frequently demanded university support for such centers. At U-Mass, participants in a 1988 sit-in called on school administrators to renovate New Africa House as a cultural center for minority students.

Racism on Campus

Racism and bigotry are back on campus with a vengeance. We can ask any of those black students who were chased and beaten at the University of Massachusetts at Amherst, who were taunted with defamatory posters at Penn State and Stanford, who were subjected to racist jokes on the University of Michigan radio station, or who were presented with a "mock slave auction" at the University of Wisconsin. Or we can ask the Jewish students who have had swastikas painted on their dormitory doors on campuses across the country, from Harvard to Occidental. Or ask the Latino students at UCLA about their reaction to the film "Animal Attraction," which was produced by a UCLA graduate student with the support of many of his faculty members and portrayed Mexican Americans in a negative light.

John Brooks Slaughter, *Los Angeles Times*, October 7, 1989.

A third strategy strives to reduce campus violence in general as a way of thwarting racial violence. Jan Sherrill, director of the Center for Study and Prevention of Campus Violence at Towson State University, in Maryland, argues that American culture condones violent means of resolving disputes as a legitimate form of male self-expression. Reagan's oft-proclaimed "values" glorified the macho response to international problems. Terrorism at a disco in Berlin? Send the Air Force to Tripoli to bomb Qadaffi. Men longed to join the president in saying, "Go ahead, make my day." A media culture of exploding cars, free-swinging cops and bone-crunching sports is reinforced by campus norms that say it's O.K. for young men to get drunk, wreck their dorm rooms and slug it out with one another. A program at Towson State's Richmond Hall has focused on reducing property damage in the dorm and violence of all kinds between students by setting strict rules and giving residents responsibility for enforcing them. As a result, there have been no racist incidents or attacks on gays or women in the dorm, which has become "a violence-free zone," according to Sherrill. It's not yet clear whether incidents elsewhere on campus will decline.

On many campuses, racism is endemic to the fraternity subculture. The house that held the slave auction at Madison, Zeta Beta Tau (Z.B.T.), is predominantly Jewish and had itself been a target of an attack: Members of Fiji crashed a Z.B.T. party, beat three persons and taunted them with anti-Semitic slurs. In another racist incident involving fraternities on campus, a Kappa Sigma party in 1986 had a "Harlem Room," with white students in blackface, watermelon punch, graffiti on the walls and garbage on the floor.

Racism among fraternities is fostered by the fact that most are completely segregated, and it is exacerbated by rituals of heavy drinking on party weekends. The Chancellor at Madison, Donna Shalala, established a Commission on the Future of Fraternities and Sororities, which is to recommend ways to reduce their racist and sexist behavior. The possibilities, Shalala said, range from attacking "substance abuse" as a cause of "misconduct" to elimination of the Greek system altogether.

Outlawing Offensive Speech

A more problematic strategy for reducing campus racism focuses on criminalizing racist speech, which constitutes the most prevalent form of harassment. At the University of Michigan, Ann Arbor, interim president Robben Fleming implemented a new code in 1988 that allows university administrators to place on probation, suspend or expel students engaged in "discriminatory" behavior, including racist speech. Under the code, the student who told the racist "jokes" over the radio would be put on probation; if he made "other blatantly racist remarks" while on probation he could be suspended or expelled. Most of the university regents support the code, *The Michigan Daily* reports, as do several deans and professors. But the student representatives of the University Council have denounced the proposal as a "terrible misuse of power," and the United Coalition Against Racism, a student group that has demanded university action against racial abuse, has voiced a similar sentiment.

At Madison, Z.B.T. was cleared by the student government disciplinary committee of all charges of violating university rules against racial discrimination. Committee chair Rana Mookherjee said of the fraternity's slave auction, "There is no rule you can write to eradicate bad taste and insensitivity." Many minority students expressed outrage at the decision; one was in tears. A spokesman for the Madison campus's Minority Coalition, Peter Chen, said, "By hiding behind the issue of free speech, the administration is making this campus safe for racism."

The protection of offensive speech will always cause frustration, but it nonetheless provides an important lesson in the meaning of the First Amendment. Campus leaders need not limit themselves to defending the First Amendment just because of constitutional barriers to criminalizing offensive speech, however. On the contrary, they have an obligation to speak out, forcefully and frequently, explaining why racist speech is objectionable. Chancellor Shalala did that: Although fraternity members have a First Amendment right to objectionable speech, she said, "using slavery as a basis for humor should be offensive to every American."

The Madison Plan

Donna Shalala began her term as chancellor in February 1988 by announcing the "Madison plan." It calls for the University of Wisconsin to double the number of minority undergraduates over the next five years; create 150 financial aid packages for low-income students; raise $4 million in private money to increase the scholarship endowment and another $4 million to endow twenty-five new minority graduate and professional fellowships; hire seventy new minority faculty members over the next three years, more than doubling the current number; and require ethnic studies courses in each college. In addition, the university will hire or promote 125 minority academic staff members over the next three years. Shalala has budgeted $4.7 million to implement this program over the next three years, part of which must come from new appropriations, which the Wisconsin legislature is considering.

Education Reflects Society

Education reflects a society where money and power dictate who gets taught, what gets taught, what kind of an environment one is taught in, and how an individual is taught. Value judgments about individuals play as great a role in education, unfortunately, as genuine ability. And it is blacks and other minorities who have suffered the most.

Anthony A. Parker, *Sojourners*, May 1990.

The Minority Coalition at Madison criticized the plan for failing to establish a strong racial harassment policy, an adequate multicultural center or antiracism workshops during student orientation. But the goals, the budget and the timetable make the Madison plan one of the most far-reaching attempts to overcome institutional racism undertaken by any major university. The University of Wisconsin's effort is important, among other reasons, because of the school's size: It has the fourth largest student body in the nation, numbering almost 44,000. It's especially heartening that Wisconsin is making such an extensive commitment at a time when people feel beaten down and defeated by eight years of losing battles against the Reagan White House.

Unfortunately, the promises made at Madison and at other progressive institutions to hire more black faculty run up against a major obstacle: the small pool of available black college teachers. These men and women are being intensely wooed, and Madison's recruitment successes will inevitably hurt the campaigns on other campuses. The shortage of black faculty is part of a larger problem—the declining number of blacks in higher education, from the undergraduate through the professorial ranks. Most talented black undergraduates opt for law or medicine or business over academia—and why not? The prospect of spending years as an isolated, underpaid, overworked assistant professor is not an inviting one.

Reflection of Society

The Madison plan addresses this problem in several ways: by pledging that the university will work with local high schools to improve their graduation rates; will in the future recruit twice as many minority students to its freshman class and provide them with financial support to help them stay through graduation; and will double the number of fellowships for graduate and professional schools, to encourage minority students to finish dissertations.

Defensive administrators at colleges and universities across the country argue that the recent spread of racism on campus shows only that the university is a part of American society, which itself seems to be increasingly racist and violent. That's true, but it shouldn't provide an excuse for educators who prefer to wait for the larger society to change. More universities need to make the kind of commitment demonstrated by Chancellor Shalala at the University of Wisconsin if they are going to overcome the racism that has stained the campus during the Age of Reagan.

"[Racial] incidents are now regularly exploited by political opportunists."

Racism in Higher Education Is Exaggerated

Edward Alexander

Edward Alexander is a professor of English at the University of Washington in Seattle. In the following viewpoint, Alexander denies that racism in higher education is a national crisis. He argues that racial incidents on college campuses are being exaggerated and exploited by minority groups in order to gain power and prestige. The author concludes that too much attention to race jeopardizes the university's mission of education.

As you read, consider the following questions:

1. Why does Alexander criticize racial-sensitivity classes?
2. What incidents does Alexander describe to support his argument that racism is exaggerated?
3. What role does Marxism play in the college racism controversy, according to Alexander?

Edward Alexander, "Race Fever." Reprinted from *Commentary*, November 1990, by permission; all rights reserved.

American universities are aflame with race fever. Official committees on "racism and cultural diversity," departmental commissioners of moral sanitation, and freelance vigilantes are in a state of high alert for signs (real or alleged) of "racism." Their Argus-eyes maintain unrelaxing surveillance of statistical charts documenting failure to meet racial quotas in hiring and enrollment, of verbal insults by "white" students against "people of color," and of classroom remarks by professors imprudent enough either to risk generalization about a group *or* to declare that generalizations about groups tell us nothing about individuals.

Incidents Are Exploited

Such diligence rarely goes unrewarded. Since many American campuses have "populations" larger than hundreds of American cities, it is hardly remarkable that incidents of behavior less than saintly, including racial harassment, should occur. What is remarkable is the way in which such incidents are now regularly exploited by political opportunists, people Joseph Epstein has labeled "the intellectual equivalent of ambulance-chasers." A few instances should suffice to illustrate the general pattern.

At Southern Methodist University (SMU) in Dallas in 1990, a freshman was "reported to university officials" for singing "We Shall Overcome" in a "sarcastic manner" during a late-night dormitory discussion. The campus was still vibrating from this shocking violation of the school's "racial-harassment rules" when it learned of a still more flagrant one, in which a white graduate student "was reported for calling a Hispanic classmate a Mexican in a derogatory manner after an intramural football game." Although the student whom the *New York Times* dubbed "the victim" of the slur received an immediate apology from the culprit, apology was also demanded, and received, by the university's judicial board and then by its "intercultural affairs office." But since Big Brother (very much like his omnipresent Big Sister, ever watchful for sexism) is not easily placated, this triune apology had to be supplemented by penance in the form of thirty hours of community service to minority organizations in Dallas.

In 1986 SMU had established a course called "Black and White." Its purpose was, as one satisfied student enrolled in it declared, to teach that "whites must be sensitive to the African-American community rather than the other way around." Sensitivity traffic is heavy, but it flows in only one direction. Any suggestion that members of a formerly despised and mistreated group may be capable of wrongdoing is punished with utmost severity. "The spirit of improvement," wrote John Stuart Mill in a famous understatement, "is not always a spirit of liberty."

There is only one sense in which these courses in sensitivity training conform to old-fashioned ideas about liberal education:

their main purpose seems to be to ventilate the moral sensibilities or, if I may change my metaphor, to flex the moral muscles in an imaginary gymnasium rather than to put one in touch with the truth about the actual world. At Emory University in Atlanta, a black student gained national attention when she reported several incidents of racial harassment, including the ransacking of her dormitory room, the scrawling of racial slurs on its walls, and the receipt of death threats in the mail. These threats, so Sabrina Collins alleged, caused her to curl into a fetal ball and to lose the power of speech. But, local prosecutors reviewing the case concluded that it was all a hoax, and that the only Emory student who participated in the harassment of Sabrina Collins was Sabrina Collins herself. Her imagination, it seems, had been fueled by an eagerness to impede an inquiry into suspicions that she had cheated in a chemistry class. This fiasco, however, did nothing to dampen the zeal of those who had been lashing the university authorities for their failure to combat the racism that had victimized Collins. "It doesn't matter . . . whether she did it or not," said the president of the Atlanta chapter of the NAACP [National Association for the Advancement of Colored People], "because of all the pressure these black students are under at these predominantly white schools. If this will highlight it, if it will bring it to the attention of the public, I have no problem with that." No problem, that is, with falsehood, with fraud, or with the doctrine that members of an oppressed group are incapable of doing wrong.

Islands of Repression

Innocents who wander into these modern Salems will quickly discover the profound truth of Abigail M. Thernstrom's description of the universities and colleges as "islands of repression in a sea of freedom." In the 1970 revised edition of *Beyond the Melting Pot*, a study of race and ethnicity in New York City, Daniel P. Moynihan and Nathan Glazer wrote that "race has exploded to swallow up all other distinctions, or so it would appear at the moment." Yet even Senator Moynihan must have been surprised by the incendiary effect of his saying to the students of Vassar College, in a February 1990 lecture, that "the United States of America provides a model of a reasonably successful multiethnic society." The blundering ear of the Vassar thought police heard Moynihan say that the U.S. was "a model of ethnic cooperation," and construed this alleged remark to be racist. For good measure they alleged (and Moynihan denied) that he had told a Dutchess County (N.Y.) official who is from Jamaica to go back to that country if he didn't like the U.S.

As is often the case in such incidents, what actually happened was far less important than the keen desire of the race-obsessed witchhunters to exploit what was *alleged* to have happened. Leaders of the Black Student Union at Vassar demanded an apology from the college administration for the remarks they themselves had foisted on Moynihan and his removal from the Eleanor Roosevelt professorship, under which rubric he had given his lecture. As the handbook of student activism clearly states that bullying, however satisfying to the militant spirit, must never be its own reward, small wonder that demands soon were also made for the establishment of a task force on racism, for the creation of a black student center, for the opening of an intercultural center, and for bountiful provision of the other desiderata of progressive race-thinking. Students who declined to join the demonstration, even if they supported its demands, were denounced by its leaders as—surprise!—racists too. One of these leaders announced, with touching candor, that he and his fellow tribunes had for some time been seeking a way to bend the college administration to their will: "This was the perfect catalyst."

Race Fever

To witness an outbreak of race fever at first hand is to have an experience, not soon forgotten, of just how lethal is the mixture of aspirants to victim status with pretenders to guilt, who compound for sins they are inclined to by damning those they have no mind to.

The University of Washington in Seattle, with 34,000 students and over 2,500 faculty, is one of the largest on the West Coast. It has had considerable experience of spectacular confrontations over the issue of race. In March 1970 the Black Student Union and the Seattle Liberation Front (led by the future editor of *Tikkun*, Michael Lerner, and described by then Washington State attorney general—now U.S. senator—Slade Gorton as an organization "totally indistinguishable from fascism and Nazism") accused the university of complicity in racism because it refused to cancel an athletic competition with Brigham Young University, a Mormon school. A mob composed of members of these two organizations and their followers invaded six university buildings, brutally beating over a dozen instructors and students who disobeyed the order to strike. Nowadays far greater results can be achieved with less arduous methods. . . .

On May 3, 1989, William P. Gerberding, president of the university, stepped on a mine while addressing an awards dinner for minority students. He made a very small "ethnic" joke while conferring the Hispanic American Recognition Award on a student in civil engineering. Perhaps, jested Gerberding, the student had acquired his interest in the highway system while "driving down the highway at 70 mph in the middle of the night to keep ahead of immigration authorities."

The honoree "didn't know if I should take it as a joke or not." But he soon received guidance from higher authority. The organization of Chicano students (Movimiento Estudiantil Chicano

65

de Aztlan, or MECHA), when it learned of the joke, informed the student that he certainly *ought* to have been offended. Ernesto Sandoval, the "Commissioner" of MECHA, summoning the indignation worthy of his title, complained that the university "had done nothing about this" and declared that an offense of such enormity could not be committed with impunity. He also stoked the fire of his wrath by remembering, now, that a year earlier Gerberding had publicly urged university students to work hard to keep pace with the Japanese—an obviously racist use of "the yellow peril."

Too Much Sensitivity

I heard a black student say that he preferred to sit at the "black table" in the dining hall because he found whites "boring." "They don't want to contend with me on anything," he said. But who can blame them? What can one expect from a group of people who have been told incessantly that they are racists, and that they must be highly circumspect in their relations with blacks lest their racism reveal itself in the form of an offensive word or two? Moreover, to the extent that the charge of "racism" is repeatedly and gratuitously tossed about . . . there is danger that the evil of genuine racism will become trivialized and hence will be ignored.

Robert L. Detlefsen, *The New Republic*, April 10, 1989.

Within a few hours, Sandoval had received a letter of apology from President Gerberding. But the letter was deemed "unsatisfactory" because it was insufficiently contrite and self-abasing. Gerberding said he would "try again." But again he failed: apology number two, though it amplified number one by heaping praise on the whole Hispanic population, still failed to utter the magical term "racism." Besides, it was not a *public* apology: "If he offended our community in public," said the commissioner, "then he can apologize to us in public."

A Public Apology

Ever willing to try harder, Gerberding agreed to apologize, now for the third time, at a public forum to be held in the aptly named Red Square in the center of the campus. He also consented to participate in a seminar especially designed for administrators found to be inadequately endowed with "ethnic and racial sensitivity." But if Gerberding thought that confessing to racism and agreeing to reeducation had opened the way to absolution, he was soon to be disillusioned. The 200 students (out of 34,000) who assembled to pass judgment on him were in no mood to be merciful.

Gerberding recited nearly all the banalities his tormentors

wanted to hear. He announced that the university's true purpose is "the celebration of diversity," which he defined (just as his audience does) entirely in racial terms: "Diversity includes all of you folks out in front of me, white, black, all in-betweens." Like them, he took it as self-evident truth that mind is a function of physiology, that the apparent fruits of intellect actually originate in genetics, and that all people belonging to a particular ethnic group either are, or should be, of one mind and will. Therefore, if you want intellectual diversity, you need a racial recipe that mixes "white, black, [and] all in-betweens" in exact proportion to their presence in the general population.

Meanwhile, the assembled embodiments and celebrants of diversity were alternately heckling and chanting, in metronomically monotonous unison, the inspiring verses: "Hey, hey! Ho, ho! Racism has got to go!" Their collective tooth-baring, their will to offend, to bully, to humiliate, comported oddly with the image of victim they so passionately claimed for themselves. Furthermore, however pleased the demonstrators might have been by Gerberding's instinctive compliance with the psychology of abdication, they wanted something tangible. As one smarmy, self-righteous lout at the front of the mob put it: "Since you can publicly admit your insensitivities and shortcomings toward people of color and racial issues, we expect your support of the Ethnic Studies Requirement as a sign of your new awareness and of our needs." Campus bullies, like Middle Eastern terrorists, hold to the conviction that no bad deed of theirs should go unrewarded.

For a year, a faculty-student Task Force on Ethnicity had been assessing a proposal that would compel every student at the University of Washington to devote one-quarter of the Humanities and Social Science credits required for a bachelor's degree to Ethnic Studies courses. The ideal (if not the actual) purpose of such courses would be to "sensitize" the American majority toward this country's minority groups and to build a curricular bulwark against the omnipresent evil of racism. But since Gerberding did not have the authority to force the hand of the committee, the anti-racism struggle now shifted to the final deliberations of the group, which the demonstrators were urged to attend (and to influence).

Are Jews a Minority?

Whether it was by accident or by the intervention of invisible powers, I entered the spectators' gallery of the crucial meeting just as the committee, which had already been in session for an hour, began to consider the Jewish question. Other "white" groups, such as Italian and Irish Americans, had, I learned, been denied most-favored-minority status at an earlier stage of the committee's deliberations. Now it was the turn of the Jews to be mea-

67

sured. Are the Jews a minority in this country? Is anti-Semitism a form of racism? Hardly abstruse questions, one might suppose; and yet they aroused intense debate. The students, representing African Americans, Native Americans, Asian Americans, and Chicano/Latino Americans—otherwise known as the "major" minorities—unanimously opposed the inclusion of Jews and anti-Semitism in the Ethnic Studies curriculum. They seemed genuinely bemused by the idea that people not in their political party should have the temerity to invade their turf and poach on the (very considerable) spoils of their anticipated victory. Their recommended solution—eventually approved by the committee—was to substitute the term "people of color" for the term "minorities" wherever it appeared in committee documents.

Students Are Tolerant

Surveys have shown that today's generation of young people has remarkably tolerant views, including widespread acceptance of interracial dating. Even though many whites may not have lived or studied with blacks, Hispanics, or other minorities in the past, they seem generally committed to equal rights and open to building friendships and associations with people whom they know have been wronged through history.

Dinesh D'Souza, *The American Scholar*, Winter 1991.

The prize for semantic juggling was won not by the students, however, but by the two professorial representatives of the Ethnic Studies program itself, both of whom have also presided over Afro-American Studies. Professor Joseph Scott could not assent to the inclusion of Jews and anti-Semitism in the proposed scheme of courses unless other "Semitic" peoples, most particularly the Palestinian Arabs, were also included. Professor Johnella Butler also opposed inclusion of Jews because Jewish persons are not necessarily of "Semitic descent" and "anti-Semitism is not institutionalized in the country."

These remarks brought a raising of the collective eyebrow and even some tittering. For it appeared that of the 37,000 who teach and learn at the University of Washington, the only ones ignorant of the fact that anti-Semites hate Jews and not "Semites" were the professors of Ethnic Studies, the officially designated historians and exorcists of racism. Some uncharitable observers, to be sure, suspected that if you touched the delicate, exotic fruit of this professorial ignorance, it would quickly lose its bloom and turn out to be not so much ignorance of the history as guilt of the sin of racism. Could the spiteful introduction of Palestinian Arabs into a discussion of American minorities be innocent? Could the assertion by a grown-up and heavily degreed woman that institutional anti-Semitism (as if that were the only kind) is absent from this country be indicative less perhaps of a susceptibility to balderdash than of a desire to make up for that absence? The more closely one observes the actions and the moral temper of the leaders of the campus campaign against racism all across this country, the more urgently does the old adage "Physician, heal thyself" rise to one's lips.

Racism and Marxism

It is hardly a secret that a majority of the more assiduous practitioners of progressive race-thinking at the universities define themselves as Marxists. At first glance this might seem surprising, because Marxism traditionally sought to explain everything by the material motives of class and property, not biology. But Marxism, as Jacques Barzun and Gertrude Himmelfarb have pointed out, is itself essentially racist in form and effect, depending as it does on a depiction of the bourgeois as, in Barzun's words, "not a human being with individual traits, but a social abstraction, a creature devoid of virtue or free will and without the right to live."

The collapse of the Marxist regimes of Central and Eastern Europe, the embarrassing fact that the first truly working-class revolution in history has been made (by Solidarity) against a *socialist* government, may have dulled the luster of economic determinism; but they have not extinguished the deep-seated modern desire to reduce human spirit and culture to matter. "Drive out nature with a fork," says [ancient Roman poet] Horace, "nevertheless she will continually return." With a little job retraining, yesterday's economic determinist becomes today's race (and "gender") determinist, seeking in physical origin and genes the key to mind, and excoriating colleagues who, in the already immortal words of Harvard's Derrick Bell, "look black and think white."

It is a sorry irony that "celebration of diversity" has become the slogan of self-proclaimed reformers of an institution called the university, a word whose origin and ideal meaning suggest that many parts have been "turned into one"—*universum*. If, as we still have good reason to believe, humanity is an infinitely varied repetition, then people of many groups, of diverse backgrounds, of a thousand dispositions can, if they practice tolerance and self-restraint, communicate with each other through the vehicle of mind. The university, in its ideal character, is predicated on the assumption that values which originate in the self or the group or the nation can be extradited and made available to those who share with the originators nothing except the human status. It aspires to Matthew Arnold's ideal of disinterestedness, the free play of the mind, unhampered by sect or party, over "the best

69

that has been thought and said in the world."

That our universities have failed to achieve the perfection of this nobly inclusive ideal, no one should deny. But will turning it on its head in favor of the superstition that members of particular groups have one mind and live solely for a political purpose really extend cultural choice and individual rights? Do we really want our universities to become training schools for prigs and Pecksniffs who pride themselves on the ability to spot racism at a distance of twenty miles, who choose their professorial "role models" according to race, and who scan their reading lists for proportional representation by race, "gender," and class, but who can no longer fathom the meaning and implication of Wordsworth's definition of the poet as "a man speaking to men"?

Identifying Racism

Part of the disagreement concerning the extent of racism in the United States comes from differing conceptions of racism. What one person may think of as reasonable or unobjectionable behavior may seem racist to another person. In this activity you will learn to recognize and evaluate types of racism.

Social scientist John E. Farley in his book *Majority-Minority Relations* broadly defines racism as "any attitude, belief, behavior, or institutional arrangement that tends to favor one race or ethnic group . . . over another." He goes on to distinguish between four kinds of racism:

1. *attitudinal racism*, or prejudice: people's attitudes and beliefs that favor one group over another. A general dislike of a certain racial or ethnic group is an example of attitudinal racism.

2. *ideological racism*: set beliefs and theories that directly state that some races are superior to others. An example is Adolf Hitler's theory of Aryan superiority.

3. *individual discrimination*: individual behaviors that lead to unequal treatment on the basis of race. Examples of this discrimination range from racially motivated violence to taxi drivers refusing to pick up minority customers.

4. *institutional racism*: racism which goes beyond individual thoughts and actions, in which social institutions such as family, church, school, and government create patterns of racial injustice and inequality, and reinforce racist ideas. Individuals involved in the institutions may be unaware that they are participating in racism. An example of institutional racism cited by Farley is the high cost of a college education in the U.S.; the result, if not the intent, of the high cost is to prevent a disproportionate number of minorities from obtaining a college degree and improving their social status.

71

Part I

In this exercise you will be asked to examine some quotations and scenarios and to determine whether they are racist, and if so, what kind of racism they represent.

The class should break into small groups. Each group should examine the following examples and determine what kind of racism, if any, is represented in each example. Beside each example place a **1** for attitudinal racism, **2** for ideological racism, **3** for individual discrimination, or **4** for institutional racism. The groups may use more than one number if appropriate, or use an **N** if they decide it is not an example of racism at all.

1. "The thought of having a black as president makes me uncomfortable."

2. In Louisiana in 1940 only 866 blacks were registered to vote. This was due in part to literacy tests in which people were required to read or copy from a printed page. Whites were often exempted from these tests. In 1940 over 50,000 white illiterates in Louisiana were registered to vote.

3. "I don't dislike blacks or Hispanics, but I'd prefer it if they didn't move next door."

4. "It has been scientifically proven that whites are the most intelligent race."

5. A study by the National Sentencing Project shows that 23 percent of black men in their twenties are in prison, on probation, or on parole. The comparable percentage for white men is 6.2 percent.

6. Mrs. Jones says she'll vote for candidate X for mayor because he is white.

7. Mrs. Arnold says she'll vote for candidate Y for mayor because he is black.

8. The suburb of Hilldale has two schools. One is the public school, which has minority students bused in from other parts of the city. The racially mixed school has a 35 percent dropout rate, and less than half of its graduates go on to college. Hilldale's other school is a private school with mostly white students. Its enrollment grew substantially after the public school increased its minority student population. The private school's yearly tuition is ten thousand dollars. It has a 5 percent dropout rate and 90 percent of its graduates go on to college.

9. Mr. Lewis flies a confederate flag in his yard on Martin Luther King Jr. Day.

10. Hispanic women are twice as likely as non-Hispanic women to be employed in service occupations.

11. A U.S. government study found that in forty cities, 90 percent of all potential home buyers were guided by real estate agents into separate black and white neighborhoods.

12. "I believe that whites must realize the U.S. is not an equal society; that they have a variety of advantages in life because of their skin color."

13. Elaine sees two black teenagers approaching her. She crosses to the other side of the street.

14. Mr. Hall, a black man, chooses to give a promotion to a black woman. When Charles, a white man, asks why he was not promoted, Mr. Hall says, "This was only fair after the past two hundred years of discrimination against us."

15. "The races should remain pure and unspoiled; interracial marriage should not be allowed."

Part II

Have the groups compare answers in a class discussion.

Part III

Have the class complete the sentence *Racism is*_____.

Periodical Bibliography

The following articles have been selected to supplement the diverse views presented in this chapter.

William B. Allen — "The New Racism Is the Old Power Grab," *Conservative Digest*, July/August 1989.

Birch Bayh — "Let's Tear Off Their Hoods," *Newsweek*, April 17, 1989.

Joanne Belknap — "Racism on Campus," *Vital Speeches of the Day*, March 15, 1991.

Howard G. Chua-Eoan — "Strangers in Paradise," *Time*, April 9, 1990.

Michael Eric Dyson — "The Two Racisms," *The Nation*, September 25, 1989.

John E. Jacob — "Racism and Race Relations," *Vital Speeches of the Day*, January 15, 1990.

William F. Jasper — "Fiercely Dependent," *The New American*, August 27, 1990.

Bernard D. Headley — "Crime, Justice, and Powerless Racial Groups," *Social Justice*, Winter 1989.

John Leo — "Our Hypersensitive Minorities," *U.S. News & World Report*, April 16, 1990.

Daniel Levitas — "A Resurgence of Bigoted Violence," *Christian Social Action*, November 1989. Available from, 100 Maryland Ave. NE, Washington, DC 20002.

Marcus Mabry — "Black and Blue, Class of '89," *Newsweek*, September 25, 1989.

Maria Mallory — "A Rust Belt Revival Tarnished by Racism," *Business Week*, July 24, 1989.

Mark Mathabane, interviewed by Bruce W. Nelan — "Taking the Measure of American Racism," *Time*, November 12, 1990.

Byron M. Roth — "Social Psychology's 'Racism,'" *The Public Interest*, Winter 1990.

Shelby Steele — "Blacks and Insecurity," *Current*, March/April 1990.

Jack E. White — "Genocide Mumbo Jumbo," *Time*, January 22, 1990.

Juan Williams — "The Fire This Time," *The New Republic*, December 10, 1990.

Is Racism Responsible for Minority Poverty?

Chapter Preface

A 1986 report by the U.S. Bureau of the Census found that one-third of black families and one-fourth of Hispanic families live in poverty. Only one-tenth of white families live in similar economic conditions. The same report stated that the median net worth of white families was $39,135, compared with $3,397 for blacks and $4,913 for Hispanics. This shocking disparity still holds true in the 1990s. Experts debate whether the cause is racism.

Observers such as economist David H. Swinton say that it is. Blacks and other minorities, Swinton argues, face racial discrimination in hiring, job promotion, and lending, even though such discrimination is illegal. Swinton also asserts that blacks and other minorities are less able than whites to counteract this situation because a history of racism has left them with a legacy of poverty and powerlessness. Minority poverty, Swinton concludes, is "the result of the historic pattern of racism and discrimination that characterizes American society."

But others, such as analyst Karl Zinsmeister, argue that racism can no longer be blamed for minority poverty. Zinsmeister points out that two-thirds of the black population in the U.S. is not poor. He believes this proves minorities can escape poverty. Instead of racism, critics like Zinsmeister believe choices such as teen pregnancy, involvement in crime, and dropping out of school cause minority poverty. Zinsmeister, comparing blacks and whites, argues: "For people who have followed the traditional American path to success—finish high school, go to college, get married—the economic playing field is now level for both races."

The viewpoints in this chapter debate the role of racism in minority poverty.

"Today's economic disparities are the result of the historic pattern of racism and discrimination that characterizes American society."

Racism Is Responsible for Black Poverty

David H. Swinton

The 1960s civil rights movement resulted in many political and legal gains for blacks and other minorities, but despite those successes blacks still lag behind whites in employment, wealth, and income. In the following viewpoint, David H. Swinton argues that the economic inequality between minorities is caused by past and present racial discrimination. He calls for civil rights activists to force whites to share economic power with blacks and other minority groups. Swinton is an economist and dean of the School of Business at Jackson State University in Jackson, Mississippi.

As you read, consider the following questions:

1. What kinds of economic gaps exist between blacks and whites, according to the author?
2. Why does Swinton argue that the civil rights movement failed to attain economic equality for blacks?
3. How does Swinton respond to those who argue that the black community should focus on self-help efforts to improve blacks' economic status?

Excerpted, with permission, from "Economic Progress for Black Americans in the Post-Civil Rights Era," by David H. Swinton, chapter 12 of *U.S. Race Relations in the 1980s and 1990s*, Gail E. Thomas, editor. Copyright © 1990 Hemisphere Publishing Corporation, a member of the Taylor & Francis Group.

Throughout American history the economic status of black, Mexican, Puerto Rican, Native American, and other non-European racial or ethnic groups has been significantly lower than that of white Americans. Their economic disadvantage has been indicated by consistently lower levels of income, wealth, business ownership, occupational status, wage rates, and employment and by higher rates of poverty and unemployment.

The historical economic disadvantage for blacks and others resulted from the fact that the dominant European-American community used its superior economic, political, and social power to exploit, segregate, ignore, discriminate against, and otherwise exclude black and other Americans of non-European descent from equal participation in the American economy. By such means, European-Americans were able to attain and perpetuate an advantaged status in the American society. The economic dominance of European-Americans had the explicit approval and support of the American government for most of American history.

The Civil Rights Movement

Individual and collective efforts to improve the economic status of black and other nonwhite Americans, at least until World War II, were undertaken largely without official government support and frequently in the face of active governmental opposition. With the implementation of fair employment policies during World War II, however, the civil rights movement began to experience some success in shifting official policy to the promotion of racial equality.

The major success of this movement after World War II is well known. Starting with the Supreme Court's 1954 *Brown v. Board of Education* decision banning official elementary and secondary school segregation, and culminating with the civil rights and social legislation of the 1960s, the civil rights movement was able to elicit the official cooperation of the U.S. government in the struggle to improve the absolute and relative economic status of black and other non-European-American ethnic groups.

By the early 1970s, the civil rights movement had left a legacy of legislation, executive orders, regulations, court rulings, and new or expanded social programs designed to promote the attainment of economic and social equality. The government's official policy had been reversed from one of at least tacit acceptance of European-American economic domination to the official promotion of racial equality.

The strategy to promote equal opportunity that emerged from the 1960s had three major components. The first was the elimination of segregation and discrimination in public activities. The second was the amelioration of the higher rates of poverty and economic disadvantage found among blacks and others. The third was the elimination of differences in human and non-human capital.

Some successes were registered in implementing programs to focus on all three strategic objectives. As a consequence, the 1960s ended amidst widespread optimism that the society was on the verge of eliminating racial inequality in economic life within a reasonable time.

Steve Sack. Reprinted with permission of *Star Tribune*, Minneapolis.

Yet, as is now well known, the promise of the late 1960s has not been realized. Today, almost 20 years after the peak of the civil rights movement, racial inequality in economic life persists. Standard economic indicators show that in most respects the economic status of minorities has not improved since the days of a short-lived trend that ended in the early 1970s. Indeed, several indicators show a declining relative economic status for blacks. The evidence is overwhelming that the achievements of the civil rights movement did not usher in the anticipated golden age of racial equality in economic life.

My primary objective is to explore the persistence of racial inequality in economic life in the post-civil-rights-movement era. The major focus will be on the unequal economic status of black Americans. There are two primary reasons for restricting my discussion to black Americans. First, blacks are the largest and the most subordinated group. Second, the historical situation of blacks is unique because they were the only major minority group to be subjected to slavery and the formal apartheid of the "Jim Crow" South. In any case I have studied blacks' economic status for nearly 20 years and have much more data, knowledge, and understanding about blacks' economic experiences than about those of the other non-European minority groups. . . .

The Persistence of Racial Inequality

The relative gaps in income and poverty rates between blacks and whites have not changed much since the early 1970s. Indeed, in some regions, income and poverty gaps have increased since 1970, while in the South there has been modest improvement. In all regions, however, the income and poverty gaps are still large. Blacks still receive less than 60¢ per $1 of income received by whites and are still roughly three times as likely to be poor in every part of the country.

The continuing disparities in income result primarily from persisting inequalities in the character of black American participation in the American economy. Black Americans continue to own and control far fewer businesses than whites. The latest data suggest that the black business sector is at least 50 times smaller than would be required for ownership parity. Total wealth holdings, as measured by the median value of wealth holdings, were over 11 times smaller than would be required for parity. Moreover, there has been no significant amelioration of the disparities in ownership of businesses or wealth since 1970.

Disparities in ownership are at the root of the persistence of economic inequality. As noted, these differences contribute directly to differences in income. They also mean that blacks have much less power and ability to determine their own economic futures. Because of their limited ownership of economic resources, blacks have been dependent on white resource owners for opportunities to participate in the American economy. The degree of black dependency did not decline in the post-1970 period.

Black dependency means that black workers have had to compete for jobs primarily in white-owned or white-controlled businesses and institutions. The outcome for blacks continues to be unfavorable occupational distributions, lower wage rates, and lower levels of employment. Overall, there has been no significant improvement in blacks' labor market status since 1970. Employed workers made small occupational gains, but these were offset by significant absolute and relative losses in employment. Wage inequality has remained about the same or a little higher than in the early 1970s. The net result of these trends is that black workers as a whole have made no significant gain in relative earnings in the post-1970 period. The failure of black workers as a whole to record any significant gains in the labor market explains a major part of the persisting economic disparities in income and poverty rates for the black population.

Thus the persisting income and poverty gaps result from the failure of the black population to make any significant gains in ownership or labor-market status. Why were there so few gains in ownership or labor-market status in the post-1970 period despite the successes of the civil rights movement? Let us turn our attention to this question.

The lowly economic status of blacks at the start of the civil rights movement resulted from the long legacy of racism, segregation, and discrimination that had left the black population with the severe economic disadvantages discussed above: low levels of business ownership and wealth and low levels of education and work experience. Moreover, blacks still were subjected to current market discrimination in gaining equal access to economic opportunities. The lack of amelioration of racial inequality in economic life suggests that the policies and programs implemented by the civil rights movement were insufficient to resolve these underlying causes of inequality. . . .

Repairing the Damages

One fatal flaw in the civil rights strategy was its failure to recognize the necessity of repairing the damages or eliminating the disadvantages that blacks had accumulated because of the history of racism and discrimination. In effect, the programs and policies developed during the civil rights era were designed to end the practice of racism and discrimination, but they paid only minimal attention to the accumulated economic disadvantages. Unfortunately, these disadvantages were real and imposed insurmountable handicaps. Poverty, lack of wealth and business ownership, and low levels of human capital made it impossible for blacks to translate nondiscrimination into racial equality.

A second major strategic flaw on the part of the civil rights movement was the failure to recognize the economic importance of unequal opportunity in establishing the white population's advantaged economic status. The distribution game in a market economy is almost zero-sum; whites were relatively advantaged precisely because blacks were relatively disadvantaged. Civil rights thinking tended to ignore the interdependencies in economic status and to commit the fallacy of composition by assuming that the relationship between merit and the determination of a single individual's economic status could be applied without change to all individuals collectively. The primary consequence of this fallacious thinking was the failure to recognize the powerful economic incentives that existed to maintain whites' advantages through discrimination and other means. The civil rights advocates generally underestimated the resistance that whites would offer to the equal opportunity agenda.

Racial Barriers to Economic Advancement

For most ethnic groups, socioeconomic mobility is a cumulative process whereby economic advancement (a better job, a raise) is translated into residential progress (a higher-status neighborhood with better schools, peer influences and social contacts), which in turn leads to additional socioeconomic gains (children receive better educations and get better jobs). This avenue for cumulative socioeconomic advancement is largely closed to blacks because of racial barriers to residential mobility.

Douglas S. Massey, *Los Angeles Times*, August 13, 1989.

Many of the failures of the civil rights strategies resulted from the fact that in making crucial design and implementation decisions, too much consideration was given to the interests of the white population that historically had discriminated against blacks. Consideration of white interests dominated the final decisions about what would be done, how it would be done, and how much would be done. Both human capital and antidiscrimination programs were designed and implemented to have minimal adverse effects on whites. . . .

In any case, the reason blacks have made little progress despite the efforts of the civil rights movement is straightforward. The efforts of this movement barely addressed the disparities in business ownership and wealth that gave whites the economic power to subordinate blacks. As a result, blacks remained dependent on whites despite the success of the movement. In addition, human capital development programs and antidiscrimination laws were insufficient to induce white-owned and white-controlled businesses and institutions to provide a significantly greater share of economic opportunities to blacks. As a consequence, the labor market and ownership disparities for blacks have not been significantly reduced. In a nutshell, this background explains the persisting economic disadvantage.

Lessons of the Civil Rights Movement

The most important lesson to be drawn from the experience of the civil rights movement in the post-1970 period is the difficulty of designing a strategy to eliminate racial inequality in economic life without altering the distribution of economic power or imposing costs on whites. The unwillingness of government officials to impose significant costs on white workers and employers probably accounts for a good share of their failure to design meaningful and effective human capital interventions and for their reluctance to promote equal opportunity. Because of this failure to implement any significant redistribution of wealth or business ownership, blacks were left without the resources for effective internal efforts. As a result, the hopes for the success of the integrationist civil rights strategy in this period received a fatal blow.

In addition, it is very difficult to implement programs to modify white racist or discriminatory behavior and to make a significant reduction in blacks' human capital disadvantages. Whites resist such programs because of their impact on the privileged position that they have attained in the American economy as a direct consequence of the economic subordination of blacks. Moreover, implementation of such efforts is even more difficult in times of economic stringency; this is an often-observed economic fact. When there are no costs or when the pie is growing, it is much easier to convince people to support programs dealing with equity concerns. The cost can be paid out of the growth dividend, and the advantaged classes need not feel the impact. This point implies that future prospects for reducing racial inequality would be aided greatly by establishing a better-performing national economy.

Strategic Thinking

We also should note the lesson that recent experience teaches about the importance of correct strategic thinking. The civil rights movement was a successful self-help movement; it focused on removing external constraints to blacks' progress, particularly those constraints arising from racism and discrimination. Yet the strategy adopted for bringing about racial equality was wrong. Civil rights strategists failed to recognize the importance of changing the distribution of power. They also failed to appreciate fully the necessity and the importance of race-specific policies to overcome historical disparities. Thus although the movement enjoyed a great deal of success in passing legislation and implementing social programs, these results proved ineffective in altering the underlying racial inequality.

Implicit in my argument in this last section is the conclusion that internal inefficiency within the black community played little or no role in blacks' failure to achieve economic equality in the post-1970 period. I suggest that this failure should be attributed entirely to the inadequacy of the ameliorative efforts. Blacks' self-help activities should continue to focus on altering the environmental constraints on black development by redistributing economic power from whites to blacks. Leverage can be applied to limited internal resources by inducing the public sector to assume the cost of reducing racial inequality in economic life.

Today's economic disparities are the result of the historic pattern of racism and discrimination that characterizes American society. The economic legacy of this past is reflected currently in blacks' limited ownership of businesses and wealth and in the accompanying disadvantages in human capital. These factors make blacks a dependent population, subject to discrimination. This situation in turn generates the continuing high level of economic inequality.

The simple logic of economic growth makes it apparent that once such historical differences are in place, it is unreasonable to expect that the disadvantaged group can overcome gaps only through internally directed self-help. Indeed, because the proportion of money saved and invested is generally higher among higher income individuals, it is logical to expect that racial inequality, once established, will continue to grow in the absence of intervention. Even in conditions of complete nondiscrimination, the result will be the same; in the face of discrimination, the gaps will increase.

Ultimately, the only intervention that can guarantee sustainable results in a free-market system is the redistribution of wealth and power. Reparations, seldom discussed in connection with solving the problem of racial inequality, probably are an appropriate approach to the adjustments required to ensure equality in a free-enterprise system. The appropriate amount of reparations would be the amount required to eliminate differences in business ownership, wealth, and human capital. An appropriate strategy for blacks in the 1990s and beyond could be the development of another social movement to obtain such reparations. The only alternative would be to change the economic system so as to break the association between current economic status and prospects for the future.

"Racism . . . has been a destructive myth, giving greater power to the odds against success than exist in reality, making it harder even to try."

The Role of Racism in Black Poverty Is Exaggerated

William Raspberry

William Raspberry is a journalist and newspaper columnist for the *Washington Post*. In the following viewpoint, he argues that blaming racism for black poverty discourages blacks from helping themselves. He argues that blacks should concentrate on finding solutions to their problems rather than trying to extract concessions from whites.

As you read, consider the following questions:

1. Why does Raspberry believe it is a myth to say that racism has crippled blacks?
2. How are blacks different from immigrants, according to the author?
3. Why does Raspberry argue that a focus on racism harms blacks?

William Raspberry, "A Journalist's View of Black Economics," *Imprimis*, March 1990. Reprinted by permission from *Imprimis*, the monthly journal of Hillsdale College. Subscription free upon request.

I am intensely interested in the subject of the economics of black America. However, I am neither a businessman, an economist, nor a social scientist. I'm a "newspaper guy."

That's not an apology. I like being a newspaper guy, and I like to think I'm a pretty good one. I point it out simply to warn you up front that what you will hear from me is neither economic analysis nor nuts-and-bolt business proposals. I like to think about things in general and my proposal is that we ought to approach this subject in that fashion.

Myths About Race

One of the things I would like us to think about is a myth: a myth that has crippled black America, sent us off on unpromising directions, and left us ill-equipped to deal with either political or economic reality.

That myth is that race is of overriding importance, that it is a determinant not just of opportunity but also of potential, a reliable basis for explaining political and economic realities, a reasonable way of talking about geopolitics, and the overwhelming basis on which to deal with the relationships between us.

When I refer to race-based explanations of the plight of black America as myth, I do not mean to suggest that all such explanations are false. My reference is to the definition of myth as a "traditional account of unknown authorship, ostensibly with a historical basis, but serving usually to explain some observed phenomenon."

Slavery and Race

The historical basis of our preoccupation with race is easy enough to see. America did not invent slavery. Slavery as an institution predates the Bible. But American slavery was peculiarly race-based. Since slavery is the basis for the very presence of black people in America, small wonder that race has assumed such importance in our mythology.

But slavery was more than just involuntary, unpaid servitude. Unlike other populations, to whom enslavement seemed a reasonable way of dealing with conquered enemies, America was never happy with the concept of one group of human beings holding another group of human beings in bondage. I suppose it was taken as a sin against God. But rather than forego the economic benefits of slavery, American slaveholders resolved the dilemma by defining blacks not as fellow human beings but more like beasts of burden. There is nothing ungodly about a man requiring unremunerated work of an animal. Didn't God give man dominion over the animals?

Now it may have been that Africans were a special kind of animal: capable of thought, and human language, and even worship.

86

But as long as whites could persuade themselves that blacks were not fully human, they could justify slavery.

Thus was born and reinforced the myth of inherent white superiority, which later became the basis for racial separation, for Jim Crow laws, for unequal opportunity and all sorts of evil. Nor is it just among whites that the myth survives.

Black Poverty Is Caused By Family Breakdown

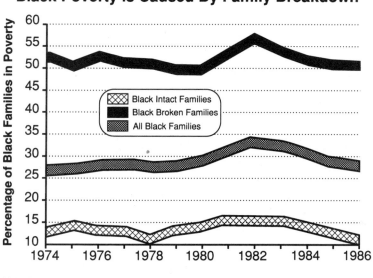

SOURCE: U.S. Census Bureau. Reprinted by permission of The Heritage Foundation.

I must say that this fact never really hit home for me until a few years ago when a reader of my column suggested it. Mary Pringle, a Virginia educator, said it occurred to her that Americans generally have lost the myths that give meaning to their lives, and that black Americans in particular suffer from the loss. The predominant surviving myth of black Americans, she said, is that of racism as the dominant influence in their lives.

Myths, she was careful to point out, are not necessarily false. Indeed, whether positive or negative, they are almost always based on actual group experience. But the nature of the operative group myth can make a profound difference in group outcomes.

"Racism is a reality, but it has been overcome by many and given way to opportunity and success." Those who have overcome it, she argued, have been moved by different myths: myths that paint them as destined for success rather than doomed to failure, myths that lead them to see themselves as members of a special group capable of overcoming all odds. That is the kind of myth that blacks need to cultivate, she said.

"Racism, though it is a reality, has been a destructive myth, giving greater power to the odds against success than exist in reality, making it harder even to *try*. What we need is a stronger, more powerful myth that is constructive and evokes a sense of identity and energy to move ahead."

I think Mary Pringle's insight is profound. As with most keen insights, once it occurs to you, you can see supporting evidence on every hand.

Positive and Negative Myths

Black youngsters in the inner cities are moved by the myth that blacks have special athletic gifts, particularly with regard to basketball. Asian youngsters are influenced by the myth that they have special gifts for math and science. Jewish youngsters accept the myth that their group has a special gift for the power of the written word.

Now all these myths are, by themselves, worthless. But when they evoke a sense of identity and the energy to move ahead, something happens. People *work* at the things they believe they are innately capable of achieving.

So it is not uncommon to see a black kid working up to bedtime, practicing his double-pump scoop, his behind-the-back dribble, his left-handed jump shot. And after a few months of work, if he has any athletic talent at all, he *proves* the myth. Asian-American youngsters, convinced that they may have special aptitude for math or science, reinforce that myth and make it reality—staying up until two in the morning working on their math and science; Jewish youngsters, convinced that they have a special gift for the written word, work at writing.

Those are all positive myths, and they are obviously powerful. But negative myths are powerful, too.

The myth that blacks cannot prevail in intellectual competition, that Chinese youngsters cannot play basketball, that Jews are specially vulnerable to guilt trips—these are negative myths whose acceptance has led to failure because they feed the assumption that failure is inevitable.

Objective reality is the arena in which we all must perform. But the success or failure of our performance is profoundly influenced by the attitudes—the myths—we bring to that reality.

Two things flow from the racism-is-all myth that we have used to account for our difficulties. The first is that it puts the solution to our difficulties outside our control. If our problems are caused by racism, and their solutions dependent on ending racism, our fate is in the hands of people who, by definition, don't love us.

The second outcome of the myth is our inclination to think of our problems in terms of a failure of racial justice. "Civil rights," which once referred to those things whose fair distribution was a governmental responsibility, now refers to any discrepancy. Income gaps, education gaps, test-score gaps, infant-mortality gaps, life-expectancy gaps, employment gaps, business-participation gaps—all now are talked about as "civil rights" issues.

The problems indicated by all these gaps are real. But describing them as "civil rights" problems steers us away from possible solutions. The civil rights designation evokes a sort of central justice bank, managed by the government, whose charge is to ladle out equal portions of everything to everybody. It prompts us to think about our problems in terms of inadequate or unfair distribution. It encourages the fallacy that to attack racism as the source of our problems is the same as attacking our problems. As a result, we expend precious resources—time, energy, imagination, political capital—searching (always successfully) for evidence of racism, while our problems grow worse.

Maybe I can make my point clearer by reference to two other minorities. The first group consists of poor whites. There are in America not just individuals but whole pockets of white people whose situation is hardly worse than our own.

And yet these poor whites have their civil rights. They can vote, live where their money permits them to live, eat where their appetites and their pocket-books dictate, work at jobs for which their skills qualify them. And yet they are in desperate straits. It doesn't seem to occur to us that the full grant and enforcement of our civil rights would leave black Americans in about the same situation that poor white people are now in. That isn't good enough for me.

There is another minority whose situations may be more instructive. I refer to recently arrived Asian-Americans. What is the difference between them and us? Certainly it isn't that they have managed to avoid the effects of racism. Neither the newly arrived Southeast Asians nor the earlier arriving Japanese-Americans, Chinese-Americans, and Korean-Americans are loved by white people. But these groups have spent little of their time and energy proving that white people don't love them.

Opportunity and Business

The difference between them and us is our operating myths. Our myth is that racism accounts for our shortcomings. Theirs is that their own efforts can make the difference, no matter what white people think.

They have looked at America as children with their noses pressed to the window of a candy store: if only I could get in there, boy, could I have a good time. And when they get in there, they work and study and save and create businesses and job opportunities for their people.

But we, born inside the candy store, have adopted a myth that leads us to focus only on the maldistribution of the candy. Our myth leads us into becoming a race of consumers, when victories accrue to the producers.

The Next Phase

In an era of abundant prosperity for many American blacks, where every measure of white racism shows it to be in sharp decline, where the crying imperative is no longer equal political rights but economic empowerment among a marginal black underclass, there is only so much white America can do. In its next phase black ambition must focus urgently upon economic activism, and black Americans must ask themselves what they can do for themselves and for their brothers. Repairing the tattered fabric of black family life, in particular, will require self-healing. The obstacle is no longer a simple "Them."

Karl Zinsmeister, *Public Opinion*, January/February 1988.

Interestingly enough, this is a fairly recent phenomenon. There was a time when we, like the more recent arrivals in this country, sought only the opportunity to be productive, and we grasped that opportunity under circumstances far worse—in law, at least—than those that obtain now.

Free blacks and former slaves, though denied many of the rights that we take for granted today, were entrepreneurial spirits. They were artisans and inventors, shopkeepers and industrialists, financiers and bankers. The first female millionaire in America was Madame C.J. Walker. At least two companies founded at the turn of the century are now on the *Black Enterprise* list of the 100 top black firms in the country.

Black real estate operatives transformed white Harlem into a haven for blacks. The early 1900s saw the founding of a number of all-black towns: Mound Bayou, Mississippi; Boley, Oklahoma; Nicodemus, Kansas; and others.

Boley at one time boasted a bank, twenty-five grocery stores, five hotels, seven restaurants, a waterworks, an electricity plant, four cotton gins, three drug stores, a bottling plant, a laundry, two newspapers, two colleges, a high school, a grade school, four department stores, a jewelry store, two hardware stores, two ice cream parlors, a telephone exchange, five churches, two insurance agencies, two livery stables, an undertaker, a lumber yard, two photography studios, and an ice plant. Not bad for an all-black town of 4,000.

As Robert L. Woodson observed in his book, *On the Road to Economic Freedom*, "The Harlem and Boley experiences, which matched aggressive black entrepreneurial activity with the self-assertion drive of the black masses, was multiplied nationwide to the point that, in 1913, fifty years after Emancipation, black America had accumulated a personal wealth of $700 million.

As special Emancipation Day festivals and parades were held that year in cities and towns across the country, blacks could take pride in owning 550,000 homes, 40,000 businesses, 40,000 churches, and 937,000 farms. The literacy rate among blacks climbed to a phenomenal 70 percent—up from 5 percent in 1863."

Over-learning the Civil Rights Lesson

What has happened since then? A lot of things, including a good deal of success that we don't talk much about. But among the things that have happened are two that have created problems for us. First is the overemphasis on integration, as opposed to desegregation and increased opportunity. Hundreds of thriving restaurants, hotels, service outlets, and entertainment centers have gone out of business because we preferred integration to supporting our own painstakingly established institutions. Indeed, aside from black churches and black colleges, little remains to show for that entrepreneurial spurt of the early decades of this century.

The other thing that has happened is that we over-learned the lessons of the civil rights movement. That movement, brilliantly conceived and courageously executed, marked a proud moment in our history. The upshot was that black Americans, for the first time in our sojourn here, enjoy the full panoply of our civil rights.

Unfortunately, that period also taught us to see in civil rights terms things that might more properly be addressed in terms of enterprise and exertion rather than in terms of equitable distribution. Even when we speak of business now, our focus is on distribution: on set-asides and affirmative action.

Self-Help

Our 1960s success in making demands on government has led us to the mistaken assumption that government can give us what we need for the next major push toward equality. It has produced in us what Charles Tate of the Booker T. Washington Foundation described as a virtual antipathy toward capitalism.

Even middle-class blacks seldom talk to their children about going into business. Instead our emphasis is on a fair distribution of jobs in business created and run by others. We ought to have a fair share of those jobs. But the emphasis, I submit, ought to be finding ways to get more of us into business and thereby creating for ourselves the jobs we need.

That is especially true with regard to the so-called black underclass who tend to reside in areas abandoned by white businesses.

In addition to figuring out ways of getting our unemployed to jobs that already exist, we need to look for ways to encourage blacks in those abandoned neighborhoods to create enterprises of their own. What I have in mind are not merely the shops and Mom and Pop stores that we still patronize (but whose owners are far likelier to be Vietnamese or Koreans than blacks), but also an entrepreneurial approach to our social problems. . . .

Many of us are succeeding, in an astonishing range of fields, and the leadership does not hesitate to point out—with perfect justification—that our success is attributable to the glorious civil rights movement: that black exertion and courage made our success possible.

Many Are Not Succeeding

But many of us aren't succeeding. Teenage pregnancy, dope trafficking, lawlessness, and lack of ambition make us doubt that they ever will succeed. But do our leaders suggest that the reasons have to do with the inadequacy of the civil rights movement, or with any lack of exertion and courage on the part of the leadership? No. When we see failure among our people, and have reason to believe that the failure is permanent, our recourse is to our mainstay myth: Racism is the culprit. Mistakenly, we credit black pride for our successes and blame prejudice for our shortfalls.

I leave it to others to suggest the specifics by which we will move to increase the economic success of black America. I will tell you only that I believe it can be done—not only because it is being done by an encouraging number of us, but also because it has been done by earlier generations who struggled under circumstances of discrimination, deprivation, and hostility far worse than anything we now face.

My simple suggestion is that we stop using the plight of the black underclass as a scourge for beating up on white racists and examine both the black community and the American system for clues to how we can transform ourselves from consumers to producers.

"The black middle class has taken advantage of the opportunities . . . in today's free market economy which has made illegal all forms of discrimination based upon race."

The Rising Black Middle Class Proves Racism Is in Decline

J.A. Parker

In the past two decades an increasing number of blacks have attained middle-class status. In the following viewpoint, J.A. Parker argues that the growing middle class is proof that racism is no longer a major problem. Minority poverty is caused more by self-defeating behavior than by racism, he asserts. Parker is president of the Lincoln Institute of Research and Education, a conservative organization studying public policy issues affecting the lives of black Americans.

As you read, consider the following questions:

1. How many blacks live in the suburbs, according to Parker?
2. How does the black middle class weaken racial stereotypes, according to the author?
3. Why does Parker criticize black civil rights leaders?

From "The Largely Unheralded Growth for the Black Middle Class," by J.A. Parker, *The Lincoln Review*, Winter 1988. Reprinted with permission.

Both established black civil rights organizations and the general media have, it seems, been engaging in a concerted effort to make the term "black" synonymous with crime, poverty, illegitimacy and drugs.

It is true, of course, that there is a serious problem within the black community in all of these areas. When civil rights groups address such problems they, all too often, fall into the trap of blaming these social ills upon "white racism," rather than examining the social pathology which exists within the nation's inner cities.

While it is essential that we face the real causes of such urban social decay it is also important that we look at a far more optimistic development which has gone largely unreported and ignored: the growth of a vibrant, healthy and productive black middle class.

Encouraging Data

The data for the black community as a whole is far more optimistic than one might imagine by reviewing either the laments of black organizations or the reporting of the press.

Real median income of black families has increased significantly since 1982 when the last economic recession ended, according to the Department of Commerce's Census Bureau.

The median income in 1986 for all black families ($17,600) and for black married-couple families ($26,580) increased by about 14 per cent from 1982. Black families with a female householder, no husband present, had a median income in 1986 of $9,300, up 9.8 per cent from 1982.

Since 1982, real family income has grown by 10.2 per cent for all white families and 11.3 per cent for white married-couple families. The median incomes of all Hispanic families and married-couple families both increased by about 9 per cent. The differences between the percentage of increases for white and black families was not statistically different from comparable Hispanic families. . . .

Moving to the Suburbs

As more and more black Americans join the middle class, they are leaving the inner cities and moving to the suburbs in increasing numbers. Across the country, the black population of the suburbs more than doubled between 1960 and 1980, going from 2.8 million to nearly 6.2 million, according to census figures. In 1980, there were 26.5 million blacks nationwide.

During the last five years of the 1970s, the average yearly net migration of blacks from cities to suburbs nationwide was 88,000, according to census figures. So far in the 1980s, census officials report, blacks have been moving to the suburbs at an even faster rate. In 1982, for example, the figure was 220,000.

In the suburbs around New York City the increase in the black population has been even greater, going from 77,000 in 1960 to 285,000 in 1980. In Westchester County, while the white population declined—from 802,722 to 729,831—between 1970 and 1980, the black population rose from 85,041 to 104,815.

High Status Jobs

The number of blacks in high status jobs has risen sharply. There are about 1.5 million black managers, business executives, and professionals today. One of the most encouraging changes since 1968 is the new prominence of black television anchors, black astronauts, black professors and authors, black leveraged buyout specialists, and black national security advisers.

Karl Zinsmeister, *Public Opinion*, January/February 1988.

Blacks are becoming increasingly active in suburban politics. In 1985, Ronald A. Blackwood became the first black elected mayor of a community in New York State when he won the post in Mount Vernon. Richard F. Jackson, Jr., a native of Peekskill, New York, served as that city's mayor after the City Council appointed him to complete the remaining term of his predecessor who had resigned. In a report on the increasing number of blacks in the New York suburbs, *The New York Times* (May 20, 1985) reported that, "In some cases, blacks said, it is the little things that show the inroads they have made in suburban life. They talk of the major department store that now carries a popular line of cosmetics for blacks, of the local newsstands that now carry and display popular black publications and the now widespread observance of Black History Month every February. John E. Harmon, a 78-year-old-historian, is the founder of the Afro-American Cultural Foundation and a resident of White Plains. He said he remembered a time when black history observances were celebrated for a week, and he almost single-handedly had to organize, publicize and sometimes finance the activities of the county. Recently, he said, observances in Westchester have attracted the county's black and white elite."

An extensive study conducted by *The Washington Post* (November 29, 1987) discovered that, ". . . this new black middle class is burgeoning in the suburbs, where the bulk of the new, white-collar, middle-class jobs are being created. . . . The majority of Washington area blacks no longer live in what people of both races have lightly referred to at times as 'Chocolate City.' The majority now live in the supposedly 'vanilla' suburbs. . . . The *Post*'s demographic analysis also shows that in terms of

95

jobs, housing and educational opportunity, Prince George's County (Maryland)—one of the most racially diverse suburban middle-class counties in the United States—is so much above the national average as to be plausibly described as the American Dream. Not only that, but Northern Virginia, long shunned by blacks as racist, is developing a black middle class with some of the highest rates of achievement in America."

Middle-Class Growth

By the second decade of the next century, the new American black middle class could be as large in percentage terms for blacks as the white middle class will be for whites, predicts Bart Landry, a professor at the University of Maryland who is the author of a recently published book, *The New Black Middle Class.*

The black middle class is expanding in such diverse places as Los Angeles, Long Island, Atlanta, Chicago and Detroit. *The Washington Post* believes that "its emergence is most obvious in the Washington area."

Among the findings of the *Post*'s study:

• The majority of the Washington area's 650,000 blacks live in its suburbs, not in the District of Columbia.

• Of the area's 300,000 prosperous blacks, almost twice as many live in mostly white neighborhoods as in mostly black ones.

• In the four largest counties—Fairfax and Prince William in Virginia and Montgomery and Prince George's in Maryland, the typical black family makes between $1,100 and $5,200 more a year than does the typical white family elsewhere in the United States.

• The typical Washington area young black adult—age 25 to 29—has more education than the typical young white elsewhere in America. In Montgomery County, the black median is higher by an entire college semester.

• Since 1980, the fastest-growing population of young blacks in absolute numbers in the region's public schools has been in Fairfax and Montgomery counties.

"There is a story there to be told. And it is a story of the success of the revolution of the last 20 years," says Milton D. Morris, director of research at the Joint Center for Political Studies, a black think tank in Washington, D.C. "It's almost as if we would rather not focus on that side of the picture, because, after all, the glass is half-empty. Many people still perceive the results as very, very tenuous. It's like, 'Yes, there are these things, but we really don't believe it's for real; we can't take it too seriously because it could disappear any minute.' But those successes, they're there. They're real. They ought to inspire us."

The black middle class has taken advantage of the opportunities that exist in today's free market economy which has made illegal all forms of discrimination based upon race, religion and ethnic origin. With segregation ended and discrimination outlawed, the only thing holding black Americans from success is the social pathology which is all too evident in the nation's inner cities. Without a work ethic and respect for education, with a skyrocketing teenage pregnancy rate and widespread drug use, many black youngsters simply are rejecting the opportunities before them. When black spokesmen blame "white racism" for what they perceive as a lack of progress, they are ignoring the real problems we face.

Blacks Have Fared Well

The best gauge of the overall status of black America is the extent of gains by the majority of the black population: the number of college-educated blacks, the size of the black middle class, the rate of black employment growth, the growth of the black business sector, and the numbers of blacks in the professions. By these important measures of progress, blacks fared extremely well during the last decade.

Joseph Perkins, *The San Diego Union*, October 2, 1990.

Washington Post reporter Joel Garreau, in his series about the black middle class, writes: "Because the majority of blacks in America are still struggling, blacks, on average, still lag behind whites in every measure of income, education and social well-being. But increasingly, averages are not fully representative of black experience in America. Generally, the black suburban middle class differs significantly in attitudes and economic behavior from the working class, which differs in turn from the poor."

George Sternleib, director of the Center for Urban Policy Research at Rutgers University, declares that, "Successful blacks are the most forgotten group of Americans there are, and the most interesting. The focus has been so much on the losers that the very people who have been able to come through have been ignored."

The University of Maryland's Bart Landry points out that the more overwhelming presence of a black middle class makes less sustainable older stereotypes which, in reality, had more to do with class than color. Such stereotypes "just do not apply," says Landry. Whites, he said, have discovered that "these people are okay, these middle-class blacks. Before they were afraid. Afraid of crime. Afraid of images of blacks who are hostile. Not good neighbors. Stereotypes that fit very poor whites as well—what whites call 'poor white trash.'"

Unfortunately, the media has a "bad news" bias, and tends to ignore good news when it appears. Murray Friedman, an historian and vice-chairman of the Civil Rights Commission points out that, "The bad news on race relations is always available. . . . A less visible but ultimately more dramatic story, however, is unfolding in the dry-as-dust statistics released recently by the Bureau of Labor Statistics. These statistics, which indicate that an important advance has taken place in race relations, haven't won much attention. The Bureau . . . notes that unemployment among blacks has dropped to 12.1%. This is its lowest level in eight years. Even more significant, the bureau's figures show that black employment has jumped by 24.9% since the recession ended in 1982. That's twice the increase in white employment over the same period and is the best-ever five-year job performance for black Americans . . . a significant number of blacks are moving up in society. Since 1981, the number of black families in the highest income bracket (more than $50,000 in 1986 dollars) increased to 8.8% from 5.1%, a rise of 58%."

A Post Civil-Rights Era

Mr. Friedman declares that, "We have entered what some now refer to as a 'post civil-rights era.' This calls for less dramatic—but no less significant approaches—than those that proved so successful in the past. The approaches must center around the battle within—strengthening the internal life of minorities and creating the economic conditions that are the most enduring basis for gaining equality. Many civil-rights leaders were trained in an older model. Some are or were ministers. They found their greatest success came from publicly identifying widespread racism in society and mobilizing the anger and frustration of their constituents in battling against it. Now, the time has come to move away from such purely racial strategies and from government palliatives and to focus more energy on jobs, the development of middle-class skills for minority underclasses and economic growth in the years ahead. In light of the current market setback and the threat of recession, the most significant question for the civil-rights movement may well be whether the recent economic advances can be maintained."

It is curious indeed that black organizations and leaders speak so little about the dramatic advances which have occurred in recent days. Economics writer Warren Brookes notes that the median income for black families rose 4.4 per cent in 1986 from a year earlier and 12.7 per cent since 1981. This is almost 46 per cent faster than white family incomes grew. It is a reversal of the 1977-81 recession, when the median income for black families fell more than 5 per cent.

There can be no doubt that hard work, a commitment to educational excellence, and a willingness to take advantage of the opportunities which exist in today's American economy can propel millions of black Americans from the underclass to the middle class. If they do not progress the reason, it seems, relates more to their own difficulties in assuming the responsibilities which are required than to any inherent bigotry in the larger society.

If black leaders and organizations genuinely seek to advance those who appear to [be] caught in a cycle of poverty it is essential that they identify the real problems which have caused this dilemma. Those who urge more welfare, more government aid, more make-work jobs—are advocating policies which will, inevitably, perpetuate the current situation.

The good news—slowly being understood by both white and black Americans—is that a vibrant black middle class has emerged, and is growing. To expand this middle class we must identify the values which have brought it into being and must work to extend those values to those who seem to lack the proper motivation necessary to achievement.

Racism Not to Blame

Professor William Julius Wilson of the University of Chicago, explores some of these questions in his book, *The Declining Significance Of Race*. He challenges those who argue that the urban poor are simply a result of a "racist" society. Dr. Wilson, who is black, declares that, "I think there is no way you can understand the current situation, the disproportionate number of blacks in the underclass, without considering the historic effects of racism. But the sharp increases in rates of social dislocation since 1970—that is, joblessness, the increase in female-headed families, welfare dependency, and related problems—cannot be placed at the foot of racism. Racism created the large black underclass and stepped aside to watch changes in the economy and other changes destroy that place. And the problem is that many liberal advocates of anti-poverty and anti-discrimination programs often tried to explain the increasing rates of social dislocation in terms of racism, but this just didn't wash."

Finally, if we truly care about the future of those black Americans who remain in poverty, we must abandon the rhetoric of the past and face the real problems of the present. Black spokesmen ill serve the needs of those in whose name they speak when they portray a false picture of the real world. They abdicate any claim to genuine leadership when they continue to do so.

"The color bar . . . has become a shifting barrier . . . curtly reminding blacks that no matter how successful they may be, they remain in some ways second-class citizens."

The Rising Black Middle Class Does Not Prove Racism Is in Decline

Richard Lacayo

A growing number of blacks in the U.S. have achieved middle-class status, but whether their experience shows that racism in America is declining remains a controversial issue. In the following viewpoint, Richard Lacayo examines the lives of middle-class blacks and argues that many still face significant racial prejudice and discrimination in their lives. He writes that racial discrimination in employment, housing, and lending still hamper blacks' economic success, and that their social interactions with other people are still marred by racism. Lacayo is a writer for the weekly newsmagazine *Time*.

As you read, consider the following questions:

1. What examples does Lacayo give of racism faced by middle-class blacks?
2. How was the black middle class changed by the end of legal segregation, according to the author?
3. Why are middle-class blacks sensitive about the ghetto poor, according to Lacayo?

Richard Lacayo, "Between Two Worlds," *Time*, March 13, 1989. Copyright © 1989 The Time Inc. Magazine Company. Reprinted by permission.

By any standard, Jarobin Gilbert is a success. A Harvard-educated linguist with degrees in international law and finance, he commands a handsome salary as a globe-trotting NBC vice president who negotiated the broadcast rights to the 1988 Olympic Games. But every so often, Gilbert is rudely reminded that for people like him, there are still some things success cannot provide—simple things, like a taxicab. Late leaving for the airport to catch an important business flight, Gilbert stood on a busy avenue futilely hailing cab after speeding cab. Finally he phoned his secretary for assistance. She got one on her first attempt. Gilbert's secretary is white. He is black. "It's pretty hard to feel like you're mainstream," he says with a sigh, "when you're wearing $2,000 worth of clothes and you can't catch a cab at night."

It has been a revolution without much fanfare, but a revolution nonetheless. While the nation's attention focused on the plight of the urban underclass, millions of black Americans marched quietly into the mainstream, creating a vibrant middle class with incomes, educations and life-styles rivaling those of its white counterpart. For them, the passions and suffering of the civil rights struggle have culminated, as they were meant to, in the mundane pleasures and pangs of middle-class life. Theirs is the infrequently told success story of American race relations.

Statistics tell some of that story. The past decade has seen a 52% increase in the number of black managers, professionals, technicians and government officials. The gap between black and white median income is wider now than it was in the late 1970s—largely because blacks did not recover from the last recession as completely as whites did. Still, roughly one-third of all black households have solidly middle-class incomes of $35,000 or more, compared with about 70% of all white households. Blacks manage the department stores that once rejected their patronage. They make decisions at corporations where once they worked only on assembly lines. They preside as mayors of cities and represent congressional districts where they were formerly denied the right to vote. They live in exclusive suburbs that once excluded them and send their children to leading schools and universities that once blackballed them.

But for all its undeniable progress, the black middle class still seems more to be poised on the banks of the mainstream than to be swimming in its current. Its members are haunted by a feeling of alienation from the white majority with which they have so much in common, a sense that somehow they still do not quite fit in. They speak again and again of "living in two worlds." In one they are judged by their credentials and capabilities. In the other, race still comes first.

Around the turn of the century W.E.B. DuBois described the

"twoness" felt by blacks, forced by segregation to see themselves both from the inside and from without, as they might appear to a hostile white world. Today the white world is less hostile. But achievement and a limited degree of acceptance have failed to remove all traces of ambiguity from the lives of the black middle class.

Racial Discrimination

Racial discrimination still prevents middle-class black families from earning as much as whites; lowers their access to mortgages, business loans and other financial services; retards their homes' rate of appreciation; prevents them from increasing their wealth effectively; and deprives them of the economic well-being enjoyed by their white middle-class counterparts.

Such inequities are partly the result of prejudice that is still prevalent now—for example, the segregation that lowers the appreciation of black homes. But today's economic inequalities are also the legacy of past discrimination that has limited educational and job opportunities, preventing blacks from competing on an equal footing with whites.

Walter L. Updegrave, *Money*, December 1989.

Rather than welcoming blacks into the mainstream, some whites feel threatened by their arrival. They seem to believe that the good life—the desirable neighborhood, the right school, the best country club—is for whites only. Blacks in token numbers may be tolerated. But when their numbers exceed a so-called tipping point, many whites go on the defensive. A generation ago, the color bar was rigid and well defined: no blacks allowed. Now it has become a shifting barrier that can suddenly materialize, curtly reminding blacks that no matter how successful they may be, they remain in some ways second-class citizens. As black psychiatrist James P. Comer wrote in his family memoir, *Maggie's American Dream*, "Being black in America is often like playing your home games on the opponent's court."

Stanley Grayson is New York City's deputy mayor for finance and economic development. His wife Patricia is a vice president at National Medical Fellowships, an organization that promotes the education of minority students in medicine. Together they earn about $200,000 annually. But more than once while she was sorting clothes in the laundry room of the luxury apartment house in which they have lived for eight years, Patricia has been approached by white residents who have tried to hire her as a maid. Her husband has seen white residents close the elevator door in his face when he tried to board. Evidently they took the well-dressed 38-year-old Grayson, one of the highest-ranking officials in New York, for a mugger. "It makes me sizzle," he says, "because it means that no matter what I accomplish as an individual, I will always be judged by what people see first, my color."

Such affronts may seem insignificant to whites, but they are reshaping the racial agenda for the next decade and beyond. The problems of the urban black underclass—unemployment, drugs, teenage pregnancy, hopeless schools—are more urgent than ever. But for the black middle class, there are new preoccupations. Not just job-creation programs, but job promotions. Not just high school diplomas, but college tuition. Not just picket lines, but picket fences. An agenda, in short, for a full partnership in the American Dream.

Superficially, middle-class blacks already seem to be living that dream. Leon and Cora Brooks have spent more than a decade at IBM, where he is a dealer account manager and she is a senior personnel specialist. They have a comfortable home in the affluent and mostly black Los Angeles neighborhood of Baldwin Hills; they have a Mercedes in the garage and a daughter at California State University at Northridge. Leon Brooks jokes, "We're a typical white family that happens to be black."

But because they happen to be black, families like the Brookses are likely to encounter galling day-to-day insults that few whites will ever face. Blatant racism among whites may be a dwindling thing, but a less candid style of prejudice persists. The bank loan officer gives a cool reception to black customers regardless of their credit rating. Shop security guards treat middle-aged black shoppers like suspected thieves. Health clubs give black applicants the runaround. Even the FBI [Federal Bureau of Investigations], which is charged with investigating complaints about discrimination, has had its difficulties. Its director, William Sessions, ordered sweeping changes in the bureau's affirmative-action program after findings that there had been discrimination against black and Hispanic agents.

The most affluent African Americans still have difficulty buying homes wherever they want to live. The suburbs are dotted with gilded ghettos such as Chicago's Chatham neighborhood and North Portal Estates in Washington, middle-class and upper-middle-class areas from which whites fled when blacks began to arrive in large numbers. A study by two University of Chicago researchers, Douglas S. Massey and Nancy Denton, shows that middle-class blacks are significantly less likely than Hispanics or Asian Americans to live among whites—so much so that an Asian or Hispanic with a third-grade education is more likely to live in an integrated neighborhood than a black with a Ph.D.

Real estate agents still frequently steer black buyers away from white areas. So-called redlining, in which banks and mortgage institutions proscribe lending in certain neighborhoods, also remains a common practice. When Michael Lomax, chairman of the Fulton County, Ga., board of commissioners and a candidate to be the next mayor of Atlanta, applied for a home-improvement loan, he was turned down at two local banks before he got his money at a third one. A subsequent investigation by the Atlanta *Journal-Constitution* discovered that banks had redlined the plush but mostly black Adams Park residential area where Lomax lives, though an average home is valued at $200,000. . . .

Unlike well-off blacks in earlier generations, the black middle class that has blossomed in the wake of the civil rights movement is not constrained by the boundaries of race. Even before the Civil War, a modest economic élite of teachers, clergy and small tradesmen had emerged among free blacks, mostly in the North. By the late 19th century, industrialization had opened the way for blacks to enter the working class in larger numbers. Their paychecks in turn spurred growth in the ranks of black professionals and shopkeepers who catered to them. But that embryonic middle class was hedged all around by barriers of segregation, blocked from most dealings with the far more lucrative white market.

The contemporary black bourgeoisie is far more tightly linked to the broader American economy. Minority entrepreneurs once made their fortunes by serving black buyers ignored by white enterprises, in the manner of Motown founder Berry Gordy and *Ebony* magazine founder John H. Johnson. The new generation is epitomized by financier Reginald Lewis. [In 1988,] his TLC Group, Inc., a leveraged-buyout firm, agreed to buy the international foods division of Beatrice Companies, Inc. (total sales in 1986: $2.5 billion). That made TLC the largest U.S. business to have a black executive at the helm.

Yet, for blacks the workplace can be a psychological minefield, seeded with racially fraught encounters that most whites never notice. If a white subordinate resists direction from a black supervisor, the manager may wonder if race is a factor in the insubordination. If a black is passed up for a promotion, he may conclude, rightly or wrongly, that race held him back,.

The problem is compounded by the fact that middle-class blacks are often relatively isolated at work, typically finding themselves greatly outnumbered by white co-workers. When the workday ends, more often than not, blacks and whites who have labored shoulder to shoulder go their separate ways. Interracial socializing off the job remains rare enough to be remarked upon when it occurs. At some colleges, black faculty feel so isolated that they have negotiated telephone allowances into their job contracts to help them stay in touch with blacks teaching at other campuses around the country. "Coming to work every day is like putting on your armor," says Jim Johnson, an associate professor of geography at the University of California, Los Angeles, where the 1,837-member faculty has just 38 blacks.

Corporate affirmative action has helped speed the integration of management—but at a cost. While such programs have helped blacks break through hiring barriers, many whites insist that their promotions are the result of special treatment. "People always say, 'He got that because he's black,'" says Bernard Kinsey, a Xerox vice president since 1983. "It's frustrating to never get the recognition for having done something." African-American executives contend that their qualifications and performance often exceed those of the whites they are competing against. Says NBC's Gilbert: "We don't give these people enough credit. Look at their backgrounds. They would have been success stories even if there were no affirmative action."

Oddly, the stereotype of the less qualified black is sometimes shared by blacks. The feeling is summed up in a wry phrase: "The white man's ice is colder." Kenneth Glover, 37, managing director for municipal finance at the Manhattan branch of Drexel Burnham Lambert Inc., recalls prospecting a well-to-do black executive as a potential client. After a telephone conversation, Glover invited the prospect to a face-to-face meeting. It broke off after only ten minutes. Later the client phoned and asked for his account to be transferred to a white investment adviser.

The going gets especially tough for blacks who have climbed near the top of the ladder. There they frequently encounter the so-called glass ceiling: they can see the next step up, but they never get invited to take it. "You have to be twice as good to get the job you want," says Robert Lee Dean, 48, a $50,000-a-year maintenance planner at a Boise Cascade plant in Jackson, Ala. . . .

Frustrated by the slow pace of change in corporate bureaucracies, many black entrepreneurs have struck out on their own. An example is Peggie Henderson, 40, who co-founded two clothing stores in Tunica, Miss., in 1979. Her family, using their own funds and $147,000 in state loans, started the Southern Group, Inc. At first the company provided two disparate services, duplicating videocassettes and distributing chemical cleaners. Recently it expanded into production. A small assembly line now turns out all-purpose cleaner and dishwashing liquid at the rate of about 50 bottles a minute. . . . Says she: "The only way the conditions of black people will improve is for us to provide jobs for ourselves. I think it's going to get worse as far as white people hiring blacks, unless we are super, super people."

Charles Blair, 41, can remember the vacation car trips of his childhood in the 1950s. Before the family took off, his father would carefully map out in advance how far they would get on each tank of gas. He had to be sure they didn't run low on a stretch of road where the service stations wouldn't sell to blacks. Those days are just a memory now—but a memory Blair wants to pass on to his two teenage sons, to help them understand the hurdles he faced in launching his own management-consulting firm in Indianapolis. "I just try to give them some sense of history," he says. And another thing, "I teach them not to feel inferior. Any barriers that seem to exist—they can find a way to do something about them.". . .

Problems in the Black Middle Class

Although middle-class blacks have seen their fortunes rise markedly since the Reagan recovery began in 1982, most are still not back to the levels of the late 1970s, before the Reagan recession. The median income for blacks in 1987 was 57.1 percent of that for whites, lower than in any year of the 1970s. Besides, gains in income are diluted by the fact that, as the Urban League's John Jacob puts it, most blacks, lacking a large savings, "are 26 weeks away from poverty." In 1984 the median net worth of black households was just $3,397, *nine percent* of the white average. Finally, the source of much black middle-class income is in some ways ominous. Fully half of all black managers and professionals are government workers, while the more lucrative jobs in private business are overwhelmingly white. Black business executives tend to be disproportionately lodged in equal-employment opportunity and community-relations posts, and are disproportionately laid off in corporate restructurings.

Morton Kondracke, *The New Republic*, February 6, 1989.

One of the most sensitive issues for the black middle class is its relationship to the ghetto poor. University of Chicago sociologist William Julius Wilson has elaborated a persuasive theory suggesting that the worsening status of the underclass is inextricably tied to the flight from the inner city of most of its upwardly mobile black population. Its departure not only deprived poor youngsters of successful role models but also knocked the props from under churches, schools and other neighborhood institutions that provided stability and support for the impoverished. Middle-class flight, together with economic shifts that have resulted in a dearth of low-skill factory jobs, dooms the inner city to social isolation and despair.

Though they may sympathize with the tragedy of the underclass, many middle-class blacks are not prepared to remain inside the ghetto. They point out that they have worked hard to spare themselves and their families deprivation. . . .

Nevertheless, the decline of the underclass imposes a psychological burden, in part because whites remain far too willing to associate all blacks with welfare dependency, crime and broken families. Moreover, many middle-class blacks feel personally guilty about the unpromising prospects of poorer blacks. That may be the most unfair burden of all, since the black middle class by itself does not have nearly enough resources to lift the underclass into the mainstream. Patricia Grayson speaks for many affluent blacks when she observes, "One person can do only so much. I think it's unfair for people to try to make successful blacks feel guilty for not feeling guilty all the time."

The truth is that *all* of the nation should feel ashamed and enraged by the sorry condition of the underclass. Its misery in the midst of an affluent society is a disgrace. While the growth and strength of the black middle class prove that the U.S. has gone far to untangle its racial conundrum, racism remains at the top of a long list of unsolved national problems. The success of middle-class blacks is mainly the product of their own hard work and tenacity. But it would not have occurred without the national consensus, embodied in civil rights legislation, to dismantle segregation and create equal opportunities for all. Further strides toward that goal depend on a renewed commitment to the elimination of prejudice—and an economy buoyant enough to ensure opportunities for all Americans.

There are already unsettling signals that the future growth of the black middle class is in jeopardy at its source. For one thing, while rates of college enrollment by black women have remained steady, the number of black males enrolled in colleges declined from 470,000 to 436,000 between 1976 and 1986. That represents a drop of 34,000 students during a period when total college enrollment grew by more than a million and the proportion of black students who finished high school climbed from 68% to 76%. Possible explanations include the shift from grants to loans in federal aid for higher education, a lack of aggressive recruitment by colleges and tougher entrance requirements.

Future progress might be stifled by an economic downturn. University of Maryland sociologist Bart Landry, author of *The New Black Middle Class*, predicts that by the end of the [century] 56.4% of all black workers and 63% of all white workers will be in the middle class—provided the economy expands at a healthy clip. If it does not, Landry warns, the expansion of the black middle class could come to a sudden halt. Says he: "During periods when the economy is tight, discrimination asserts itself."

"High dropout rates, low salaries, and job discrimination have plagued many Latinos, ensnaring them in a cycle of poverty, alienation, and underachievement."

Racism Causes Hispanic Poverty

Rafael Valdivieso and Cary Davis

Hispanics—people with Latin American and Spanish-speaking heritage—are a rapidly growing minority group in the U.S. In the following viewpoint, Rafael Valdivieso and Cary Davis describe the Hispanic population in the U.S. and argue that racial discrimination in employment and education causes many Hispanics to live in poverty. Valdivieso is vice president for research at the Hispanic Poverty Development Project, an organization which encourages the analysis of public policies affecting Hispanics in the U.S. Davis is director of administration and a research demographer for the Population Reference Bureau, a research organization focusing on national and global population trends.

As you read, consider the following questions:

1. How many different Hispanic groups do Valdivieso and Davis describe?
2. What disadvantages do Hispanics face in the U.S. because of their background, according to the authors?
3. What government policies do Valdivieso and Davis recommend concerning Hispanics?

From "U.S. Hispanics: Challenging Issues for the 1990s," by Rafael Valdivieso and Cary Davis, *Population Trends and Public Policy*, no. 17, December 1988. Reprinted with permission of the Population Reference Bureau.

The number of Hispanic residents in the United States reached 20 million in 1988. After blacks, they are the nation's largest minority. Most Americans know that the number of Hispanics is increasing rapidly, but few really know much about the Hispanic community or appreciate the diversity among Latino groups. Nor do they realize the impact the Hispanic population will have on the nation's schools and labor force in the future.

The very term "Hispanic" is a label with a nebulous meaning, applied by the general population to an ever-changing group of U.S. residents. The terms Hispanic or Latino generally refer to individuals whose cultural heritage traces back to a Spanish-speaking country in Latin America, but also include those persons with links to Spain, or from the southwestern region of the U.S., once under Spanish or Mexican control.

Hispanics are found in every U.S. state, in every type of profession, and may be of any race—but the tendency to generalize about them as a group is fueled by the fact that the majority speak Spanish, live in the Southwest, and occupy the lower end of the social hierarchy.

Many Hispanics face similar problems which—because of their increasing numbers—U.S. policymakers must address. High dropout rates, low salaries, and job discrimination have plagued many Latinos, ensnaring them in a cycle of poverty, alienation, and underachievement. Public policies and programs dealing with education, welfare, and labor relations can help Hispanics lead more productive, independent lives. . . .

Stark Contrasts

The growing Hispanic presence in the U.S. has blinded many Americans to the real diversity that exists within this community. The categories of "Hispanics" used by the Census Bureau largely reflect the countries of origin for recent migration streams: Mexicans; Puerto Ricans; Cubans; Central and South Americans; along with the catchall "Other Hispanics."

Latinos of Mexican ancestry have long been the largest U.S. group covered by the umbrella term Hispanic. In 1988, Mexicans accounted for 62 percent of all Hispanic Americans. About 13 percent of U.S. mainland Hispanics were Puerto Rican in 1988; 5 percent were Cuban; 12 percent Central and South American; and 8 percent "Other Hispanic." Except for the "Other" category, all the groups have made their major numerical impact on the U.S. since World War II. . . .

Latinos have many characteristics that set them apart from other Americans, but which are also common to other disadvantaged minorities and to earlier immigrant groups. In general, Hispanics have less education, lower incomes, and higher rates of unemployment and poverty than the general population. They have been painted with a broad brush of ethnic stereotyping—hated for their differences and feared because of their growing presence.

Hispanic Median Weekly Earnings as a Percentage of White Median Weekly Earnings, Ages 16-34, for Selected Metropolitan Areas 1987 vs. 1979

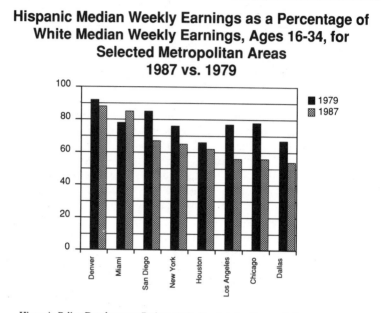

Hispanic Policy Development Project, 1990. Reprinted with permission.

Because many Hispanics have darker skin than the average non-Hispanic, and because most speak Spanish, they are an easy target for discrimination. Public concern and misinformation about illegal immigration has tarnished the image of all Hispanics because most illegals are from Latin America. Many blame Hispanics for the flow of illegal drugs from Latin America.

Hispanics have faced discrimination in schools and housing, and in obtaining jobs and promotions. They have suffered harassment by police and been discouraged from political participation. Many earlier immigrant groups suffered from similar injustices. However, in part because substantial immigration from Latin America is still occurring, Hispanics continue to experience ethnic discrimination.

Slow Educational Progress

Low educational achievement has been a major barrier to the advancement of Hispanics in U.S. society. Hispanics have made modest gains in educational attainment since 1970, yet education

110

still stands out as one of the quality-of-life indicators most at odds with the non-Hispanic population. More than 3 out of 5 (62 percent) Latinos age 25 to 34 had completed four years of high school by March 1988, but a much higher proportion (89 percent) of non-Hispanics had completed high school.

Although good schools can break the cycle, research consistently shows that the success of children in school can usually be predicted from the educational status of their parents. The Latino adults most likely to have school-age children are in the 25-to-34 age bracket. In 1988, this group was over three times as likely to have not completed high school as other Americans.

Some U.S. Latino groups are more likely than others to have high school diplomas. In 1988, nearly 83 percent of Cuban Americans age 25 to 34 had completed high school compared to only 67 percent of Puerto Ricans and 54 percent of Mexican Americans.

Only 12 percent of Hispanics in the 25-to-34 age bracket had completed four or more years of college, less than half the percentage of non-Hispanics. The range within Hispanic groups is even more striking, from a low of 8 percent of Mexican Americans to a high of 24 percent of Cuban Americans with four or more years of college.

Although many Hispanic students are handicapped by a limited knowledge of English, this alone does not explain poor academic performance. Among Hispanics, Cuban students are the most likely to speak Spanish at home, yet have the highest educational levels. Clearly, for these students the benefits of the middle class, professional background of the majority of U.S.-Cuban parents outweigh the "disadvantage" of having to learn English as a second language.

While college attendance is crucial for overall advancement of Hispanics, increasing the percentage who finish high school is a necessary first step. The high dropout rate not only hurts Hispanics, it constitutes a massive waste of human resources sorely needed in this era of keen international economic competition. Moreover, because educational attainment is strongly associated with social and economic status, the high dropout rate is certain to contribute to Latino poverty in the future.

Low-Paying Jobs

In 1988, Hispanics made up only 7 percent of the U.S. civilian labor force. The Hispanic share, however, is likely to increase as the non-Hispanic population ages and the number of working-age Hispanics continues to grow.

Hispanic men, in fact, are more likely to be employed or seeking work than other American men, 79 percent versus 74 percent, although only about 71 percent of Puerto Rican and Other Hispanic males are in the labor force.

111

Hispanic women, and Puerto Ricans in particular, are less likely to be working than other women. Only 51 percent of female Hispanics, and 40 percent of Puerto Rican women, were in the labor force in 1988 compared to 56 percent of non-Hispanic women. Some observers feel that this difference reflects the traditional Latin American disapproval of women working outside the home. However, this gap may be closing: The percentage of younger Hispanic women who are working exceeds that of young non-Hispanics.

Combating Racism

Perhaps no area is more worthy of business concern than the destructive and destabilizing racial and ethnic prejudice, discrimination, and violence erupting today in major metropolitan centers. And it is not all taking place down these mean streets. Increasingly—even in polite company—it is becoming "acceptable" to make bigoted comments.

Communities that divide themselves sharply along racial and ethnic lines are not communities that will succeed in integrating Hispanics or any other group into their economic mainstreams. In fact, they are communities at risk of destroying all sense of community.

Hispanic Policy Development Project, *A More Perfect Union*, 1990.

Because of their relatively low educational levels and language problems, Hispanics tend to enter poorly-paid jobs with little chance of advancement. In 1988, only 28 percent of Hispanic men were in the upper-level managerial, technical, and administrative categories compared to 48 percent of non-Hispanic men. Cuban men are an exception to this; 51 percent held higher-status positions.

Not only are Hispanics overrepresented in low-paying, semiskilled jobs but they work in economic sectors vulnerable to cyclical unemployment and in some industries, like manufacturing, that are threatened with a long-term decline. Hispanics are as likely as non-Hispanics to be in the labor force, yet they are more likely to be unemployed. In 1988, 8.5 percent of Hispanics were out of work compared to only 5.8 percent of other Americans.

High Poverty Rates

The low-status occupations and high unemployment among Hispanics translate into low incomes and high poverty rates. Median family income for Hispanics in 1987 was only $20,300, two-thirds of the non-Hispanic median income of $31,600. In real dollars, this income gap between Hispanics and other Americans actually grew between 1978 and 1987, primarily because Hispanics still have not recovered from the economic recession of 1980 and 1981.

Within the Hispanic community, income levels reveal marked differences. Cuban family income in 1987, at $27,300, approached the non-Hispanic median. Puerto Rican families, at the other extreme, had average annual incomes of only $15,200, one-half of the non-Hispanic median and more than $5,000 less than the next highest Hispanic group.

Since Hispanic families are relatively large, these incomes must support more household members. The average family size for non-Hispanics in 1988 was 3.1, compared to 3.8 for all Hispanics and 4.1 persons for Mexican Americans.

Also, Hispanic families are less likely than others to be headed by a married couple and much more likely to be headed by a single parent, usually the mother. Consequently, fewer Hispanic families have the potential earning power provided by two working parents. Married-couple families account for only 70 percent of all Hispanic families, compared to 80 percent of non-Hispanic families. Nearly one-quarter, 23 percent, are headed by an unmarried or separated woman, while 16 percent of non-Hispanic families are female-headed. A whopping 44 percent of Puerto Rican families are headed by single females, double the Hispanic and almost triple the non-Hispanic average.

Children at Risk

These statistics highlight the handicaps faced by many Latino children. With large families, low incomes, and a high proportion of single-parent families, the success of a significant proportion of the next generation is at risk. In 1987, 26 percent of all Hispanic families had incomes below the poverty threshold, compared to only 10 percent of non-Hispanic families. In single-parent families headed by an Hispanic female, over half (52 percent) were below the poverty line, exactly equal to the proportion of black families headed by a single female in poverty.

Within Hispanic groups, poverty rates range from a high of 38 percent for Puerto Rican families to a low of 14 percent for Cuban. Perhaps most discouraging, two-thirds of female-headed Puerto Rican families were poor in 1987.

Poverty rates for Hispanics actually increased between 1978 and 1987, while rates for white and black Americans have decreased. The number of poor Hispanics grew from 2.9 million in 1979 to 5.5 million in 1987, a 90 percent increase.

Poor Hispanics are less likely to benefit from federal welfare programs than poor black Americans, but more likely than non-Hispanic whites. The percentage of poor Hispanics served by federal welfare programs fell slightly between 1980 and 1988, partly as a result of federal budget cuts. The only major program that reaches a majority of poor Hispanics is the subsidized school lunch program, received by 92 percent of poor Hispanic children in 1988. In the same year, only 30 percent of poor Hispanics received cash assistance; 13 percent lived in public housing; 49 percent received food stamps; and 42 percent received Medicaid.

High poverty rates are likely to persist among Hispanics in the 1990s. Actions to curb the high poverty levels must deal primarily with:

• Education and job training;
• Discrimination in hiring and promotion; and
• Access to welfare programs by the Hispanic poor, especially single-parent families.

Each of these issues requires the attention of policymakers and community leaders from the national to the local level. . . .

As we enter the 1990s, U.S. Hispanics constitute an increasing share of our school children and entry-level job seekers; yet they remain a disadvantaged minority. The Latinos' growing presence suggests that policymakers should seek ways to:

• Ease their transition into mainstream society;
• Ensure their maximum productivity through improved education and training; and
• Encourage their participation in the decision-making and political processes.

Perhaps the recognition that improving the position of Hispanics is in the best interest of all Americans offers policymakers the best incentive to focus more attention on Hispanic concerns.

"Hispanics are making far more progress in this society than is generally believed."

Hispanic Poverty Is Not Caused by Racism

Linda Chavez

Linda Chavez is a former staff director of the U.S. Civil Rights Commission and is currently a senior fellow at the Manhattan Institute for Policy Research, a conservative New York-based research organization. In the following viewpoint, she argues that the vast majority of Hispanics are not impoverished, but are instead succeeding economically and socially in the U.S. She states that poverty statistics for Hispanics are relatively high because many of them are recently arrived immigrants. Chavez asserts that government programs based on the assumption that Hispanics are a disadvantaged minority are flawed and may actually harm Hispanics.

As you read, consider the following questions:

1. Why does Chavez contend that statistics measuring Hispanic poverty undervalue Hispanic progress?
2. What two distinct groups of Hispanics reside in the U.S., according to the author?
3. According to Chavez, why are Puerto Ricans poorer than other Hispanic groups?

Linda Chavez, "Tequila Sunrise." Reprinted, with permission, from the Spring 1989 issue of *Policy Review*, the flagship publication of The Heritage Foundation, 214 Massachusetts Ave. NE, Washington, DC 20002.

Hispanics are one of the fastest growing groups in the United States and may within 50 years represent the largest single ethnic group in the country. Today, 19.5 million Hispanics live in the U.S., making up almost 8 percent of the overall population. If current rates of immigration and fertility continue, by the middle of the 21st century one out of three Americans will be of Hispanic descent. What happens to Hispanics is therefore important not only for the well-being of members of that group but for the future of this country. Fortunately, despite the popular belief that Hispanics are faring poorly, the evidence—properly examined—suggests that most Hispanics are making clear progress into the economic and social mainstream.

Appearance of an Underclass

As a group, Hispanics are more likely than the general population to be poor, unemployed, under-educated, and living in families headed by women. The Census Bureau reported that the wage gap between median earnings of Hispanic families and those of non-Hispanic whites had actually grown between 1986 and 1987, with Hispanics earning only 66 percent of what non-Hispanics earned. More than a quarter of all Hispanic families lived below the poverty line in 1987.

Statistics like these have led to speculation that Hispanics are becoming an underclass. The response of many Hispanic leaders has been to argue for government programs to solve the problems that seem to plague the Hispanic community. Rafael Valdivieso, vice president of the Hispanic Policy Development Project, summarized the position of many Hispanic leaders in a recent publication he co-authored with Cary Davis for the Population Reference Bureau: "High dropout rates, low salaries, and job discrimination have plagued many Latinos, ensnaring them in a cycle of poverty, alienation, and underachievement. Public policies and programs dealing with education, welfare, and labor relations can help Hispanics lead more productive, independent lives."

The federal government has for the last 20 years premised its policy toward Hispanics on just such analyses, and the states have followed suit. The result has been the creation of programs that treat Hispanics as a more or less permanently disadvantaged minority group. When the programs fail to produce the desired results—as the statistics policymakers rely on seem to demonstrate—more money and additional programs are requested. This approach is doomed to failure because the assumptions on which it rests are simply wrong. Hispanics are making far more progress in this society than is generally believed, but the indications of that success are hidden behind statistics that ignore important differences among Hispanics.

116

Most analysts concede interethnic differences between Hispanic subgroups. For example, average (mean) family income and median education attainment for Cuban Americans is almost the same as for the general population, while that of Mexican Americans and Puerto Ricans lags far behind. (Since Cubans make up barely 5 percent of the entire Hispanic population, statistics on Cuban income or education have a negligible effect on those of the total group, however.) More important than interethnic differences between Hispanics are differences related to individual nativity and length of time in the United States.

Hispanic Integration

To be sure, at various times and places Hispanics have been subjected to something quite close to racial discrimination. But the evidence on the integration of Hispanics into American society indicates that they generally do not face the same problems as blacks—the efforts of Hispanic leaders to persuade their people and the American public to the contrary notwithstanding.

Peter Skerry, *The Wall Street Journal*, April 27, 1990.

In assessing Hispanic progress, it is important to know whether the group being measured at point A is essentially the same as the group being measured at point B. When we find, for example, that median family income for Hispanics in the United States went up only $1,300 (in constant 1987 dollars) between 1982 and 1987 while median family income for non-Hispanics went up $3,500 in the same period, we assume that progress for individual Hispanics is proceeding at a much slower rate than for other Americans. Our assumption rests on the notion that the Hispanic group being measured in 1982 is essentially the same as the group being measured in 1987. The problem is, it's not. Between 1982 and 1987, the Hispanic population of the United States grew by nearly 25 percent. Almost half of this growth came from immigration by foreign-born Hispanics. Approximately one-third of all Hispanics are foreign-born and at least one-third of these came here within the last five years. Not surprisingly, the presence of these new immigrants distorts the picture of Hispanic progress.

Double Handicap

Most Latin immigrants come to the United States in their late teens and early twenties to enter the labor force. Most start with two handicaps in the U.S. job market: on average, they have less formal education than their native-born counterparts and they do not speak English fluently. The median education attainment

117

for Mexican immigrants is 6.1 years, barely half the median education attainment of the total U.S. population. But, perhaps even more important in impact on immigrants' earnings is lack of English fluency. Intuitively, the link between poor English language skills and low wages seems clear. The only kind of jobs that require little or no English occur in low-paid occupations or in ethnic enclaves where supervisors speak the language of immigrant employees.

A recent study of all immigrants by Francisco L. Rivera-Batiz confirms this view. Using information from a 1985 National Assessment of Educational Progress Young Adult Literacy Assessment Survey, Rivera-Batiz establishes "strong and statistically significant positive connections between English reading proficiency and wages." He shows that average hourly wages for immigrants rise from $5.36 an hour for those who have been in the United States less than five years to $6.24 after five years and $7.03 after 10 years. "The increase in wages . . . is directly associated with the increased English proficiency [on reading scores] from 192 to 202 to 288 exhibited by corresponding groups of immigrants." (A score of 300 reflects adept English reading skills; thus immigrants appear to approach English reading fluency after 10 years in the United States.

Another study by Walter McManus, William Gould, and Finis Welch specifically links English proficiency to higher wages among Hispanic males. McManus et al. assert that "among those [Hispanics] for whom the language questionnaire identifies no deficiencies in English, we find no important earnings differences from native-born Anglos."

Educational Advances

Any analysis that treats Hispanics without regard to their nativity or time of arrival in the United States will show depressed education and wage levels for the entire group. The Census Bureau's Population Characteristics Series of its Current Population Reports provides information on Hispanics that is broken down by age, sex, and Hispanic subgroup, but not by nativity or length of stay in the United States. The decennial census, however, solicits information on the nativity of respondents. In an analysis of 1980 census data for the Russell Sage Foundation, Frank Bean and Marta Tienda report important differences in the status of native-born and foreign-born Hispanics. In 1980, for example, the median education attainment of adult, native-born Mexican Americans was 11.1 years compared with 12.0 years for non-Hispanic whites. By comparison, foreign-born Mexican immigrants had a median education attainment of only 6.1 years. The combined education attainment of all Mexican-origin Hispanics was 9.1 years. Including both native- and foreign-born Mexican-origin persons in the same category makes it appear that Mexican Americans are more educationally deprived than they actually are.

Other studies that separate data on native-born Hispanics produce similar results. The RAND Corporation reports that native-born Hispanics are staying in school in California at the same rate as the statewide average. The dropout rate among native Hispanics in California is about 20 percent, not the 40 or 50 percent rate generally reported for all Hispanics. Bean and Tienda confirm that the dropout rate differential for foreign-born Mexicans nationally is twice that of native-born Mexican Americans and that non-English-speaking Hispanic students are three or four times more likely than Hispanics who speak English to drop out of school before graduation.

These studies suggest that the Hispanic population of the United States really consists of two distinct subsets: new immigrants and native-born Hispanics or Latin immigrants who have been in the United States at least 10 years. The latter group is making impressive progress in American society. Native-born Mexican Americans earn 75 percent of the median family income of non-Hispanic whites in 1980, up from 69 percent in 1970. Even this gap can be explained in part by their relative youth. The median age of Hispanics in 1980 was 23 years, compared with 30 years for the total population. (As already noted, the earnings of fully English-proficient Hispanic men are equal to those of non-Hispanics.) But most important, even immigrant Hispanics, who show larger initial wage gaps, quickly close those gaps. As Barry Chiswick has stated in an American Enterprise Institute publication, after 15 years in the United States, Mexican immigrants earn wages equivalent to their native-born counterparts; after 18 years, Cuban immigrants (who have higher median education attainment than Mexicans) earn wages equivalent to non-Hispanic whites.

Jewish Parallel?

Individual members of the first subset of Hispanics are constantly moving into the next group, but the way we report the status of the Hispanic population tends to obscure this important fact. The result is a picture of Hispanic progress as more or less stagnant—and a call for programs to treat Hispanics as a permanently disadvantaged minority group rather than as an aspiring immigrant and first-generation population that is on the road to success in the United States.

The tendency to base assumptions about future progress for an ethnic group on the basis of information from a snapshot view of their current status is certainly not unique to Hispanics. Thomas Sowell recounts in his book, *Ethnic America*, the ways in which contemporary analysts assessed Jews in New York in the early 1900s:

The remarkable achievements—especially intellectual achievements—of later generations of Jews cannot simply be read back into the immigrant generation. These children often had serious educational problems. A 1910 survey of a dozen cities found two-thirds of the children of Polish Jews to be below the normal grade for their age. . . . A 1911 study showed that 41 percent of the 5,431 Russian-Jewish children surveyed were behind the "normal" grade level. . . . As late as World War I, soldiers of Russian—mostly Jewish—origin averaged among the lowest mental test scores of any of the ethnic groups tested by the U.S. Army. These results led a leading contemporary authority on tests to declare that this disproved "the popular belief that the Jew is highly intelligent." Like many confident "expert" conclusions, this one failed to stand the test of time.

Such thinking not only can motivate ethnic prejudice but varieties of it can direct well-meaning but misguided policy. The notion that Hispanics are failing to move into the economic and social mainstream provides the basis of support for programs as wide-ranging as bilingual education for elementary and secondary school children to ballots printed in Spanish for Hispanic voters to affirmative action programs for Hispanics in public and private education and employment. These programs are necessary, so the reasoning goes, because Hispanics lag behind the general population in all socioeconomic indicators and will not "catch up" without government-directed efforts. Little attention is paid to the fact that Hispanics are making precisely the kind of progress one would expect from a group so heavily dominated by non-English-speaking immigrants—slow but steady movement into the middle class by successive generations born in the United States.

Puerto Rican Exception

Not all Hispanic subgroups fare equally well. Puerto Ricans (not surprisingly, since they are citizens by birth) do not fit the immigrant pattern of Mexican-, Caribbean-, and Central or South American-origin Hispanics. They suffer the highest rates of poverty, unemployment, female-headed households, and out-of-wedlock births. Although Puerto Ricans cannot be divided into the usual foreign-born/native-born categories for comparisons of earnings levels and education, they can be divided into island-born and mainland-born. For Puerto Ricans, only education attainment seems to be positively affected by nativity—in 1980, educational levels were higher by three years for mainland-born Puerto Ricans, making them equal in education attainment to non-Hispanics.

One clue to understanding why Puerto Ricans fare so poorly is their low labor force participation. Only 74 percent of Puerto Rican males worked or were looking for work in 1980, compared with 84.5 percent of white men. Puerto Rican men born on the mainland were even less likely to work: only 67 percent participated in the labor force. By contrast, other Hispanics were as likely or more likely to participate in the labor force than the general population; foreign-born Mexican-origin males had the highest rate, 88 percent.

Hispanics Face Less Discrimination

In the early years of the [civil rights] movement, Hispanics—mostly Mexican-Americans and Puerto Ricans—could claim that, like blacks, they had suffered discrimination and were entitled to the same anti-discrimination programs. Even then, however, the case was weak. Bias against Mexican-Americans was never as pervasive as it was against blacks. As early as 1931 attempts to establish segregated schools for Latino children were struck down in court. In Texas—certainly the most hostile environment Mexican-Americans faced—Jim Crow laws did not apply to Mexican-Americans. Nor did political leaders turn their backs on Hispanic voters. From the late nineteenth century on, Mexican-American votes were an important source of Democratic power in Texas. And Hispanics successfully ran for statewide office even in states with few Hispanic voters. Since 1900 six Hispanics have been elected governor in three states, New Mexico, Arizona, and Florida; it took until 1989 for the first black to be elected governor of any state, Douglas Wilder in Virginia. Hispanic leaders bristle at the suggestion that Hispanics have faced less discrimination in this society than blacks—but it's true.

Linda Chavez, *The New Republic*, November 19, 1990.

A corollary to Puerto Ricans' low labor force participation is their high rate of dependence on public assistance. Puerto Rican women are more likely to be on welfare than are white, black, or other Hispanic women, according to Bean and Tienda.

Even among Puerto Ricans, however, the prognosis is not totally dim. Though fewer Puerto Ricans work, those who hold jobs are doing as well or better than other Hispanics. According to the Current Population Survey for March 1988, 32 percent of Puerto Rican men and 65 percent of Puerto Rican women who were employed held white-collar jobs; 15 percent of the men and 20 percent of the women were employed in managerial and professional roles.

These figures suggest two Puerto Rican communities, one made up of persons who have jobs and are doing well and another of those who are out of the labor force and are struggling economically. Charles Murray in his book *Losing Ground* made an eloquent case that welfare policy was largely responsible for a similar pattern among blacks. Welfare may indeed be the culprit in the bifurcated Puerto Rican community. Unlike most Hispanic immigrants, Puerto Ricans have had access to federal welfare programs before coming to the United States.

The Puerto Rican experience suggests we ought to proceed cautiously in creating programs to "help" Hispanics. Hispanic leaders who call for ever more government involvement in the lives of Hispanics should consider the law of unintended consequences. Too often the helping hand of government becomes a vise of dependency. Surely no one wants to derail the progress ordinary Hispanic men and women are making now on their own.

Recognizing Stereotypes

A stereotype is an oversimplified or exaggerated description of people or things. Stereotyping can be favorable. However, most stereotyping tends to be highly uncomplimentary and, at times, degrading.

Stereotyping grows out of our prejudices. When we stereotype someone, we are prejudging him or her. Consider the following example: Mr. Smith believes all ethnic minorities in the U.S. are drug abusers who would rather steal money and deal drugs than do an honest day's work. If Mr. Smith sees young black, Hispanic, or Asian men idle, he tells them to get a job. He disregards the possibilities that they may not be able to find work for a variety of legitimate reasons or may have a job but work a different shift than Mr. Smith. Instead, he labels them as lazy criminals. Why? He has prejudged all minorities and will keep his stereotype consistent with his prejudice.

Part I

The following statements relate to the subject matter in this chapter. Consider each statement carefully. *Mark S for any statement that is an example of stereotyping. Mark N for any statement that is not an example of stereotyping. Mark U if you are undecided about any statement.*

S = *stereotype*
N = *not a stereotype*
U = *undecided*

123

1. The majority of corporate presidents in the U.S. are white.

2. All whites carry prejudices against blacks.

3. Blacks are the most oppressed minority in the United States.

4. Asians adjust to American life easier than other minorities because they are intelligent and motivated.

5. Blacks are to blame for their own poverty because they all use drugs and have illegitimate children.

6. One-third of all blacks live in poverty.

7. All Hispanics and Asians have large families.

8. American Indians tend to be poor and uneducated.

9. American Indians are peaceful and live in harmony with the earth and its creatures.

10. Blacks succeed in professional sports because of their superior physical prowess.

11. Most blacks tend to vote for Democratic candidates in presidential elections.

12. Test scores indicate that Asians score higher in math than blacks and whites.

13. Asian children are naturally proficient at math and science.

14. Blacks are arrested more frequently than members of any other racial group because they break laws more often.

15. Racial bias against Hispanics was never as strong as it was against blacks.

16. Whites are more educated than blacks.

Part II

Based on the insights you have gained from this activity, discuss these questions in class:

1. Why do people stereotype one another?

2. What are some examples of positive stereotypes?

3. Why are stereotypes harmful?

4. What stereotypes currently affect members of your class?

Periodical Bibliography

The following articles have been selected to supplement the diverse views presented in this chapter.

George M. Anderson — "Housing Discrimination: A White Collar Crime," *America*, March 31, 1990.

John Sibley Butler — "The Need for Black Business," *Current*, January 1991.

Linda Chavez — "Rainbow Collision," *The New Republic*, November 19, 1990.

William Granville Jr. — "From Gangland to Corporate America," *The Freeman*, June 1990. Available from The Foundation for Economic Education, Irvington-on-Hudson, NY 10533.

Dorothy Height — "Self-Help—A Black Tradition," *The Nation*, July 24-31, 1989.

Norman Hill — "Blacks and the Unions," *Dissent*, Fall 1989.

William J. Kolshenyk — "Pride and Prejudice," *Conservative Digest*, July/August 1989.

Morton M. Kondracke — "The Two Black Americas," *The New Republic*, February 6, 1989.

Richard D. Lamm — "Confronting Minority Failure," *Vital Speeches of the Day*, May 1, 1989.

Joseph Perkins — "Boom Time for Black America," *Policy Review*, Summer 1988.

Ishmael Reed — "The Black Pathology Biz," *The Nation*, November 20, 1989.

James P. Scanlan — "The Perils of Provocative Statistics," *The Public Interest*, Winter 1991.

Peter Skerry — "Hispanic Job Discrimination Exaggerated," *The Wall Street Journal*, April 27, 1990.

Shelby Steele — "On Being Black and Middle Class," *Commentary*, January 1988.

Roberto Suro — "Hispanics in Despair," *The New York Times*, November 4, 1990.

Martin Tolchin — "Minority Poverty on Rise but White Poor Decline," *The New York Times*, September 1, 1988.

Margaret B. Wilkerson and Jewell Handy Gresham — "The Racialization of Poverty," *The Nation*, July 24-31, 1989.

Does Affirmative Action Alleviate Discrimination?

Chapter Preface

For more than two centuries, minorities have suffered from the effects of discrimination in employment and education. In an effort to remedy this situation, the federal government established affirmative action programs that prohibited discrimination. President Lyndon Johnson's executive order in 1965 required federal contractors to adopt affirmative action guidelines to ensure that applicants were employed without regard to their race, creed, color, or national origin. The Equal Employment Act of 1972 further applied affirmative action principles to colleges and universities in order to increase minority enrollment.

As a result of these laws, affirmative action has increased minority opportunities and income. For example, U.S. Census Bureau data show that the percentage of black families earning more than $25,000 increased almost 8 percent from 1970 to 1987. These improvements have caused civil rights supporters to herald affirmative action as an important and necessary program. Benjamin Hooks, executive director of the National Association for the Advancement of Colored People, credits the policy for the increase in the number of minority politicians, doctors, lawyers, and other professionals.

But while affirmative action has helped some minorities, critics argue that it stigmatizes minorities with self-doubt. Critics assert minority employees tend to feel they may have been hired because they are members of a minority, not because of their qualifications. As Shelby Steele, an author and critic of affirmative action, writes, "The quality that earns us [minorities] preferential treatment is an implied inferiority."

Has affirmative action helped or hurt minorities? Do racial preferences discriminate or reduce discrimination? These questions and other issues are addressed in the following chapter.

"Affirmative action is simply any action taken to ensure, or affirm, equal opportunity for oppressed or previously disadvantaged groups."

Affirmative Action Benefits Minorities

Benjamin L. Hooks

Supporters of affirmative action say that without it, racial discrimination in employment and education would continue unchecked. In the following viewpoint, Benjamin L. Hooks argues that mandatory racial preferences are needed because equal opportunities have been denied to minorities. Hooks believes affirmative action requirements force institutions like corporations and schools to comply with civil rights laws. Hooks is executive director of the National Association for the Advancement of Colored People.

As you read, consider the following questions:

1. What does Hooks believe is ironic about critics of affirmative action?
2. According to the author, why did the system of preferential goals and timetables originate?
3. What examples does Hooks cite as evidence of the benefits of affirmative action?

Benjamin L. Hooks, "'Self-Help' Just Won't Do It All," *Los Angeles Times*, July 10, 1990. Reprinted with permission.

Weary of colonial rule, the angry activists stood on the banks of Boston Harbor on a cold December evening, lugged about 340 crates to the river's edge and pitched more than $10,000 worth of tea into the brisk, bustling waters.

The action of American patriots at the Boston Tea Party—which helped launch the American Revolution—was, incredibly, a pitch for affirmative action.

America's 18th-century revolutionaries were affirming their right to self-determination and equal opportunity. Surely, we have not forgotten their rallying call, "No taxation without representation." Or Patrick Henry's impassioned, noble cry, "Give me liberty or give me death."

This is why we bristle at the current "controversy" over the value and benefits of modern-day affirmative action.

Critics Are Wrong

Affirmative action critics suggest that such policies have not benefited poor blacks, have impeded the development of coalitions for social programs and have inhibited black Americans through a deep sense of inferiority.

These notions would be comical if they weren't so dangerous.

The irony is that that these well-trained—if misguided—academicians have the opportunity to espouse such nonsense is itself due to affirmative action.

Would they have been trained at some of the nation's leading colleges without it? Would they be professors at predominantly white universities? Would they not feel the racist sting of Jim Crow's piercing whip? Would they be published in some of America's most influential periodicals?

They fail to realize that affirmative action is simply any action taken to ensure, or affirm, equal opportunity for oppressed or previously disadvantaged groups.

What's wrong with that? If a society discriminates against a people for centuries—enslaves them, lynches them, oppresses them, denies them access to jobs, homes, a good education, the political process, etc.—the just way to offer remedy is to give that people an equal opportunity.

Goals and Timetables

The affirmative action debate often gets mired in the issue of numerical goals and timetables, which are often disparagingly called quotas by critics and opponents.

The NAACP [National Association for the Advancement of Colored People] has never promoted the concept of so-called quotas. In fact, goals and timetables would never have been necessary if corporate and municipal leaders had been willing to follow the letter and spirit of the law.

129

Goals and timetables came about because of the failure of parties to be sincere in their efforts to provide equal opportunity. They were built in by judges who tired of the stances of interposition and nullification. The "we can't find any" argument was most often an attempt by corporate and municipal leaders to skirt the law. So judges had to construct goals and timetables to keep parties from making a mockery of the federal court. Critics who negate or ignore white America's duty to help solve black America's problems misrepresent the issue, mislead the public and subvert the struggle.

Society Must Be Fair

While we recognize that heightened "self-help" efforts among blacks will lessen our plight—and we at the NAACP promote such efforts—we believe what the Kerner Commission said more than 20 years ago still rings true:

"What white Americans have never fully understood—but what the Negro can never forget—is that white society is deeply implicated in the ghetto. White institutions created it, white institutions maintain it and white society condones it."

Discrimination Breeds Inequality

Blatant discrimination and subtle bias against women and racial minorities continue to breed inequality and close doors of opportunity. And the racially charged rhetoric of "quotas" and "reverse discrimination" used by our leaders is destroying the national will to open those doors. . . .

In 1964, a year after Dr. Martin Luther King shared his "dream," he explained the reasoning behind affirmative action in "Why We Can't Wait":

"It is impossible to create a formula for the future which does not take into account that our society has been doing something special *against* the Negro for hundreds of years. How then can he be absorbed into the mainstream of American life if we do not do something special *for* him now?". . .

Affirmative action is necessary if women and racial minorities are to achieve equality in our nation. Affirmative action works. The problem is not with affirmative action, but with our national leadership.

Mark Lloyd, *The Christian Science Monitor*, January 18, 1991.

In their near-exclusive focus on what blacks should do, critics largely overlook the responsibility of government, big business and the courts in what is purported to be a fair and democratic society.

When blacks have done all they can to save themselves, white society must still do the right thing. If racism, discrimination and unequal opportunity prevail, lone efforts by blacks will remain virtually ineffective.

Certainly, critics who suggest that black Americans need to develop their individual skills and must not eternally regard themselves as victims are not totally wrong. Neither are they wrong when they urge young blacks to study, be disciplined and conscientious, and to reject the notion that achievement somehow diminishes blackness.

But they are totally wrong when they suggest, implicitly or otherwise, that acknowledged black leaders are not pushing these concepts as well. We are. So, at best, these critics are doing no more than parroting our views.

I make hundreds of speeches a year in which I preach the gospel of hard work, discipline and achievement. Other leaders do the same. To suggest otherwise is a gross distortion and disservice.

While self-responsibility and self-determination must play heightened roles in our communities, we believe government cannot shirk its role.

I hasten to add that I am curious as to how this issue evolved as a controversy in the first place. Goals and timetables are as American as apple pie.

You must pay your taxes by April 15. You must not drive more than the posted speed limit. You must register to vote or apply for a passport by certain dates. Car manufacturers must ensure their cars meet certain emissions standards by certain times.

America operates by goals and timetables—and we all acknowledge and accept that. It is only when it comes to human resources that we bristle at this concept.

Affirmative Action's Beneficiaries

Naturally, we at the NAACP promote the concept of self-help. And the fact is that blacks have committed to self-help since the slave ships first docked on America's shores.

In America, we see the benefits of that self-help concept and affirmative action efforts. We have black mayors, elected officials, police officers, firefighters, journalists, judges, doctors, lawyers, captains of industry and thousands of other professionals.

More importantly, we have office clerks, secretaries, laborers, court employees and literally millions of everyday working people whose jobs are indirectly and directly linked to affirmative action and self-help.

These would have been the people mired inextricably in poverty and despair were it not for coalition-building and affirmative action.

The critics who benefited from but oppose affirmative action obscure the legacy of exclusion and discrimination that prompted such remedial efforts. They should be ashamed.

As the U.S. Commission on Civil Rights once noted, just as medical treatment is based on the diagnosis of an illness, affirmative action stems from diagnosis of a social sickness.

The remedy cannot be divorced from the illness. Critics write much about some "corrosive effect" of affirmative action but very little about the racism, oppression and discrimination that necessitates it—and which is much more corrosive and destructive.

We shall at the NAACP always promote self-help, but will never waver in our push to insist that government play its role and do its part. For how long? For as long as necessary.

"I think . . . blacks . . . now stand to lose more from [affirmative action] than they gain."

Affirmative Action Hurts Minorities

Shelby Steele

Critics maintain that the policies of affirmative action do more harm than good. Shelby Steele is one critic who argues that affirmative action does not help those minorities who need the most assistance—low-income blacks. He states that since some minorities are hired due to racial preferences, they suffer from an "implied inferiority," in which their qualifications are questioned by non-minorities. Steele is the author of *The Content of Our Character* and an English professor at San Jose State University in California.

As you read, consider the following questions:

1. What effect has affirmative action had on median incomes of both black and white families since the 1970s, according to Steele?
2. Does the author believe blacks can be justly repaid for the past sufferings of their race?
3. What does Steele mean by the term "glass ceiling" in the corporate environment?

From "A Negative Vote on Affirmative Action," by Shelby Steele, *The New York Times Magazine*, May 13, 1990. Copyright © 1990 by Shelby Steele. Reprinted with special permission from St. Martin's Press, Inc., New York.

In a few short years, when my two children will be applying to college, the affirmative-action policies by which most universities offer black students some form of preferential treatment will present me with a dilemma. I am a middle-class black, a college professor, far from wealthy, but also well removed from the kind of deprivation that would qualify my children for the label "disadvantaged." Both of them have endured racial insensitivity from whites. They have been called names, have suffered slights and have experienced firsthand the peculiar malevolence that racism brings out of people. Yet they have never experienced racial discrimination, have never been stopped by their race on any path they have chosen to follow. Still, their society now tells them that if they will only designate themselves as black on their college applications, they will probably do better in the college lottery than if they conceal this fact. I think there is something of a Faustian bargain in this.

Of course many blacks and a considerable number of whites would say that I was sanctimoniously making affirmative action into a test of character. They would say that this small preference is the meagerest recompense for centuries of unrelieved oppression. And to these arguments other very obvious facts must be added. In America, many marginally competent or flatly incompetent whites are hired every day—some because their white skin suits the conscious or unconscious racial preference of their employers. The white children of alumni are often grandfathered into elite universities in what can only be seen as a residual benefit of historic white privilege. Worse, white incompetence is always an individual matter, but for blacks it is often confirmation of ugly stereotypes. Given that unfairness cuts both ways, doesn't it only balance the scales of history, doesn't this repay, in a small way, the systematic denial under which my children's grandfather lived out his days?

Moral Symmetry

In theory, affirmative action certainly has all the moral symmetry that fairness requires. It is reformist and corrective, even repentant and redemptive. And I would never sneer at these good intentions. . . .

Yet good intentions can blind us to the effects they generate when implemented. In our society affirmative action is, among other things, a testament to white good will and to black power, and in the midst of these heavy investments its effects can be hard to see. But after 20 years of implementation I think that affirmative action has shown itself to be more bad than good and that blacks—whom I will focus on in this essay—now stand to lose more from it than they gain.

In talking with affirmative-action administrators and with

blacks and whites in general, I found that supporters of affirmative action focus on its good intentions and detractors emphasize its negative effects. It was virtually impossible to find people outside either camp. The closest I came was a white male manager at a large computer company who said, "I think it amounts to reverse discrimination, but I'll put up with a little of that for a little more diversity." But this only makes him a half-hearted supporter of affirmative action. I think many people who don't really like affirmative action support it to one degree or another anyway.

I believe they do this because of what happened to white and black Americans in the crucible of the 1960's, when whites were confronted with their racial guilt and blacks tasted their first real power. In that stormy time white absolution and black power coalesced into virtual mandates for society. Affirmative action became a meeting ground for those mandates in the law. At first, this meant insuring equal opportunity. The 1964 civil rights bill was passed on the understanding that equal opportunity would not mean racial preference. But in the late 60's and early 70's, affirmative action underwent a remarkable escalation of its mission from simple anti-discrimination enforcement to social engineering by means of quotas, goals, timetables, set-asides and other forms of preferential treatment.

More Blacks in Poverty

The apparent economic impact of affirmative action has been to help the already upwardly mobile black middle and upper class but to drive more blacks below the poverty line, producing a far more rapid rise in income inequity among blacks than among whites.

Warren T. Brookes, *The Washington Times*, May 24, 1990.

Legally, this was achieved through a series of executive orders and Equal Employment Opportunity Commission guidelines that allowed racial imbalances in the workplace to stand as proof of racial discrimination. Once it could be assumed that discrimination explained racial imbalances, it became easy to justify group remedies to presumed discrimination rather than the normal case-by-case redress.

Even though blacks had made great advances during the 60's without quotas, the white mandate to achieve a new racial innocence and the black mandate to gain power, which came to a head in the very late 60's, could no longer be satisfied by anything less than racial preferences. I don't think these mandates, in themselves, were wrong, because whites clearly needed to do better by blacks and blacks needed more real power in society. But as they came together in affirmative action, their effect was to distort our understanding of racial discrimination. By making black the color of preference, these mandates have reburdened society with the very marriage of color and preference (in reverse) that we set out to eradicate. . . .

Implied Inferiority

The fact is that after 20 years of racial preferences the gap between median incomes of black and white families is greater than it was in the 1970's. None of this is to say that blacks don't need policies that insure our right to equal opportunity, but what we need more of is the development that will let us take advantage of society's efforts to include us.

I think one of the most troubling effects of racial preferences for blacks is a kind of demoralization. Under affirmative action, the quality that earns us preferential treatment is an implied inferiority. . . .

The effect of preferential treatment—the lowering of normal standards to increase black representation—puts blacks at war with an expanded realm of debilitating doubt, so that the doubt itself becomes an unrecognized preoccupation that undermines their ability to perform, especially in integrated situations.

Exploiting the Past

I believe another liability of affirmative action comes from the fact that it indirectly encourages blacks to exploit their own past victimization. Like implied inferiority, victimization is what justifies preference, so that to receive the benefits of preferential treatment one must, to some extent, become invested in the view of one's self as a victim. In this way, affirmative action nurtures a victim-focused identity in blacks and sends us the message that there is more power in our past suffering than in our present achievements.

When power itself grows out of suffering, blacks are encouraged to expand the boundaries of what qualifies as racial oppression, a situation that can lead us to paint our victimization in vivid colors even as we receive the benefits of preference. The same corporations and institutions that give us preference are also seen as our oppressors. At Stanford University, minority-group students—who receive at least the same financial aid as whites with the same need—took over the president's office demanding, among other things, more financial aid.

But I think one of the worst prices that blacks pay for preference has to do with an illusion. I saw this illusion at work recently in the mother of a middle-class black student who was going off to his first semester of college: "They owe us this, so don't think for a minute that you don't belong there." This is the logic by which many blacks, and some whites, justify affirmative action—it is something "owed," a form of reparation. But this logic overlooks a much harder and less digestible reality, that it is impossible to repay blacks living today for the historic suffering of the race. If all blacks were given a million dollars tomorrow it would not amount to a dime on the dollar for three centuries of oppression, nor would it dissolve the residues of that oppression that we still carry today. . . .

Subtle Discrimination

Several blacks I spoke with said they were still in favor of affirmative action because of the "subtle" discrimination blacks were subject to once they were on the job. One photojournalist said, "They have ways of ignoring you." A black female television producer said: "You can't file a lawsuit when your boss doesn't invite you to the insider meetings without ruining your career. So we still need affirmative action." Others mentioned the infamous "glass ceiling" through which blacks can see the top positions of authority but never reach them. But I don't think racial preferences are a protection against this subtle discrimination; I think they contribute to it.

In any workplace, racial preferences will always create two-tiered populations composed of preferreds and unpreferreds. In the case of blacks and whites, for instance, racial preferences imply that whites are superior just as they imply that blacks are inferior. They not only reinforce America's oldest racial myth but, for blacks, they have the effect of stigmatizing the already stigmatized.

I think that much of the "subtle" discrimination that blacks talk about is often (not always) discrimination against the stigma of questionable competence that affirmative action marks blacks with. In this sense, preferences make scapegoats of the very people they seek to help. And it may be that at a certain level employers impose a glass ceiling, but this may not be against the race so much as against the race's reputation for having advanced by color as much as by competence. This ceiling is the point at which corporations shift the emphasis from color to competency and stop playing the affirmative-action game. Here preference backfires for blacks and becomes a taint that holds them back. Of course one could argue that this taint, which is after all in the minds of whites, becomes nothing more than an excuse to discriminate against blacks. And certainly the result is the same in either case—blacks don't get past the glass ceiling. But this argument does not get around the fact that racial preferences now taint this color with a new theme of suspicion that makes blacks even more vulnerable to discrimination. In this crucial yet gray area of perceived competence, preferences make whites look better than they are and blacks worse, while doing nothing whatever to stop the very real discrimination that blacks may encounter. I don't wish to justify the glass ceiling here, but only suggest the very subtle ways that affirmative action revives rather than extinguishes the old rationalizations for racial discrimination.

Preferences Don't Teach Skills

I believe affirmative action is problematic in our society because we have demanded that it create parity between the races rather than insure equal opportunity. Preferential treatment does not teach skills, or educate, or instill motivation. It only passes out entitlement by color. . . .

I think we need social policies that are committed to two goals: the educational and economic development of disadvantaged people regardless of race and the eradication from our society—through close monitoring and severe sanctions—of racial, ethnic or gender discrimination. Preferences will not get us to either of these goals, because they tend to benefit those who are not disadvantaged—middle-class white women and middle-class blacks—and attack one form of discrimination with another. Preferences are inexpensive and carry the glamour of good intentions—change the numbers and the good deed is done. To be against them is to be unkind. But I think the unkindest cut is to bestow on children like my own an undeserved advantage while neglecting the development of those disadvantaged children in the poorer sections of my city who will most likely never be in a position to benefit from a preference. Give my children fairness; give disadvantaged children a better shot at development —better elementary and secondary schools, job training, safer neighborhoods, better financial assistance for college and so on. A smaller percentage of black high school graduates go to college today than 15 years ago; more black males are in prison, jail or in some other way under the control of the criminal-justice system than in college. This despite racial preferences.

"More [affirmative action] is needed, not only to compensate blacks for the effects of past discrimination, but also to reduce present and future discrimination."

Affirmative Action Should Be Strengthened

Stanley H. Masters

Advocates of affirmative action say it is necessary to counter historical discrimination against blacks. In the following viewpoint, Stanley H. Masters argues that whites in America have profited from blacks' lack of opportunities. As a result, says Masters, whites owe blacks increased opportunities in jobs and education. He maintains affirmative action is needed to reduce present and future discrimination. Masters is an economics professor at the State University of New York at Binghamton, and the author of *Black-White Income Differentials*.

As you read, consider the following questions:

1. According to Masters, in what terms do most white males view ethical issues?
2. Why doesn't the author think a competitive economy will eliminate discrimination?
3. Why does Masters believe the Reagan administration generally opposed affirmative action?

Excerpted from "The Social Debt to Blacks: A Case for Affirmative Action," by Stanley H. Masters. Reprinted by permission of Greenwood Publishing Group, Inc., Westport, CT, from *The Wealth of Races* edited by Richard F. America. Copyright © 1990 by Richard F. America.

Blacks and whites have lived together in this country for over 300 years. Throughout this period, the white community has dominated the black community economically. To what extent have whites profited from the inferior economic position of blacks? To what extent do whites owe blacks reparations for white gains that have come at the expense of blacks? As used here reparations refer to actions that favor blacks over whites, actions that create greater opportunities for blacks than will be available through either market competition or through those government policies such as Title VII of the Civil Rights Act of 1964, designed to make the labor market color-blind. . . .

Historical Overview

Let us begin with how blacks and whites first arrived in this country. The ancestors of most whites came to the United States voluntarily. Initially, the main impetus was religious freedom, but soon the motivation of most immigrants was economic opportunity for themselves and their children. The ancestors of most blacks did not come here voluntarily but were brought forcibly by whites. The slave trade would not have originated and continued if it were not profitable for white shipowners.

Although the slave trade was abolished in the early nineteenth century, the institution of slavery continued and prospered. The slave population continued to increase, with some whites in the business of breeding blacks. Many white planters made great fortunes, based partly on their ownership of slaves. In the long run, however, it is doubtful that either the planter class or the South as a whole benefited from slavery. The costs of the Civil War most likely outweighed the previous gains.

After the Civil War, blacks provided a cheap form of wage labor. The presence of many blacks with relatively little skill and almost no physical capital hurt poor whites by providing competition for their labor, thus reducing wage rates. The existence of such cheap labor, however, aided those whites with greater skill and physical capital. While blacks made some gains in schooling and occupational status in the generation after the Civil War, Jim Crow laws soon reversed this trend. As a result of increasing racial barriers to occupations and declining relative quality of black schooling, less skilled whites gained at the expense of blacks in the late nineteenth century.

The Twentieth Century

Opportunities for blacks increased in the twentieth century, especially during periods of high labor demand, such as World War I and World War II. During and after World War II, a significant proportion of blacks left the South for Northern cities. This migration occurred partly because of the declining demand for unskilled labor in Southern agriculture and partly because of the demand of Northern employers for cheap labor to replace the previous stream of European immigrants.

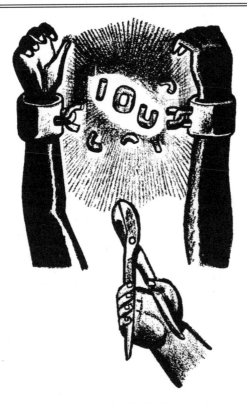

David Suter, *Time*, December 31, 1990. Reprinted with permission.

In the 1960s federal legislation outlawed discrimination in employment and many other areas. Partly for this reason, there was some improvement in the relative economic position of blacks in the late sixties and early seventies. These gains did not continue during the eighties, however. In fact, there has been a decline in the relative family income of blacks. In part, this decline in the relative income of black families has occurred because of the large increase in low-income single-parent families. Blacks have also been hurt disproportionately by the low aggregate demand for labor in the economy over most of the past ten years and by the economic decline of the large Northern cities where many blacks live.

For the past decade there has been relatively little racial differential in the average earnings of women. Among men, however, the average black earns only about two-thirds as much as the average white. Although the earnings rate is somewhat higher for young men who are employed, unemployment is very high among young blacks, about 50 percent for teenagers.

This history, though admittedly very brief and sketchy, highlights several periods when whites have profited at the expense of the elementary human rights of blacks. The most dramatic examples of exploitation are the slave trade bringing blacks to this country, the slave economy of the antebellum South, and the suppression of the economic and political rights of blacks in the period after Reconstruction. Unless it can be shown that the effects of such exploitation have been largely eliminated in subsequent years, there is a strong moral argument for some kind of reparation from whites to blacks.

Reparations from all whites to all blacks for the current effects of previous exploitation runs counter to other equity considerations, however. First, the most flagrant abuses against blacks occurred many years ago. Most people do not wish to be held accountable for the sins of their distant ancestors. Second, not all whites in this country are descended from exploiters and not all blacks are descended from slaves. Most of us see ethical issues primarily in individualistic terms rather than in terms of groups, at least among most white males.

With this background in mind, let us now focus on the nature of discrimination in a capitalistic economy. . . .

A Human Capital Approach to Racial Inequalities

In a competitive economy, a worker's income will depend on his or her productivity. According to human capital theory, a worker's productivity is closely related to skills learned at home, at school, and on the job. Children whose parents have little education or income generally will be at a disadvantage.

During slavery, blacks were not allowed to read or write. After slavery, most blacks began with very little capital, either human or physical. In much of the South, only the most rudimentary public education was available to blacks, even in the early twentieth century. As James P. Smith has shown, the poor educational opportunities available to blacks in the early twentieth century directly affected the average earnings of blacks until the last few years. Yet the indirect effects continue today and will continue for many years in the future since the educational opportunities of parents also affect those of their children.

Several writers, including Anthony Downs, Glenn C. Loury, and Linda Datcher, have emphasized that education and other forms of human capital developed by children depend not only on their family background, but also on the community. If income and educational levels are low, and if family discipline is weak, perhaps because of overcrowding or the prevalence of single-parent families, then it will be difficult to operate schools effectively. Children may also develop bad work habits and hostile attitudes toward authority.

Loury has shown that, even if there are no differences in preferences or abilities between two racial groups, if one group starts out with lower income and if individuals prefer to live in a community with a disproportionate number of their race, then competitive economic forces will never eliminate racial inequality. Differences in neighborhood preferences by race lead to racial segregation and those growing up in the poorer communities are at a disadvantage, thus perpetuating the initial racial inequality from generation to generation. In the absence of some special efforts to assist blacks, sizable racial differences in economic opportunity will remain, even if the economy were entirely competitive. . . .

Housing and Statistical Discrimination

Community factors are likely to affect the socialization of children, both within and outside of school. If, for whatever reason, poor families have more disruptive children than middle or upper income families, then clearly it is in the interest of nonpoor families to have housing segregation by income and wealth. In our society, race is even more important than income in defining group membership, with race serving as an easily visible proxy for economic status. Thus, it is not surprising that there is great housing segregation by race. Since there does appear to be at least a moderate correlation in our society among race, income, and socially disruptive behavior, it is likely that housing segregation by race has benefited middle and upper class whites.

Black Jobs Increase

Affirmative action *per se* has had its effect: black jobs shifted toward firms with contracts with the federal government. Between 1970 and 1980, black employment in non-federal contractor firms that report to the EEOC [Equal Employment Opportunity Commission] grew by 5 percent. Among federal contractors, total black employment expanded by more than 15 percent.

Nathan Glazer, *The Public Interest*, Winter 1988.

Statistical discrimination against blacks makes it more difficult for blacks to compete for top jobs. Conversely, such discrimination increases the availability of top jobs for whites. Therefore, upper income whites benefit from statistical discrimination. Given rigidity in wage rates and high levels of unemployment, statistical discrimination probably benefits most whites.

These arguments are based on the assumption that housing

segregation and statistical discrimination have not affected the total economic pie that can be divided up among the races. By underutilizing black abilities and increasing racial conflict, discrimination probably reduces the size of the pie. Thus, it is not clear whether, on balance, whites have gained from discrimination. If some kind of reparations can reduce future discrimination against blacks, however, then any positive effect of reduced discrimination on total income strengthens the case for reparations.

The Need for Reparations

We have seen why market forces are not likely to eliminate discrimination and racial inequality. Since the 1960s, however, we have had important federal legislation outlawing many kinds of discrimination. In particular, Title VII of the Civil Rights Act of 1964 prohibits employment discrimination by race. Given this legislation, is there still need for reparations?

Although Title VII has surely helped reduce labor market discrimination, there is considerable controversy concerning empirical estimates of the effects of this legislation. On a priori grounds, there are several reasons to be pessimistic that such legislation can effectively eliminate discrimination, however. First, litigation is very expensive and time consuming. Thus, many likely victims of discrimination do not seek redress in the courts. Second, it is often difficult to prove discrimination, especially statistical discrimination. For example, just how far does an employer have to go in justifying the job relevance of tests or other screening devices that give an advantage to whites relative to blacks? Finally, not all racial inequality results from labor market discrimination. For example, Loury's model, discussed above, places considerable emphasis on the role of housing segregation by race.

In conclusion, whites appear to have benefited from the inferior opportunities of blacks, at least in terms of greater relative opportunities. Neither market forces nor antidiscrimination legislation can be expected to eliminate discrimination or economic inequality by race. Consequently, we need to consider some form of reparations from whites to blacks. Such reparations might compensate for the effects of past discrimination against blacks and thus also eliminate some of the mechanisms that continue to perpetuate such discrimination.

Affirmative Action as Reparation

Many kinds of reparation might be considered. Since incomes are determined primarily in the labor market, we should focus on policies in this area. Affirmative action policies can be viewed as reparations since such policies give preference to blacks for jobs where blacks are currently underrepresented. . . .

If blacks or other minorities are underrepresented in certain jobs, relative to their availability in the employer's labor market, then an affirmative action employer is under an obligation to make an extra effort to increase their representation in such jobs. This extra effort is one form of reparation, at least as far as the term is defined here. Affirmative action is required of most government contractors, it is often required by the courts when an employer has been found guilty of discrimination; and it also has been chosen voluntarily by many employers. In recent years, however, affirmative action has been criticized increasingly as a form of reverse discrimination against white males. Partly for this reason, the Reagan administration generally opposed affirmative action requirements and reduced enforcement efforts in this area.

Effective Antidote

Affirmative action, even weakly and spottily deployed, opens doors of opportunity that would otherwise be slammed tight. As a result, the country is better and stronger. It surely is one of the most effective antidotes to the widespread habit of undervaluing the capacities of minorities and women.

Roger Wilkins, *Mother Jones*, July/August 1990.

If affirmative action is vigorously pursued (and does not degenerate into a bureaucratic exercise in paperwork), it can redress some of the problems we have discussed above. First, affirmative action directly increases employment opportunities for blacks in many high-paying jobs. Second, if affirmative action is handled wisely, it can help break down the racial stereotypes that underlie statistical discrimination. In this way affirmative action today can increase the employment opportunities of blacks in the future, even if affirmative action is no longer practiced at that time.

Criticisms of Affirmative Action

Given these advantages of affirmative action, why is this concept under so much attack today? First, some believe that labor market discrimination has largely disappeared so that affirmative action is unnecessary. As we have seen, however, there is little reason to believe that either market competition or government antidiscrimination policies, such as Title VII, have eliminated such discrimination. While, in theory, affirmative action could do so, empirical studies suggest that government affirmative action policies have not had large effects.

Second, closely related to this first criticism is the view that affirmative action represents reverse discrimination against white males. Even if racial inequality today does result from past discrimination, opponents of affirmative action believe it is unfair to penalize present white workers for the sins of their fathers. In part, this is a value judgment. . . .

Third, opponents of affirmative action argue that it reduces economic efficiency by requiring firms to hire unqualified workers. Rigid quotas may have this effect. Yet affirmative action requirements are couched in terms of good faith efforts by employers. If the employer can show that he or she has made a reasonable effort to recruit, select, and train minorities, but still has not been able to employ many minority workers, then employers will have met affirmative action requirements. . . .

Recruit Blacks Who Will Succeed

Fourth, if affirmative action does lead to the employment of unqualified minorities, the failure of such workers to succeed in their jobs may reinforce rather than reduce the racial stereotypes that underlie statistical discrimination. . . . While this danger is real, it can be reduced by trying to recruit and promote blacks that do appear likely to succeed and by giving them whatever training and support are necessary as they take over on the job.

Finally, some have argued that, while affirmative action may have helped increase the job opportunities of well-educated blacks, it has done little to help lower class blacks, a group that has been especially hard hit by reduced job opportunities and less generous welfare benefits in recent years. . . .

Preferences Needed at All Levels

The criticism of affirmative action as not doing very much for lower class blacks appears to be largely valid. The problem lies not in the theory of affirmative action but in its application. Affirmative action is considered appropriate when blacks are underrepresented relative to their availability in the workforce. . . .

Focusing affirmative action on top jobs where blacks are underrepresented has helped overcome the particularly high levels of discrimination that do exist for such positions and does increase the incentive for blacks to achieve high levels of education. Nevertheless, in my view, some preference in recruiting, hiring, training, and promoting blacks is necessary at all occupational levels, not just those that require the most human capital. . . .

Neither market competition nor legislation to try to make the employment process color-blind is likely to eliminate labor market discrimination against blacks. More is needed, not only to compensate blacks for the effects of past discrimination, but also to reduce present and future discrimination.

"Efforts to end . . . racism . . . by using affirmative action are . . . doomed to failure."

Affirmative Action Should Be Abandoned

Steven Yates

Affirmative action is often criticized as a policy that penalizes one ethnic group for the actions of group members hundreds of years ago. In the following viewpoint, Steven Yates argues that groups of people are not collectively capable of sensation or consciousness. Consequently, he believes one race of people cannot owe reparations, such as racial preferences, to another race. Yates also maintains that affirmative action discriminates against white males and fuels racial tensions. The author is a philosophy professor at Auburn University in Alabama.

As you read, consider the following questions:

1. What does the author mean by the term "shackled runner"?
2. What does Yates say are the two results of hiring a minority because of his or her race?
3. Why is affirmative action reverse discrimination, according to Yates?

Steven Yates, "Affirmative Action: The New Road to Serfdom," *The Freeman*, December 1990. Reprinted by permission.

For over 20 years, policies calling for "affirmative action" for women and minorities have been part of American political life, and a source of enormous controversy. Advocates say the policies are morally justified, and necessary for the continued advancement of women and minorities in a society long characterized by racial prejudice and gender bias.

In this article I wish to examine this issue anew. Do the claims made on behalf of affirmative action hold up? How much substance is there to the charge that "affirmative action" is a euphemism for reverse discrimination? Moreover, has affirmative action benefited women and minorities in the ways originally intended, or have such policies worked to their detriment in some respects, as well as to the detriment of our organizations? Finally, to what extent is affirmative action compatible with the principles of a free and open society?

There are two aspects to the issue. *First*, many philosophers, legal scholars, and others have tried to defend affirmative action goals and policies on moral grounds alone. I will argue that these defenses as well as the responses to the reverse discrimination charge rest on dubious assumptions, and that sometimes these can be mined from the writings of its advocates themselves. But as it turns out, affirmative action has remained mostly untouched by such failures. *Second*, affirmative action and related policies like forced busing to achieve "racial balance" in public schools have usually been imposed not as a result of intellectual arguments but through political force (or threat of force), from the upper echelons of government downward, usually through the courts. It is in this sense that affirmative action is a serious threat to a free society. . . .

Society's Obligations

The starting point of the claim that affirmative action is morally justified is clear enough. Our society does have a legacy of discrimination against blacks, other minorities, and women, arbitrarily keeping them out of jobs, restaurants, and good schools, while concentrating power and influence in the hands of white males of European descent. As a result, many members of these groups are educationally and economically well behind white males and show few signs of catching up. Affirmative action's proponents conclude from this that today society has obligations to these groups by offering them special advantages not available to white males. Or to make the point another way, *preferential treatment* of minorities and women is called for, and morally justified.

Arguments defending preferential treatment diverge at this point. Some are *backward looking* in the sense that their point of reference is the legacy of discrimination itself. What may be called the *argument from compensatory justice* holds that because blacks, women, and others were discriminated against in the past and excluded from full participation in the economic life of American society, reparation is owed these groups today. The way to make reparation includes offering them preferential treatment. This, we are told, will "balance the books."

But what of the fact that Title VII of the Civil Rights Act of 1964 explicitly repudiates preferential treatment?

Indirect Victims

Advocates of this backward-looking approach to affirmative action reply as follows: Simple nondiscrimination is not enough. First, socially inculcated biases, which are the legacy of generations, are difficult to eradicate and may not even be recognized as such by the perpetrators. Second, most members of past-victimized groups are still far behind most white males in their ability to compete for educational and employment opportunities. Hence even though blacks (to take the most obvious example) are no longer *direct* victims of legally sanctioned discrimination today, their descendants are nevertheless *indirect* victims.

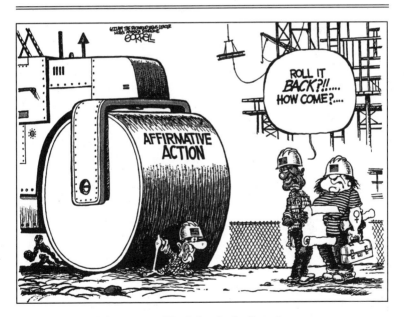

Reprinted with special permission of North America Syndicate, Inc.

This is sometimes called the *shackled-runner* argument, in the sense that these "runners" cannot compete effectively today because of "shackles" placed on them by their heritage. Since their immediate ancestors suffered direct discrimination while the white males of the time did not, they were born with disadvantages mostly nonexistent in the dominant white culture. According to the shackled-runner argument, the fact that today's white males did not do the "shackling" does not affect the fact that they were born in an environment free from a history of discrimination, thus suggesting a justification for preferences even if they sometimes lead to a more qualified white male being passed over for a job or promotion. Backward-looking arguments, then, see compensation as a means to justice, and mandate reparation in the form of preferential treatment of members of past-disadvantaged groups as the primary means of compensation.

Forward-looking arguments have as their reference point not past discrimination per se but rather a certain kind of society that presumably would have existed had there been no past discrimination or oppression. In this society the educational, political, and economic influence of all social groups would have been roughly equal, with no one group dominant. We may call this the *argument from social justice*.

The Moral Mandate

For advocates of this position, the moral mandate is not so much to make reparation but rather to increase the strength of these groups to the point where all have equal access to educational facilities and positions of power, and are represented in the work force in proportion to their percentage in the population. Affirmative action programs are then justified on the grounds that they help fulfill these demands of social justice, and again this holds even when they occasionally result in the selection of a woman or minority job applicant (or candidate for admission to a college or university program) over a white male with superior paper credentials; for it is reasonable that the group which has long been unjustifiably dominant be expected to make the sacrifices.

But wouldn't this last be detrimental to organizations? Not necessarily, it is asserted; it might even be to their advantage. For the larger and more diverse the applicant pool for a desirable position, the more potential talent to draw on and the greater the likelihood of a firm or university being able to hire first-rate employees or faculty members. With regard to universities in particular, long at the center of affirmative action-related controversies, the diversity achieved through preferential faculty hiring and admissions policies should help further one of the aims of the university: the quest to uncover and communicate knowledge, which (given that "knowledge" is no longer something over which white males of European descent can claim a monopoly) should rightly include perspectives that can be had only from incorporating diverse points of view into the curriculum.

Furthermore, black faculty members can serve as role models for black students, representing examples of black success; in this sense, being black can be considered by itself a bona fide qualification for a certain kind of university position. Consequently, it is maintained, preferential treatment of women and minority groups is practical as well as on solid ground morally.

This completes what is, I believe, a fair statement of the most important arguments of those favoring preferential treatment. Despite their long-standing support in the academic world and endorsement by the courts, there are good reasons for denying that they succeed. Let us consider some criticisms.

The Failure of Moral Arguments

The major complaint against preferential policies is that they inevitably lead to reverse discrimination against young white males and hence only perpetuate the very sort of injustice they purport to redress; let us call this the *reverse discrimination counter-argument*. Justice, in this view, requires equal treatment under the law for all citizens. Preferential treatment violates this by going beyond the original, carefully worded provisions in Title VII of the Civil Rights Act of 1964; in practice it violates rather than helps bring about equality of opportunity. Thomas Sowell expresses this as follows: " 'Equal opportunity' laws and policies require that individuals be judged on their qualifications as individuals *without regard* to race, sex, age, etc. 'Affirmative action' requires that they be judged *with regard* to such group membership, receiving preferential or compensatory treatment in some cases to achieve a more proportional 'representation' in various institutions and occupations."

Pure Poison

Affirmative action is pure social poison. The sooner the Supreme Court rules it unconstitutional under the "equal protection of the laws" clause of the Fourteenth Amendment the better it will be for all of us, of whatever skin color.

Jeffrey Hart, *The Manchester Union Leader*, November 7, 1989.

Philosopher Thomas Nagel, a long-time defender of preferences, readily concedes that preferential treatment "is a departure from the ideal—one of the values finally recognized in our society is that people should be judged so far as possible on the basis of individual characteristics rather than involuntary group membership." Nagel therefore recommends the practice as a temporary measure to be abandoned once its goal of increasing the strength of previously disadvantaged groups is achieved.

Nagel maintains that this goal outweighs the complaints of white males who occasionally lose out.

Considerations suggested by the shackled-runner argument indicate, contrary to Sowell, that preferential treatment does not run counter to equal opportunity but is actually a necessary condition for it. What ultimately justifies preferential treatment in the present, continues Nagel, is that it "further[s] a social goal of the first importance," that of the removal of the race- and gender-based caste system that prevailed in the United States prior to the Civil Rights era and which still persists in muted form. According to Nagel, despite the seeming "element of individual unfairness" present, preferential treatment programs do not involve the sense of racially based contempt or gender-based superiority that characterized discrimination in the past; rather, they flow from the mandate of "increasing the social and economic strength of formerly victimized groups."

Will this kind of reply do? There are several reasons for thinking not, and many of Nagel's own remarks indicate serious problems with the response to the reverse discrimination counterargument as well as related problems.

Saddling the Beneficiaries

It is often taken for granted that affirmative action has benefited blacks and women in particular, and is said to be needed for other groups as well (e.g., the elderly and the handicapped). But in fact it saddles its alleged beneficiaries with the stigma of having obtained a position not by virtue of abilities or qualifications but because of involuntary group membership.

This can have two immediate adverse results. First, co-workers are apt to regard those workers with a certain amount of skepticism that wouldn't have been there had merit been the major criterion in hiring. This will be all the more so in universities: will a person be in a position to serve as a good "role model" if his students suspect that the only reason for his being there is affirmative action? Second, alleged beneficiaries might come to regard *themselves* with suspicion and lose self-confidence. Nagel summarizes: "Even those who would have made it anyway fall under suspicion, from themselves and from others: it comes to be widely felt that success does not mean the same thing for women and minorities."

In recent years this situation has become much worse. The rise of racial tensions throughout American society and particularly on college campuses during the past several years has been the subject of intense scrutiny. Most observers take the line that such tensions are a by-product of Reagan-era conservative politics which, they allege, were hostile (or, at best, indifferent) to the interests of minorities. They add that racial disturbances on campuses, including "hate speech" and even violence by white

152

students aimed at black students, indicate a residuum of racism that the civil rights movement has so far failed to eradicate. But if one listens to what is being said by the more politically astute of the white students, it becomes clear that their target is not minorities but the preferential treatment of minorities. . . .

The point is, preferential treatment invariably favors members of some groups at the expense of members of others, and this can hardly help but produce resentment and hostility among those sacrificed. At least some of the hostility will be aimed at the favored groups. . . .

Who Benefits?

But preferential treatment cannot help blacks who don't have the qualifications even to be considered for a desirable position or college admission. It is more likely to work in favor of those who both happen to be in the right place at the right time and whose qualifications seem to be at least marginal. Consequently, preferential treatment works most in favor of those least handicapped by past discrimination and benefits little, if at all, those presumably most handicapped.

A parallel situation exists for white males. White males who are financially very well off—who we may assume for the sake of argument are the main beneficiaries of past discrimination— can often obtain jobs and promotions through connections and thus circumvent affirmative action policies. On the other hand, white males who themselves come from impoverished or lower-class backgrounds are often in no position to benefit from preferential policies of any kind. Furthermore, these men are usually the ones to be sacrificed since they have minimal resources to fight back. . . .

These considerations all help point the way to a major objection to the moral defenses of affirmative action: their main emphasis is on *groups* or group identity instead of on *individuals* and individual merit. In the world of affirmative action, an individual is not an autonomous agent in his or her own right but a member of a group for classification. Indeed, groups are often seen as moral entities, agents, or victims of morally reprehensible acts by other groups. Thus blacks as a group or women as a group are often deemed victims of discrimination; white males as group are deemed responsible and forced to make restitution. . . .

Do Rights Apply to Groups?

Affirmative action seems inevitably to benefit individuals who typically are not the ones who have suffered the worst forms or even significant amounts of racial or sexual discrimination, and the white males sacrificed are typically too young or economically vulnerable to have had any role in instituting or perpetuating discriminatory practices or to have benefited from them.

153

That there is something seriously wrong with this reification of groups should be evident by noting that despite claims that reparation is owed to groups (e.g., blacks) because the groups were wronged by past acts of discrimination, reparation can only be made to the groups by providing recompense to individual members, with the only criterion frequently being that those receiving the reparation happened to be in the right place at the time.

This brings us to the crux of the issue: do moral categories (rights, obligations, and so on) apply at all to involuntary and mostly unstructured human collectives such as races, genders, and age brackets? Such entities aren't capable of sensation or consciousness. They do not think or act. In other words, they are not agents, where an *agent* is understood as an entity that can set goals, direct its own actions, or be harmed by the actions of others. So if a capacity to act or be acted on is a necessary condition for moral attributes, then the claim that certain groups owe, or are owed, reparation for past wrongs is unintelligible.

Moral wrongs can be committed only by individuals, and only individuals can be owed reparation for acts committed against them. Given this, we need only add the obvious fact that both the worst perpetrators of racial discrimination in the past and their most maligned victims are no longer alive either to make reparation or to receive such recompense; it is no more just to make today's white males pay reparation than it would be to penalize this year's incoming freshman class for acts committed by last year's graduated seniors. This, I submit, is the main basis of the charge that affirmative action amounts to unjust reverse discrimination against white males. . . .

The Failures of Affirmative Action

Efforts to end whatever institutional racism still exists by using affirmative action are counterproductive and doomed to failure: (1) they discriminate in reverse against white males, and hence perpetuate the basic injustice of discrimination on the basis of involuntary group identity; (2) this fuels racial tensions by producing resentment on the part of those who lose out; (3) affirmative action further harms its intended beneficiaries by insinuating that double standards are needed for their advancement, suggesting, to my mind, that affirmative action orthodoxy is closer to a kind of racism than its advocates would care to admit; finally and perhaps most important of all, (4) the aims of affirmative action are impossible to realize without massive increases in centralized state power.

The institutionalization of double standards in such a way that no one could violate them and get away with it would require a massive governmental machinery. This supervision would ultimately lead to a controlled, fascistic economy instead of a free economy.

"The black underclass warrants special priority . . . because of its special history."

Poor Blacks Should Receive Special Treatment

Stephen Steinberg

Stephen Steinberg teaches sociology and urban studies at Queens College and at the City University of New York. His writings include the book, *Ethnic Myth*. In the following viewpoint, he argues that racism plays an integral part in the creation of black poverty, and that programs to help the urban poor should focus on blacks. He argues that blacks deserve special consideration because of past and present racial injustices.

As you read, consider the following questions:

1. How has racial stereotyping of blacks changed in recent years, according to Steinberg?
2. What evidence does the author use to demonstrate the effectiveness of affirmative action programs?
3. How does Steinberg respond to those who argue that poverty programs should be directed at all the poor regardless of race?

From "The Underclass: A Case of Color Blindness," by Stephen Steinberg, *New Politics*, vol. 2, no. 3, Summer 1989. Reprinted with permission.

William Julius Wilson is in the forefront of those who see the underclass as the byproduct of economic dislocations that have transformed the urban economy, wiping out literally millions of jobs in manufacturing and related fields. These dislocations, which are themselves the product of larger transformations in the global economy, have had an especially severe effect on blacks since they are concentrated in cities and job sectors most affected by deindustrialization. Thus many blacks remain trapped in poverty, perhaps more so than any other group in American history.

Furthermore, Wilson sees this endemic unemployment and underemployment as the root cause of the "tangle of pathologies" associated with the underclass—unstable marriages, out-of-wedlock children, welfare, crime, drugs, and so on. Wilson's agenda for change is consistent with his analysis. Because the causes are not race-specific—that is, based on patterns of deliberate racial exclusion—neither can the resolution be race-specific. Thus, he proposes "a universal program of reform" that would attack unemployment and underemployment. Essentially, Wilson's agenda involves a renewal and expansion of the forgotten war on poverty. Thus, Wilson calls for (a) macroeconomic policy to promote growth and generate jobs, and (b) improved welfare and social services, including job training, for those who need it. . . .

Wilson's emphasis on economic structures and labor markets has enlarged the scope of analysis well beyond the antiquated race relations model, which presupposed that racial inequality was solely a function of race prejudice. Wilson seems to be saying that even if Gunnar Myrdal had his way, and all whites were exorcised of their distorted and malicious racial beliefs, the underclass would be about as badly off as they are today. Without doubt, the underclass is more than a product of race and specific patterns of racial exclusion.

A problem arises, however, when class analysis is carried to a point that obscures the role that racist structures play not only in the production of the underclass, but in its perpetuation as well.

The Racist Sources of the Underclass

The first thing that needs to be said is that the very existence of a ghetto underclass is evidence of institutionalized racism. Ultimately, the ghetto underclass is the stepchild of slavery itself, linked to the present by patterns of racial segregation and inequality that are still found in all major institutions, including ghetto schools. Thus, the cumulative effect of past and present racism may well result in an underclass that lacks the necessary education and skills to compete for the better jobs, even if employers were not personally motivated by racial prejudice. That less than half of black men of working age are part of the labor force speaks for itself. This is a measure of the extent to which American labor markets are perpetuating patterns of racial inequality.

Feiffer © 1987 Jules Feiffer. Reprinted with permission of Universal Press Syndicate. All rights reserved.

But black workers *are* being discriminated against directly, to a far greater extent than Wilson acknowledges. The fact of a large black middle class, relatively immune from racial stereotypes and acts of overt discrimination, is not really germane. Indeed, white society has come to recognize the new face of black America, and has responded by elaborating and refining racism to take class into account. Instead of blanket stereotypes that once applied to all blacks, whites have learned to discriminate between those respectable blacks who are reasonably tolerated, and those other blacks who bear the stigma of the ghetto and are still objects of racial stereotyping, fear, and scorn. This elaboration of a once-monistic system of beliefs may well be part of a long term attenuation of racist ideology, with parallels to other ethnic groups (as when lace-curtain Irish were distinguished from shanty Irish, uptown Jews from downtown Jews, and so on). Nevertheless, the fact that middle-class blacks may encounter less racism does not mean that ghetto blacks are so fortunate.

Indeed, Wilson does not adequately explain why blacks—who were never heavily represented in the manufacturing sector in the first place—have not found more jobs in the rapidly expanding service sector. Along with others, he assumes that there is a "mismatch" between the educational and skill levels of black workers and the demands of a postindustrial labor market. As Wilson writes: "Basic structural changes in our modern industrial economy have compounded the problems of poor blacks because education and training have become more important for entry into the more desirable and higher-paying jobs and because increased reliance on labor-saving devices has contributed to a surplus of untrained black workers." Of course, Wilson is right with respect to the *most* desirable and *highest*-paying jobs in the service sector. However, the vast majority of the new jobs in the service sector do not require a great deal of education and skills. This is true not only of the lowest-paying jobs, but also of coveted jobs in major service industries, such as hospital and health care, hotels, restaurants, transportation, and sales. These are precisely the job areas where recent immigrants have made significant inroads, undoubtedly at the expense of blacks.

Job Discrimination

The problem with the mismatch hypothesis is that it seriously underestimates the color line in the world of work. There is, as Norman Fainstein has argued in a recent paper, a pattern of "employment ghettoization" whereby blacks are excluded from whole job sectors, especially those decently paid jobs that require minimal education and skills. On the basis of a detailed analysis of labor market data, Fainstein came to the following conclusion:

> . . . the economic situation of blacks is rooted more in the character of the employment opportunities in growing industries than in the disappearance of "entry-level" jobs in declining industries. Unlike the immigrants of yesterday, the problem for blacks is not so much inadequate educations as the channeling of the educated into relatively poor jobs and the exclusion of many of the uneducated from work altogether.

Thus, Fainstein shows that blacks who have attended college have a rate of unemployment as high as that for whites who have dropped out of high school. At the other end of the spectrum, less educated blacks have great difficulty in finding jobs that generally do not require much education. The restaurant industry is a case in point. Blacks are generally excluded from entry-level jobs with career ladders, such as waiters and cooks in full-service restaurants, and relegated to menial, low-paying, and dead-end jobs.

In a 1985 study of closed labor markets in New York City, Walter Stafford also provides detailed documentation of labor market segregation. He found that 68 percent of all blacks work in only 20 of the city's 212 industries covered in the study—mainly hospitals, banks, insurance companies, telephone communications, and department stores. On the other hand, blacks have virtually no representation in 130 out of 193 industries in the city's private sector. Those blacks who are employed in core industries are generally found in clerical positions. Blacks are rarely found in supervisory positions anywhere in the service economy.

Other data indicate the extraordinary dependence of blacks on public-sector employment. A total of 149,080 blacks in New York City—a full third of all black workers—were employed by the government in 1980. This number increased by some 21,000 employees since 1970, despite overall shrinkage in the size of the government work force. On a national level, over 470,000 blacks are employed by the federal government, and another 835,000 are employed by state and local governments. Without this public-sector employment, which in large measure reflects affirmative action policy, much of the black middle class simply would not exist.

Clearly, this pattern of employment ghettoization cannot be blamed solely on a mismatch between workers and jobs. It is equally the result of patterns of discrimination that leave whites with a virtual monopoly on whole job sectors, especially in the expanding service economy. To the extent that blacks—tenth-generation Americans—do suffer from a deficit of education and skills, this must be seen in historical context. To tell these descendants of slaves and quasi-slaves that they would be hired in industry if such jobs existed, or in white-collar jobs if only they were qualified, amounts to a preposterous negation of history.

This is why I take issue with Wilson's categorical distinction between past and present racism, leading to the conclusion that the current problems of blacks have more to do with class than with race. These class disabilities are real enough, but they are the byproduct of past racism, they are reinforced by present racism, and they constitute the basis for perpetuating racial divisions and racial inequalities. Wilson acknowledges all of this in principle, but still reaches the conclusion that race—that is, race *per se*—is of declining significance. . . .

An Assault on Poverty

Needless to say, all poverty is contemptible, and it is easy and tempting to call for a color-blind assault on poverty. The problem with the color-blind left, like the color-blind right, is that it is willing to pay lipservice to the unique oppression of blacks, but is unwilling to address it outside of a larger social agenda. In my view, by virtue of their unique oppression, blacks have historical and moral claim to have their grievances redressed before those of other groups. Blacks should not have to queue up with the other displaced workers in the nation's rust belt. For their underclass status is not merely the result of plant shutdowns. It is the end product of three centuries of racial oppression.

From a national standpoint, too, the black underclass warrants special priority, again because of its special history. For the black underclass represents not just economic dislocation, income maldistribution, and social injustice; it represents all that, *and* racism. The black underclass is the present-day manifestation of America's greatest crime, and is a blot on American democracy. At stake is not just social and economic justice, but the very soul of the nation.

The Case for a Race-Specific Policy

Just as Wilson's analysis led him to "a universal program" for change, the foregoing analysis suggests the need for a race-specific public policy. Several elements of such a policy are outlined below:

1. We need a national commitment to eliminate ghettos. It is remarkable how we, as a nation, have become inured to the odious moral connotations of this term. We talk about "ghettos" with the same neutrality that we talk about "suburbs." Ghettos are nothing less than the shameful residue of slavery. It took one century after this nation declared its own freedom from colonial domination to abolish slavery. It took another century, and a protracted and bloody civil rights struggle, to end official segregation. It is time for a third stage that will eliminate racial ghettos, and destroy the less visible barriers that manifest themselves in a host of inequities ranging from lower incomes to higher mortality.

2. The elimination of ghettos would entail large-scale programs of urban reconstruction, like those proposed by Wilson and others. These programs, however, should have the specific purpose of eliminating ghettos, lest they become a pork barrel for a myriad of "urban" and "minority" constituencies. Furthermore, in my view, these economic policies must not ignore the racial and cultural dimensions of the underclass. For economic policy to work, it is imperative that local groups and individuals be empowered so that the process of reconstruction can occur from within, rather than being imposed from outside. Only community-based groups can bridge the chasm that separates the underclass from mainstream society, and marshal the cultural and spiritual resources to effect meaningful change. . . .

3. We should not be diverted by the adamant opposition to affirmative action, and the split in the liberal coalition over this issue. Affirmative action has been hotly contested because it is the most radical development in race policy since Reconstruction. It is radical because it legitimated the principle of compensation for past wrongs, and provided a fool-proof mechanism for achieving racial parity—one which has achieved significant results in major employment sectors.

For example, in 1973 the American Telephone and Telegraph Company, one of the largest employers in corporate America, entered into a six-year agreement with the Equal Employment

160

Opportunities Commission to correct prior discriminatory employment practices. By 1982 the percentage of minority craft workers had increased from 8.4 percent to 14 percent. The proportion of minorities in management increased at an even higher rate—from 4.6 percent to 13.1 percent.

Raw numbers point up the impact of affirmative action even more vividly. The number of black employees at IBM increased from 750 in 1962, to 7,251 in 1968, to 16,546 in 1980. Under threat of litigation, governmental agencies have pursued affirmative action programs even more aggressively. To take one key example, since the late 1960s the number of black police officers nationally increased by 20,000. These diverse examples testify to the profound impact that affirmative action has had on black representation in both the private and public sectors.

These examples also rebut the claim, made by Wilson and others, that affirmative action primarily benefits those who are "already advantaged." As William Taylor has pointed out: "The focus of much of the effort has been not just on white collar jobs, but also on law enforcement, construction work, and craft and production jobs in large companies—all areas in which the extension of new opportunities has provided upward mobility for less advantaged minority workers.

The Black Poor Are Different

No matter how much more politically palatable general programs might be, the black poor need programs designed specifically for them because some of the black poor are different. I speak primarily of the poor in single-parent homes, particularly those in which the parents themselves are no more than children. . . .

I do not mean that the black poor are different in the eyes of God or that they differ from other classes or races at birth in their innate potential. I do mean that the racially inflicted economic, cultural and psychological damage they suffer is unique and hideously destructive and requires specially tailored remedies.

Roger Wilkins, *The New York Times*, August 22, 1989.

Having laid the groundwork and survived the harrowing legal battles, we should not turn away from affirmative action as a strategy for rectifying past wrongs. On the contrary, affirmative action should be extended into all areas of our economy and society. Wilson is right to worry that its benefits will not filter down to the underclass, but this is not an insurmountable problem. Our statisticians have demonstrated their skill at classifying who belongs to the underclass. The challenge is to make this designation a ticket to a good job, instead of what Richard McGahey

161

has called "poverty's voguish stigma.". . .

In my view, it is vitally important to acknowledge that two groups—Indians and blacks—have suffered a unique oppression in America. To be sure, other groups have suffered prejudice and discrimination, and countless injustices. But what is there to compare with wars of extermination, the appropriation of Indian land, and the banishing of the surviving population to reservation wastelands? What claims are the moral equivalent to two centuries of slavery, and another century of second-class citizenship, codified in the nation's laws and pervading every social institution? More is involved here than historical and moral truth. The whole justification—indeed, the only justification—for race-specific public policy is that certain groups have been victims of crimes of such magnitude and with such enduring consequence that "equal opportunity" is not enough, and special remedial policies become necessary.

In the final analysis, this is what is most disturbing about Wilson's thesis regarding "the declining significance of race" and his advocacy of universal, as opposed to race-specific, public policy. It absolves the nation of responsibility for coming to terms with its racist legacy, and takes race off of the national agenda.

"The problems of the ghetto underclass can be most meaningfully addressed by a comprehensive program that . . . features universal as opposed to race- or group-specific strategies."

Poor Blacks Should Not Receive Special Treatment

William Julius Wilson

Blacks form a significant portion of the urban poor. Some people have argued that blacks should receive special treatment in the form of affirmative action and other race-specific programs because past and present racism has left them economically disadvantaged. In the following viewpoint, William Julius Wilson challenges this idea. He argues that racism plays a relatively minor role in perpetuating poverty, and that economic and welfare policies should be geared to benefit all the poor, not just blacks. Wilson is the Lucy Flower Distinguished Service Professor of Sociology and Public Policy at the University of Chicago. His books include *The Declining Significance of Race* and *The Truly Disadvantaged*, from which this viewpoint is excerpted.

As you read, consider the following questions:

1. What two kinds of racial discrimination does Wilson describe?
2. What are the limits of civil rights laws in dealing with the poor, according to the author?

Excerpted, with permission, from *The Truly Disadvantaged* by William Julius Wilson, published by the University of Chicago Press. Copyright © 1987 by the University of Chicago. All rights reserved.

Why have the social conditions of the ghetto underclass deteriorated so rapidly in recent years? Racial discrimination is the most frequently invoked explanation, and it is undeniable that discrimination continues to aggravate the social and economic problems of poor blacks. But is discrimination really greater today than it was in 1948, when black unemployment was less than half of what it is now, and when the gap between black and white jobless rates was narrower?

As for the poor black family, it apparently began to fall apart not before but after the mid-twentieth century. Until publication in 1976 of Herbert Gutman's *The Black Family in Slavery and Freedom*, most scholars had believed otherwise. Stimulated by the acrimonious debate over the Moynihan report, Gutman produced data demonstrating that the black family was not significantly disrupted during slavery or even during the early years of the first migration to the urban North, beginning after the turn of the century. The problems of the modern black family, he implied, were associated with modern forces.

Discrimination Past and Present

Those who cite discrimination as the root cause of poverty often fail to make a distinction between the effects of *historic* discrimination (i.e., discrimination prior to the mid-twentieth century) and the effects of *contemporary* discrimination. Thus they find it hard to explain why the economic position of the black underclass started to worsen soon after Congress enacted, and the White House began to enforce, the most sweeping civil rights legislation since Reconstruction.

The point to be emphasized is that historic discrimination is more important than contemporary discrimination in understanding the plight of the ghetto underclass—that, in any event, there is more to the story than discrimination (of whichever kind). . . .

In the early 1960s there was no comprehensive civil rights bill and Jim Crow segregation was still widespread in parts of the nation, particularly in the deep South. With the passage of the 1964 Civil Rights Bill there was considerable optimism that racial progress would ensue and that the principle of equality of individual rights (namely, that candidates for positions stratified in terms of prestige, power, or other social criteria ought to be judged solely on individual merit and therefore should not be discriminated against on the basis of racial origin) would be upheld.

Programs based solely on this principle are inadequate, however, to deal with the complex problems of race in America because they are not designed to address the substantive inequality that exists at the time discrimination is eliminated.

On the other hand, the competitive resources developed by the *advantaged minority members*—resources that flow directly from the family stability, schooling, income, and peer groups that their parents have been able to provide—result in their benefiting disproportionately from policies that promote the rights of minority individuals by removing artificial barriers to valued positions.

Nevertheless, since 1970, government policy has tended to focus on formal programs designed and created both to prevent discrimination and to ensure that minorities are sufficiently represented in certain positions. This has resulted in a shift from the simple formal investigation and adjudication of complaints of racial discrimination to government-mandated affirmative action programs to increase minority representation in public programs, employment, and education.

However, if minority members from the most advantaged families profit disproportionately from policies based on the principle of equality of individual opportunity, they also reap disproportionate benefits from policies of affirmative action based solely on their group membership. This is because advantaged minority members are likely to be disproportionately represented among those of their racial group most qualified for valued positions, such as college admissions, higher paying jobs, and promotions. Thus, if policies of preferential treatment for such positions are developed in terms of racial group membership rather than the real disadvantages suffered by individuals, then these policies will further improve the opportunities of the advantaged without necessarily addressing the problems of the truly disadvantaged such as the ghetto underclass. The problems of the truly disadvantaged may require *nonracial* solutions such as full employment, balanced economic growth, and manpower training and education (tied to—not isolated from—these two economic conditions).

The Need for Welfare

It would be ideal if problems of the ghetto underclass could be adequately addressed by the combination of macroeconomic policy, labor market strategies, and manpower training programs. However, in the foreseeable future employment alone will not necessarily lift a family out of poverty. Many families would still require income support and/or social service such as child care. A program of welfare reform is needed, therefore, to address the current problems of public assistance, including lack of provisions for poor two-parent families, inadequate levels of support, inequities between different states, and work disincentives. A national AFDC [Aid to Families with Dependent Children] benefit standard adjusted yearly for inflation is the most minimal required change. We might also give serious consideration to programs such as the Child Support Assurance Program developed by Irwin Garfinkel and colleagues at the Institute for Research on Poverty at the University of Wisconsin, Madison. This program, parts of which are currently in operation as a demonstration project in the state of Wisconsin, provides a guaranteed minimum benefit per child to single-parent families regardless of the income of the custodial parent. The state collects from the absent parent through wage withholding a sum of money at a fixed rate and then makes regular payments to the custodial parent. If the absent parent is jobless or if his or her payment from withholdings is less than the minimum, the state makes up the difference. Since all absent parents regardless of income are required to participate in this program, it is far less stigmatizing than, say, public assistance. Moreover, preliminary evidence from Wisconsin suggests that this program carries little or no additional cost to the state.

Class vs. Race

The issue today is not race, but class. The insistence on applying race-specific solutions to economic problems has snatched defeat from the jaws of our civil rights victories.

Robert L. Woodson, *The Heritage Lectures*, February 6, 1990.

Neither the Child Support Assurance Program under demonstration in Wisconsin nor the European family allowances program is means-tested; that is, they are not targeted at a particular income group and therefore do not suffer the degree of stigmatization that plagues public assistance programs such as AFDC. More important, such universal programs tend to draw more political support from the general public because they are available not only to the poor but to the working- and middle-class segments as well. Finally, the question of child care has to be addressed in any program designed to improve the employment prospects of women and men.

Disproportionate Benefits

If the truly disadvantaged reaped disproportionate benefits from a child support enforcement, child allowance program, and child care strategy, they would also benefit disproportionately from a program of balanced economic growth and tight labor-market policies because of their greater vulnerability to swings in the business cycle and changes in economic organization, including the relocation of plants and the use of labor-saving technology. It would be shortsighted to conclude, therefore, that universal programs (i.e., programs not targeted at any particular group) are not designed to help address in a fundamental way some of the problems of the truly disadvantaged such as the ghetto underclass.

Universal Programs

By emphasizing universal programs as an effective way to address problems in the inner city created by historic racial subjugation, I am recommending a fundamental shift from the traditional race-specific approach of addressing such problems. It is true that problems of joblessness and related woes such as poverty, teenage pregnancies, out-of-wedlock births, female-headed families, and welfare dependency are, for reasons of historic racial oppression, disproportionately concentrated in the black community. And it is important to recognize the racial differences in rates of social dislocation so as not to obscure problems currently gripping the ghetto underclass. However, as discussed above, race-specific policies are often not designed to address fundamentally problems of the truly disadvantaged. Moreover, as also discussed above, both race-specific and targeted programs based on the principle of equality of life chances (often identified with a minority constituency) have difficulty sustaining widespread public support.

Does this mean that targeted programs of any kind would be necessarily excluded from a package highlighting universal programs of reform? On the contrary, as long as a racial division of labor exists and racial minorities are disproportionately concentrated in low-paying positions, antidiscrimination and affirmative action programs will be needed even though they tend to benefit the more advantaged minority members. Moreover, as long as certain groups lack the training, skills, and education to compete effectively on the job market or move into newly created jobs, manpower training and education programs targeted at these groups will also be needed, even under a tight labor-market situation. For example, a program of adult education and training may be necessary for some ghetto underclass males before they can either become oriented to or move into an expanded labor market. Finally, as long as some poor families are unable to work because of physical or other disabilities, public assistance would be needed even if the government adopted a program of welfare reform that included child support enforcement and family allowance provisions.

For all these reasons, a comprehensive program of economic and social reform (highlighting macroeconomic policies to promote balanced economic growth and create a tight labor-market situation, a nationally oriented labor-market strategy, a child support assurance program, a child care strategy, and a family allowance program) would have to include targeted programs, both means-tested and race-specific. However, the latter would be considered an offshoot of and indeed secondary to the universal programs. The important goal is to construct an economic-social reform program in such a way that the universal programs are seen as the dominant and most visible aspects by the general public. As the universal programs draw support from a wider population, the targeted programs included in the comprehensive reform package would be indirectly supported and protected. Accordingly, *the hidden agenda for liberal policymakers is to improve the life chances of truly disadvantaged groups such as the ghetto underclass by emphasizing programs to which the more advantaged groups of all races and class backgrounds can positively relate.*

I am reminded of Bayard Rustin's plea during the early 1960s that blacks ought to recognize the importance of fundamental economic reform (including a system of national economic planning along with new education, manpower, and public works programs to help reach full employment) and the need for a broad-based political coalition to achieve it. And since an effective coalition will in part depend upon how the issues are defined, it is imperative that the political message underline the need for economic and social reforms that benefit all groups in the United States, not just poor minorities. . . .

A Comprehensive Program

The problems of the ghetto underclass can be most meaningfully addressed by a comprehensive program that combines employment policies with social welfare policies and that features universal as opposed to race- or group-specific strategies. On the one hand, this program highlights macroeconomic policy to generate a tight labor market and economic growth; fiscal and monetary policy not only to stimulate noninflationary growth, but also to increase the competitiveness of American goods on both the domestic and international markets; and a national labor-market strategy to make the labor force more adaptable to changing economic opportunities. On the other hand, it highlights a child support assurance program, a family allowance program, and a child care strategy.

I emphasize that although this program also would include targeted strategies—both means-tested and race-specific—they would be considered secondary to the universal programs so that the latter are seen as the most visible and dominant aspects in the eyes of the general public. To the extent that the universal programs draw support from a wider population, the less visible targeted programs would be indirectly supported and protected. The hidden agenda for liberal policymakers is to enhance the chances in life for the ghetto underclass by emphasizing programs to which the more advantaged groups of all class and racial backgrounds can positively relate.

Before such programs can be seriously considered, however, the question of cost has to be addressed. The cost of programs to expand social and economic opportunity will be great, but it must be weighed against the economic and social costs of a do-nothing policy. As Sar A. Levitan and Clifford M. Johnson have pointed out, "The most recent recession cost the nation an estimated $300 billion in lost income and production, and direct outlays for unemployment compensation totaled $30 billion in a single year. A policy that ignores the losses associated with slack labor markets and forced idleness inevitably will underinvest in the nation's labor force and future economic growth." Furthermore, the problem of annual budget deficits of almost $200 billion (driven mainly by the peacetime military buildup and the Reagan administration's tax cuts), and the need for restoring the federal tax base and adopting a more balanced set of budget priorities have to be tackled if we are to achieve significant progress on expanding opportunities.

The Doors of Opportunity

With the passage of civil rights laws, one-third of black Americans—those prepared by family status, education, or economic circumstances—walked through the doors of opportunity once they were opened. For unprepared blacks, however, removing racial barriers did not enable them to join the mainstream of the American economy. Their problems were and *remain* economic; continued attempts to apply race-specific solutions to their problems do nothing to advance economic progress for poor blacks.

Robert L. Woodson, *The World & I*, January 1990.

In the final analysis, the pursuit of economic and social reform ultimately involves the question of political strategy. As the history of social provision so clearly demonstrates, universalistic political alliances, cemented by policies that provide benefits directly to wide segments of the population, are needed to work successfully for major reform. The recognition among minority leaders and liberal policymakers of the need to expand the War on Poverty and race relations visions to confront the growing problems of inner-city social dislocations will provide, I believe, an important first step toward creating such an alliance.

a critical thinking activity

Distinguishing Bias from Reason

When dealing with controversial subjects, many people allow their emotions to dominate their powers of reason. Thus, one of the most important critical thinking skills is the ability to distinguish between statements based upon emotion or bias and those based upon a rational consideration of the facts. For example, consider the following statement: "Affirmative action lowers academic standards because it favors minority students who have inferior academic skills." This statement is biased because it is based on the emotional, unproven belief that minority students are not as skilled as white students. In contrast, the statement "The grades and SAT scores of minority college students are lower than those of whites. Because of this, minorities often perform poorly in college" is a reasonable statement. The data concerning grades and scores provides the factual basis for the author's opinion.

Another element the reader should take into account is whether an author has a personal or professional stake in advancing a particular opinion. For example, a minority employee may defend affirmative-action policies. Since affirmative action has helped minorities achieve better employment and income, the reader should ask whether this interest influences the author's statement. A critical reader should always be alert to an author's background and credentials when attempting to identify bias. Note also that it is possible to have a strong interest in a subject and still present an objective case. A minority employee who has encountered job discrimination or been helped by affirmative action is in an excellent position to give an opinion on the effectiveness of affirmative action.

The following statements are adapted from opinions expressed in the viewpoints in this chapter. Consider each statement carefully. *Mark R for any statement you believe is based on reason or a rational consideration of the facts. Mark B for any statement you believe is based on bias, prejudice, or emotion. Mark I for any statement you think is impossible to judge.*

If you are doing this activity as a member of a class or group, compare your answers with those of others. Be able to defend your answers. You may discover that others come to different conclusions than you do. Listening to the rationale others present for their answers may give you valuable insights in distinguishing between bias and reason.

R = a statement based upon reason
B = a statement based upon bias
I = a statement impossible to judge

1. White institutions create, maintain, and condone the ghetto.

2. Minority-hiring goals and timetables would never have been necessary if corporate and municipal leaders had been willing to follow the letter and spirit of civil-rights laws.

3. Affirmative action's critics never consider the decades of discrimination that minorities have endured.

4. Preferential treatment has never taught skills, educated, or instilled motivation in minorities.

5. Affirmative action is a testament to white goodwill and to black power.

6. Affirmative-action programs are needed to help counteract a legacy of discrimination against Asians, other minorities, and women in the United States.

7. Affirmative action favors those who both happen to be in the right place at the right time and whose qualifications are marginal at best.

8. Preferential treatment favors members of some groups at the expense of members of other groups.

9. Because affirmative action encourages the hiring of minorities, young white males suffer the most from the effects of affirmative action.

10. The white community has planned and conspired for years to economically dominate the black community.

11. Upper-income whites already benefit from affirmative action because they have historically received more favorable treatment based on their race.

12. Because white middle-class families are wealthier and black middle-class families are poorer than they were twenty years ago, the need for affirmative action is greater now than ever before.

13. Affirmative-action policies have been imposed through political force, usually through the courts, proving that the government wants to eliminate unlawful discrimination.

14. Affirmative action has helped increase high-paying employment opportunities for Hispanics, and can thus do the same for other minority groups.

Periodical Bibliography

The following articles have been selected to supplement the diverse views presented in this chapter.

Business Week	"Affirmative Action Ain't Broke, So . . . ," June 26, 1989.
Matthew Cooper	"Hyping the 'Quota' Wars," *U.S. News & World Report*, December 24, 1990.
Michael E. Dyson	"Deaffirmation," *The Nation*, July 3, 1989.
Terry Eastland	"Toward a Real Restoration of Civil Rights," *Commentary*, November 1989.
Alan Farnham	"Holding Firm on Affirmative Action," *Fortune*, March 13, 1989.
Ted Gest	"Are Quotas on the Way?" *U.S. News & World Report*, May 28, 1990.
Andrew Hacker	"Affirmative Action: The New Look," *The New York Review of Books*, October 12, 1989.
Hendrik Hertzberg	"Wounds of Race," *The New Republic*, July 10, 1989.
June Jordan	"Where Is the Rage?" *The Progressive*, October 1989.
Michael Kinsley	"What's Really Fair," *Time*, November 19, 1990.
Frederick R. Lynch	"Surviving Affirmative Action," *Commentary*, August 1990.
Thurgood Marshall	"The Supreme Court and Civil Rights," *USA Today*, March 1990.
Tom Mathews	"Quotas," *Newsweek*, December 31, 1990.
National Review	"Real Rights," July 14, 1989.
Daniel Seligman	"The Whole Point of Affirmative Action," *Fortune*, July 2, 1990.
Margaret C. Simms	"Rebuilding Set Aside Programs," *Black Enterprise*, September 1990.
Bill Turque	"Black Conservatives Quarrel Over Quotas," *Newsweek*, December 24, 1990.
Roger W. Wilkins	"In Ivory Towers," *Mother Jones*, July/August 1990.

Should Minorities Emphasize Their Ethnicity?

Chapter Preface

In his book *The Content of Our Character*, black professor and writer Shelby Steele argues that the main problem facing blacks today is not white racism but the fact that blacks are placing too much emphasis on establishing a black identity that separates them from other Americans. Many blacks, he writes, "cling to an adversarial, victim-focused identity and remain preoccupied with white racism. . . . This sort of identity is never effective and never translates into the actual uplift of black people." Steele contends that there are countless opportunities for blacks who focus on individual achievement rather than on promoting a group identity.

Steele's views have been criticized by many blacks who argue that it is imperative that blacks maintain a separate ethnic identity based on their shared African and slave heritage. As political science professor Manning Marable writes, "We are witnessing the development of a substantial segment of the African-American population which is 'post-black'—without any cultural awareness, historical appreciation, or political commitment to the traditions, customs, values, and networks that have been the basis for black identity in America." For Marable and others, promoting one's own ethnic identity is as important for blacks as fighting for civil rights.

The debate over whether assimilation or preserving ethnic identity best aids minorities in American society also affects other minority groups who face prejudice and discrimination, including Hispanics and American Indians. The viewpoints in this chapter examine these issues.

"Racial integration . . . has produced the symbols of progress and the rhetoric of racial harmony without the substance of empowerment for the oppressed."

Blacks Should Emphasize Their Ethnicity

Manning Marable

Manning Marable is a professor of political science and sociology at the University of Colorado at Boulder, a newspaper columnist, and author of several books including *Black Politics* and *How Capitalism Underdeveloped Black America*. In the following viewpoint, Marable argues that, by attempting to assimilate into white society, blacks have lost their sense of community and identity, but have not succeeded in improving their lives or ending racism. He concludes that integration is not a viable solution for the problems blacks face in the U.S.

As you read, consider the following questions:

1. What assumptions about integration have proven false, according to Marable?
2. How does the author differentiate between race and ethnicity?
3. What does Marable believe is necessary for racial peace?

From "The Rhetoric of Racial Harmony," by Manning Marable, *Sojourners*, August/September 1990. Reprinted with permission from *Sojourners*, PO Box 29272, Washington, DC 20017.

America's society is more thoroughly integrated today in terms of race relations than at any point in its entire history. Since 1964, the number of black elected officials has increased from barely 100 to 7,000. The number of African Americans enrolled in colleges and universities has quadrupled; the number of black-owned banks and financial institutions has increased tenfold; the percentage of African Americans in the middle class and professions has significantly expanded.

Perhaps the most striking changes in public perceptions of race have occurred in popular culture, social institutions, and the media. American music, theater, public education, sports, and the arts are now heavily influenced by the rhythms and patterns of African-American life. Black images in commercial advertisements are commonplace. Blacks remain underrepresented in the ownership and management of cultural and social institutions, but are nearly omnipresent as employees and prominent public representatives, particularly in the state sector.

Problems Persist

Despite these symbols of racial advancement, in recent years incidents of racist harassment, vigilante violence, and social disruption have escalated. Hundreds of African-American students have been victimized by intimidation or outright threats on university campuses across the country. White youth are forming "white student unions" at several institutions to push back affirmative action and the preferential recruitment of minorities as faculty and students.

Civil rights organizations point to a disturbing pattern of legal indictments and political harassment of black elected officials, and to the growth of violent incidents aimed against black-owned property and individuals in urban areas. Racial tensions in cities such as New York have culminated in a series of massive public demonstrations by both blacks and whites, with both sides accusing the other of "racism." A quarter century removed from the historic Civil Rights Act of 1964, which abolished legal racial discrimination in public accommodations, and the Voting Rights Act of 1965, which extended the electoral franchise to all Americans regardless of race, the goal of racial harmony and integration seems more distant than ever before.

What explains the racial paradox, the emergence of a black middle class and acceptance of black cultural achievements within the context of a deepening crisis of race relations in the society as a whole? Any analysis of the contemporary status of African Americans in the United States must begin with analysis of the accomplishments and the contradictions of the civil rights movement of the 1950s and 1960s.

The leaders of the desegregation social protest movement a

generation ago mobilized millions with one simple demand—
"freedom." In the context of the "Jim Crow" or racially segregated society of the South in the post-World War II period, freedom meant the elimination of all social, political, legal, and economic barriers that forced black Americans into a subordinate
status.

Implicit in the demand for desegregation were several assumptions. Desegregation would increase opportunities for blacks in
business, government, and society overall. Desegregated educational institutions would promote greater racial harmony and understanding between young people from different ethnic communities, which in turn would promote residential integration.
Affirmative action policies, the strategy of compensating for past
discrimination against minorities, would gradually increase the
numbers of African Americans, Hispanics, and other people of
color in administrative and managerial positions.

It was assumed that as African Americans escaped the ghetto
and were more broadly distributed across the social class structure and institutions of society, racial tensions and bigotry
would decline in significance. As blacks were more thoroughly
integrated into the economic system, it was thought, the basis
for racial confrontation would diminish.

The thesis above was fundamentally flawed in several key respects. First, desegregation did not benefit the entire black community uniformly. Black professionals and managers, those who
had attended colleges and technical schools, were the principal
beneficiaries. Working-class African Americans also benefited:
Incomes increased as new opportunities were created in upper-
income levels of the labor force, and their children for the first
time had access to higher education.

Race and Class

But opportunity in a capitalist society is always a function of
social class position, which means ownership of capital, material resources, education, and access to power. For the unemployed, the poor, and those without marketable skills or resources, for those whose lives were circumscribed by illiteracy,
disease, and desperation, "race" continued to occupy a central
place as a factor in their marginal existence.

Legal desegregation contributed to the popular illusion that
the basis for racial discrimination and conflict no longer existed.
The abolition of racially separate residential districts, hotels,
schools, and other public institutions convinced many white
Americans that the "Negro question" had finally been firmly resolved. Black American leaders such as Martin Luther King Jr.
had always insisted upon the achievement of a "colorblind society." The passage of antidiscriminatory legislation had eliminated all basic impediments to the socioeconomic and cultural

177

advancement of African Americans, according to this view.

Thus, as many black leaders continued to speak out against current social injustices, or pointed to the growing economic disparities between blacks and the majority of middle-class whites, their complaints were easily dismissed as anachronistic, self-serving rhetoric. By raising the issue of racism, many whites now believed, blacks themselves must be "racist."

The American civil rights leadership and the black political establishment now find themselves in a quandary largely of their own making. Their failure to develop a body of politics representing a qualitative step beyond the discourse and strategies of the civil rights movement of a generation ago is directly linked to the poverty of their theoretical outlook.

Race and Ethnicity

The central theoretical and conceptual weakness of this largely middle-class, African-American leadership is its inability to distinguish between *ethnicity* and *race*, and to apply both terms to the realities of American capital, power, and the state. African-American people are both an ethnic group (or more precisely, a national minority) and a racial group. Our ethnicity is derived from the cultural synthesis of our African heritage and our experiences in American society, first as slaves and subsequently as sharecroppers, industrial laborers, the unemployed, and now as the core of the post-industrial urban underclass in the semi-destroyed central cities of North America.

Integration and the Next Generation

Unlike the generation of blacks who reached maturity before, and during, the early '70s, my generation has no memory of credible black leaders, such as Malcolm X or Martin Luther King Jr. Nor do we have a relationship with those indigenous institutions, such as the black church, that developed as a consequence of racism and segregation. The debilitating effects of racism and segregation notwithstanding, blacks had been able to instill a sense of self and community. But the practice of integration created the illusion of equality with the wider culture, effectively wresting control of the black freedom movement by holding it hostage to federal good will and weakening or destroying those institutions that influenced blacks' worldview.

Anthony A. Parker, *Sojourners*, August/September 1990.

As black scholar W.E.B. DuBois observed nearly a century ago, black Americans are both African and American, "two souls, two thoughts, two unreconciled strivings; two warring ideals in one dark body, whose dogged strength alone keeps it from being torn asunder." This central duality is at the core of our ethnic consciousness, forming the fundamental matrix for all expressions of African-American music, art, language patterns, folklore, religious rituals, belief systems, the structure of our families, and other culture manifestations and social institutions. Blackness in the cultural context is the expression and affirmation of a set of traditional values, beliefs, rituals, and social patterns, rather than physical appearance or social class position.

Race is a totally different dynamic, rooted in the structures of exploitation, power, and privilege. "Race" is an artificial social construction that was deliberately imposed on various subordinated groups of people at the outset of the expansion of European capitalism into the Western Hemisphere five centuries ago. The "racial" consciousness and discourse of the West was forged above the bowels of slave ships, as they carted their human cargoes into the slave depots of the Caribbean and the Americas. The search for agricultural commodities and profits from the extreme exploitation of involuntary workers deemed less than human gave birth to the notion of racial inequality.

In the United States, a race is frequently defined as a group of individuals who share certain physical or biological traits, particularly phenotype (skin color), body structure, and facial features. But race has no scientific validity as a meaningful biological or genetic concept. Beyond this, the meaning of race shifts according to the power relations between the racial groups.

For instance, in apartheid South Africa, Japanese people were considered by the regime as "white," whereas Chinese were classified as being "colored." In Brazil, a person of color could be "white," "mulatto," or "black," depending upon the individual's vocation, income, family connections, and level of education. . . .

Race Is Situational

Race, therefore, is not an abstract thing, but an unequal relationship between social aggregates, which is also historically specific. The subordinated racial group finds itself divorced from the levers of power and authority within the socioeconomic order. The oppressed racial group's labor power, its ability to produce commodities, is systematically exploited, chiefly through abnormally low wage rates. It is denied ownership of the major means of production. It lacks full access to sources of capital and credit. The racial group's political status is marginal or peripheral, as full participation and legislative representation are blocked.

Finally, dominant and subordinate racial categories are constantly reinforced in the behaviors and social expectations of all groups by the manipulation of social stereotypes and through the utilization of the legal system to carry out methods of coercion. The popular American myth of the Negro's sexual promiscuity, prowess, and great physical attributes, for example, was designed to denigrate the intellectual abilities and the scientific and cultural accomplishments of blacks. . . .

To be white in the United States says nothing directly about an individual's culture, ethnic heritage, or biological background. A society created to preserve "white culture" either would be very confused or tremendously disappointed. White culture does not exist. White power, privileges, and prerogatives within capitalist society do exist.

Whiteness Is Power

Whiteness is fundamentally a statement of the continued patterns of exploitation of subordinated racial groups which create economic surpluses for privileged groups. To be white means that one's "life chances," in the lexicon of American sociologists, improve dramatically. Any white person, regardless of personal appearance, income, or education, usually finds it much easier to establish credit, purchase better homes, and initiate businesses than the average non-white person.

To be white in the United States statistically means that police officers rarely harass you, that your life expectancy is significantly longer than non-whites, and that your children will probably inherit property and social position. Blackness in American racial terms has meant a hundred different insults, harassments, and liabilities experienced daily, living with the reality that a black university graduate will make less money in his or her lifetime than the average white graduate of secondary school; experiencing higher death rates due to the absence of adequate health care facilities in one's neighborhood; accepting the grim fact that, in 1990, a young white American male's statistical likelihood of becoming a victim of homicide is roughly one chance in 186, while a young black male's statistical chances are one in 20.

The ambiguity and confusion concerning the crucial differences between race and ethnicity within the United States are directly attributable to the uneven merger of the two concepts as they related to black Americans. People of African-American nationality, whose cultural patterns and social traditions were derived in part from Africa, were overdetermined externally as the subordinate racial category. Physical appearance and phenotype were convenient, if not always predictable, measures for isolating the members of the oppressed racial group, "the blacks."

For white Americans this racial-ethnic overdetermination did not occur for several reasons. White Americans originated from many different countries and cultures, ethnic intermarriage was frequent, and the rigid economic and legal barriers that confined blacks behind the walls of the ghetto usually did not exist. By the mid-20th century, millions of white Americans had no clear ethnic or cultural identity beyond vague generalizations. Their sense of aesthetics was derived largely from the lowest cultural common denominator—the mass media and the entertainment industry.

Whites' racial identity was ruptured from ethnicity, and was only politically or socially relevant as it affected issues of direct personal interest—such as whether a Hispanic or African-American family intended to purchase a home in their neighborhood, or whether their employer planned to initiate an affirmative-action hiring program for minorities. Whiteness was fundamentally a measure of personal privilege and power, not a cultural statement.

Absorbing Black Culture

White capitalist America's cultural vacuity, its historical inability to nurture or sustain a vibrant "national culture," drawing upon the most creative elements of its various ethnic constituencies, helps to explain the present paradox of desegregation. Millions of white Americans, devoid of their own cultural compass, have absorbed critical elements of African-American music, dance, literature, and language. They now accept black participation in professional athletics and extend acclaim to African-American film stars and entertainers. In a desperate search for collective identity, whites have mimicked blacks in countless ways, from the black-faced minstrels of the 19th century to the contemporary white musical groups singing reggae and rap.

But whites' affinity and tolerance for blackness are largely cultural, not racial. Many whites have learned to appreciate African-derived elements of music, dance, and religious rituals, but would not endorse the sharing of power or material privileges, which would undermine the stratification of race. . . .

Integration Without Understanding

The central characteristic of race relations in the 1990s is "interaction without understanding." White students purchase the latest taped recordings of black singers and cheer the latest exploits of black athletes, while they bitterly reject the imposition of course requirements mandating classes in African-American politics, history, or literature. White employers encourage the recruitment of black junior executives in their firms, but would shudder at the prospect of minorities moving into their exclusive neighborhoods or joining their elite private clubs. White religious leaders espouse pious platitudes about ethnic understanding and racial reconciliation, while doing relatively little to bring their white, upper-class congregations into close contact with the gritty problems of the ghetto. Racial integration, within

181

the framework of capitalism, has produced the symbols of progress and the rhetoric of racial harmony without the substance of empowerment for the oppressed.

Perhaps the greatest irony in this post-civil rights situation is that African Americans born after 1960 frequently have great difficulty identifying the realities of contemporary oppressive race and class structures because of the transformation of white racial etiquette. No white politician, corporate executive, or religious leader now uses the term "nigger" in public. African Americans coming to maturity in the 1980s and 1990s have never personally experienced Jim Crow segregation. They cannot express how they feel to be denied the right to vote because their electoral rights are guaranteed by law. They have never personally participated in street demonstrations, boycotts, picket lines, and seizures of government and academic buildings. Few have tasted the pungent fumes of tear gas or felt the fiery hatred of racist mobs. The absence of a personal background of struggle casts a troubled shadow over the current generation of black Americans who are poorly equipped to grapple with the current complexities of racial and class domination.

Cultural Literacy

Integration also crippled African Americans in the context of their "cultural literacy." Under traditional racial segregation, the strict barriers that were established forced a wide variety of professions and social classes into intimate interaction. Black physicians had to look for patients in the black community. African-American attorneys depended upon black clients. Black storeowners looked to blacks for patronage.

Black social organizations, civic associations, and religious institutions reflected the broad spectrum of social class, from custodians and sanitation workers to school teachers and civil servants. The sense of shared suffering and collective cooperation provided the basis for an appreciation of the community's racial identity and heritage. African-American history was taught in segregated schools and churches, and pictures of prominent black leaders were frequently displayed.

Denied access to the white media, blacks established their own network of race-oriented publications. A separate cultural and artistic underground developed in the cities, creative enclaves that produced the classical legacy of modern jazz and the urban blues.

But as the racial boundaries were liberalized and as white public discourse became largely race-neutral, the terrain for black cultural awareness diminished. Young African Americans no longer were forced to confront their ethnicity or cultural history. In effect, we are witnessing the development of a substantial segment of the African-American population which is "post-black—without any cultural awareness, historical appreciation, or political commitment to the traditions, customs, values, and networks that have been the basis for black identity in America. . . .

The challenges of race, class, and power confronting black Americans are far more complicated than Martin Luther King Jr. ever anticipated when he stood on the steps of the Lincoln Memorial at the August 1963 March on Washington, D.C., delivering his "I Have a Dream" speech. The objective should not be the realization of a utopian, colorblind society, but a democratic social order that seeks to achieve several goals.

Integration into What?

Integration begs the question—integration into what? What kind of society prefers selective assimilation to transformation? The answer is one which still seeks to cover-over the fundamental questions of justice and compassion. Integration has served that cover-up.

The reign of insatiable materialism over human dignity in American society destroys the souls of rich and poor alike. And the acceptance of an economic system based on theft from the poor at home and around the world will continue to keep masses of people at the bottom. In a white-controlled society, a disproportionate number of those will be people of color.

Jim Wallis, *Sojourners*, August/September 1990.

First, democratic principles must be extended from the electoral system into the structures of the economy and social order, making a job or guaranteed income a human right. Also, public health-care facilities, housing, and access to transportation must be available to all. Finally, ethnicity must be distinctly separated from race, which would preserve America's diverse cultural and ethnic heritages while abolishing all forms of institutional discrimination that are justified by the perpetuation of racial categories. We must destroy "race" without uprooting culture and ethnicity.

"A new model is needed, one that returns to the . . . goals of integration and equal rights."

Blacks Should Not Emphasize Their Ethnicity

Joe Klein

Joe Klein is a writer for *New York*, a weekly magazine. In the following viewpoint, he argues that racial tensions between whites and blacks have increased because of lack of contact between the two groups. Black leaders should not concentrate on obtaining special treatment and programs for blacks, he contends, because such programs only lead to more separation between blacks and whites. He states that the goal for blacks should instead be assimilation within white society.

As you read, consider the following questions:

1. Why is the topic of race seldom discussed, according to Klein?
2. According to the author, why was the goal of integration abandoned in the 1960s?
3. Why is there peer pressure against academic success among black students, according to Klein?

Adapted from "Race: The Issue," by Joe Klein. Copyright © 1991 News America Publishing Incorporated. All rights reserved. Reprinted with the permisssion of *New York* magazine.

Race is an issue politicians go to great pains to avoid. It has been deemed unfit for open discussion, in all but the most platitudinous manner, for many years. The public is, oddly, complicit in this: People seem to sense that the topic is so raw, and their feelings so intense, that it's just too risky to discuss in mixed company. "It never comes up," says another mayoral hopeful. "Crime does all the time, but it's rarely linked to race. I get questions and comments in public meetings about everything under the sun—but never about race."

In private, though, race seems the *only* thing people are talking about these days. . . . The radio talk shows . . . are full of it. The subject dominates fancy dinner parties in Manhattan; it comes up on supermarket lines in Queens and around kitchen tables in Brooklyn; it has suddenly become permissible to vent frustrations, to ask questions and say things—often ugly things—that have been forbidden in polite discourse for many years.

The Central Question

And the central question, at least among whites, is. . . . Why have so many blacks proved so resistant to *incubation*? Why, after 25 years of equal rights—indeed, of special remedial treatment under law—do so many remain outside the bounds of middle-class society? Why do even educated blacks seem increasingly remote, hostile, and paranoid? In a society besotted with quick fixes and easy answers to every problem, is this the one that will prove insoluble?

Even though none of the candidates will say it publicly, race is *the* central issue in 1989's mayoral campaign. But then it was the great unspoken in 1988's presidential election as well—remember Willie Horton? It is, and always has been, the most persistent and emotional test of America's ability to exist as a society of equals. In New York, the challenge is immediate and explosive: Race is at the heart of all of the city's most critical problems—crime, drugs, homelessness, the crises in public education, public health, children's services. All have been exacerbated by racial polarization and antagonism. And also by a conspiracy of silence—by a fear of speaking candidly about the causes and possible solutions to these problems.

The silence may well be about to end. Each new outrage— Howard Beach, Tawana Brawley, the constant drumbeat of crack killings, cops blown away, the jogger raped, the black woman raped and thrown off the Brooklyn rooftop (one of the legion of black victims ignored by white society)—each new barbarity nudges people closer to the moment when the discussion of how black and white Americans can come to terms with each other is reopened.

It is a public debate that was closed down abruptly nearly

twenty years ago. The country has been drifting toward disaster ever since. "There is an illness in the community now, a psychosis," says John Lewis, the Georgia congressman and one of the true heroes of the civil-rights movement. "We need to bring all the dirt and all the sickness out into the open. We need to talk again about building what Dr. King called a *beloved community*—a truly integrated society of blacks and whites."

Integration seems an impossibly romantic notion now. Even to propose it as the solution to the racial morass raises derisive hoots in the black community and patronizing shrugs and smiles from whites. Serious talk of integration ended when "black power" began to flourish and *equal rights* was supplanted by *affirmative action* as the rallying cry of the movement. Aggrievement—the notion that blacks deserved special compensatory treatment—replaced assimilation at the top of the activists' agenda. Integration withered as a goal; "community control" replaced it. The movement imploded—and white America was only too happy to let it happen. Liberals quickly, romantically—and quite irresponsibly—acceded to the new black demands; conservatives were quietly relieved that blacks no longer wanted *in*. Only a few brave souls raised the obvious question: How could blacks be included in American society if they insisted on separating themselves from it? For the most part, interracial debate ended.

"White America ceded control of the *definition* of the problem to blacks in the late sixties and early seventies," says Glenn Loury, a black professor of political economy at Harvard's Kennedy School. "But not control of the solution. A situation of mutually reinforcing cowardice has resulted."

Twenty years later, having suffered a generation of black "power" and white indifference, race relations are at a dead end. The usual litany of achievement—the growth of a black middle class, the integration of public life—isn't very convincing. The horrific desperation of the black underclass demands that the racial debate be reopened, and the only logical place for it to begin is where it left off: at the moment when the civil-rights movement resegregated itself. "We made a serious mistake when the movement turned against its first principle: integration," John Lewis laments. "The seeds that were planted twenty years ago have borne very bitter fruit."

The Move from Integration

The shift from integration to "black power" seems a strange, counterproductive inversion now—and yet it seemed perfectly logical at the time. How did it happen—and happen so quickly? The death of Martin Luther King Jr. is often cited as a turning point—Lewis mentions it—but Stokely Carmichael proclaimed "black power" two years before King's death, and Malcolm X was drawing large crowds well before that. The separatist impulse had

186

always been there, ever since emancipation—and so its revival in the mid-sixties was no great surprise. The surprise was the speed with which it moved from a handful of radicals at the periphery to the heart of the civil-rights movement. The irony was that it occurred at a moment when civil-rights legislation—bills that *mandated* integration—were flying through Congress and the leading integrationist, Martin Luther King, was winning the Nobel Peace Prize. Never had America seemed so open to the idea of inclusion.

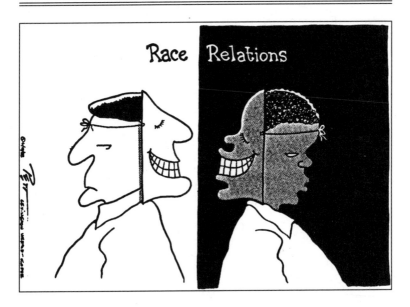

Joel Pett/*Lexington Herald-Leader.* Reprinted with permission.

And yet the legislation itself—particularly the Voting Rights Act of 1965—contained the seeds of separatism. As Bayard Rustin, a stalwart integrationist until his death in 1987, pointed out early on, "What began as a protest movement is now being challenged to translate itself into a political movement." This meant a shift from nonviolent demonstrations to "the building of community institutions or power bases" to elect black politicians.

There wasn't much percentage in integration for the black mayors and aldermen who soon won election across the black belt in the South and in the urban slums up North. For people like Charles Evers, running for mayor of Fayette, Mississippi, black electoral *power* was a far more immediate concern than the gauzy ideal of "black-and-white together." Their agenda was naturally compensatory: If the streets on the white side of town were paved, equality meant paving them on the black side of town. Like all good politicians, the new black officials pandered to their core constituencies. This was classic ethnic politics, a healthy impulse—but it put the black pols into closer rhetorical proximity with the militant separatists: Both were calling for "black power."

Northern black leaders wanted a piece of the action, too—but they were locked into larger, white-dominated government entities. For them, the naked choice was between power and integration: By separating from the white system—by demanding "community control" of school districts in New York, for example—they could gain a measure of power from the white politicians who ran the town. As Nicholas Lemann observed in *The Atlantic*, the "community action" component of the federal war on poverty reinforced this tendency by funneling money to a new generation of community leaders, instead of to the established city authorities—even Lyndon Johnson, it seemed, believed in black power.

There was, less obviously, a certain security in separatism as well. If the schools (and neighborhoods) remained black, there was a good chance blacks would run them. Integration challenged blacks as profoundly as it did whites. It meant competing against *the man* for the top jobs. And a great many blacks were convinced—despite all the new laws and King's Nobel Prize and a president who said "We shall overcome"—that the competition would be as unfair as it always had been. There were, quite understandably, more than a few who quietly wondered if the racists were right and secretly feared that they couldn't compete. "That impulse was nothing new," said a labor leader deeply involved in the civil-rights movement. "The black teachers in the South were pretty solidly against integration in the 1950s."

So the militants provided the new black class of political leaders with a philosophical rationale for their natural impulses to accumulate power and avoid competition: White society was fundamentally racist, and so integration was pointless. Blacks were victims of a systematic oppression and deserved special treatment—affirmative action, quotas, more programs of every sort—in recompense. This was quite satisfying intellectually. Many fair-minded Americans agreed: Blacks *had* been treated abominably. Their restraint in the face of the most noxious provocation had been remarkable. Even when the great urban riots began in the mid-sixties, these seemed an understandable—if not justifiable—response to white prejudice.

Special Treatment

But a line was crossed when blacks demanded—and then got—special treatment. A price was paid, most immediately in heightened antagonism from the white working class, which felt threatened by the new rules. But eventually by the blacks themselves: By defining themselves as victims and separating themselves by race, they had guaranteed their continued isolation from white society. "This . . . is the tragedy of black power in America today," wrote Shelby Steele, the brilliant black essayist, in *Harper's*. "It is primarily a victim's power. . . . Whatever gains this power brings in the short run through political action, it undermines in the long run. Social victims may be collectively entitled, but they are all too often individually demoralized."

When aggrievement was proclaimed the central, psychic fact of black life, the most aggrieved and alienated—the most amoral, the criminals—became the definers of "true" blackness in the media and also in the streets. White liberals, guilt-ridden (I write from experience), accepted this spurious definition at face value. Far worse, though: For a brief, truly revolting moment, white radicals celebrated the most antisocial blacks as culture heroes. Criminality was romanticized. Slums were now called "ghettos," which assumed a romantic communalism and immediacy of oppression that simply didn't exist.

The radical looniness reached its apex with the celebration of the Black Panthers and of Eldridge Cleaver's hopelessly perverted *Soul on Ice*, in which black-on-white rape was described as a political act. (As a young reporter in Boston at the time, I interviewed a white rape victim who coolly described her post-violation reaction: "I went to the free clinic to get a tetanus shot, and then went home and reread Eldridge Cleaver, so I could better understand what happened.") There was something incredibly careless—and so ironic as to feed the worst black paranoia—about both the white radicals' celebration and the liberals' acceptance of this pathological behavior. By romanticizing these irresponsible activities—criminality, sexual "freedom," drug use, and general lack of ambition—whites were lending support to a subtle system of oppression that had existed since slavery times.

Old Solutions

"One can think of the lower-class Negroes as bribed and drugged by this system," wrote John Dollard in his landmark 1937 study *Caste and Class in a Southern Town*. "The effect of the social set-up seems to be to keep Negroes infantile, to grant them infantile types of freedom from responsibility. . . . The evidence is unmistakable that the moral indolence allowed to Negroes is perceived by them and their white caste masters as a compensating value and gain [for forced labor in a plantation or share-cropping system]."

The words seem rather harsh now, after a quarter-century of euphemisms. But John Dollard wrote as a firm advocate of "Negro" rights; he described a pattern of oppression and prescribed a solution. He made a clear distinction between the determinedly proper black middle class, struggling to assimilate, and the rural underclass, which had not yet shed the behavior patterns imposed by their former slave masters. Then he concluded,

"The dominant aim of our society seems to be to middle-classify all of its members. Negroes, including lower-class Negroes, are no exceptions. Eventually they must all enter the competition for higher status which is so basic and compulsive an element in our way of life. This will mean . . . approximating more nearly the ideal of restraint, independence and personal maturity which is implicitly attached to our demands for individual competition and mobility."

This was considered radical race-mixing in the thirties; 30 years later, black activists had come to see any derogation of lower-class black morality as white paternalism. When Daniel Patrick Moynihan wrote a report—in the spirit of Dollard—on the instability of black family structure in 1965, he was pilloried. A sociological ice age ensued. . . .

Meanwhile, the pathology metastasized. When Moynihan wrote his report in 1965, a "staggering" 26 percent of nonwhite children were born out of wedlock; now the figure is 61 percent. The technology of underclass indolence also has exploded: The Saturday-night knife fights on the black side of the tracks that Dollard says the rednecks found so amusing have become shoot-outs with semi-automatic weapons; "white lightning" has become crack. Sex remains sex—but mixed with hypodermic needles spells AIDS.

Is Racism the Cause?

A great many blacks and white liberals will argue that these spiraling pathologies are the result of racism, the hopelessness and frustration that are part of growing up desperately poor and "knowing" that the system won't cut you any slack. This is undoubtedly true, as is William Julius Wilson's belief that the departure of the black middle class from the cities to the suburbs removed role models, disciplinarians, and other socializing forces from the slums, hastening the collapse of the social order. "You can't imagine how removed these kids are from life as we know it," says Andrew Cuomo, who runs a program for homeless families. "They have no contact with *anyone* who has succeeded in the system. They don't have an uncle who's a lawyer or an aunt who's a teacher. They see no point to succeeding. The line you hear most often is 'Stay in school so you can go to work in McDonald's.'"

This terrible deprivation no doubt would have existed if sociologists had been free to ply their trade in the slums, and if the civil-rights movement had kept integration as its goal, but the militant know-nothingism of the black nationalists certainly hasn't helped any. Sadly, when "black power" filters to the streets, it's often little more than a rationale for failure: More than a few scholarly studies, notably one by John U. Ogbu and Signithia Fordham in *The Urban Review*, have shown that there is enormous peer pressure against academic success in black high schools. It is considered "acting white."

The taunts that Ogbu and Fordham describe seem no worse than those endured by generations of Jewish, Irish, and Italian nerds, but the sanctions are cosmic: The black kid who succeeds in school is not only a traitor to the race but a sucker besides. He, or she, is busting his butt for a job at *McDonald's*. There is tremendous pressure on these kids—even those from strict, stable middle-class homes, as some of the children involved in the April 1989 Central Park rape apparently were—to prove their blackness by misbehaving.

White society offers very few incentives to the black teenagers who resist peer pressure and play "our" game. Indeed, they are treated with the same disdain visited upon the potential hoodlums. In a stunning bit of television, Ted Koppel gave six star black high-school students a camera and sent them out into the white world, asking for change of a dollar. The reactions were depressing. Most whites simply ignored the kids. White women were startled when approached; one seemed to jump back, then hastened to the other side of the street.

A Vicious Spiral

Given the levels of criminality now, these reactions are also understandable. They are part of the vicious spiral of racism and reaction that has been allowed to spin out of control during the years of silence. The pattern is clear: The more violent the streets become, the more race-sensitive whites become, and the blacks, in turn, grow more isolated and angry. The rape of the jogger in Central Park seems to have ratcheted the cycle another turn toward anarchy. . . .

There is also a new outbreak of the half-crazed paranoia and conspiracy-theorizing that have become quite popular in the black media. *The City Sun,* considered a "respectable" black weekly, published a truly vomitous account of the incident, including a fantasy description of the victim's body as "the American Ideal . . . a tiny body with round hips and pert buttocks, soft white thighs, slender calves, firm and high breasts."

The author of this trash went on to opine that—if you omit the question of whether the rape actually occurred—the children who committed the Central Park abomination were being subjected to the same sort of treatment as the Scottsboro boys, the blacks falsely convicted of raping a white woman in Alabama 50 years ago. This sort of nonsense is of a piece with the increasing numbers of blacks nationally who, according to one pollster, believe that the drug crisis is a conspiracy on the part of white society to "commit genocide" against blacks. "The really disturbing thing is that the more solid the black middle class becomes," this pollster said, "the more its fundamental views of the issues seems to diverge from middle-class America.". . .

There have been two paradigms for dealing with dilemmas of race, and neither has worked. Conservatives have ignored the problem, left the solution to "market forces" or, worse, to social Darwinism. Liberals seem to have abandoned critical thought entirely, allowing militants to dictate their agenda, scorning most efforts to impose sanctions on antisocial behavior by underclass blacks.

The New Segregation

Some might argue that neo-segregationism is acceptable because minorities choose to set themselves apart, while classical segregation, on the other hand, was offensive because it was imposed on minorities by majoritarian society.

I would argue that such an analysis is superficial. The real danger in neo-segregationism lies in the fact that if carried too far, it can promote political alienation—and in its most extreme manifestation, separatism. We have only to look at Northern Ireland, Lebanon and Sri Lanka to understand what a lack of unity does to a country.

Richard Estrada, *The Dallas Morning News*, March 24, 1989.

A new model is needed, one that returns to the original movement goals of integration and equal rights while addressing the deterioration that has taken place in black family structure and community institutions over the past twenty years. Integration— that is, *assimilation* into the middle-class economy—can be the only possible goal. The society has to "emphasize commonality as a higher value than 'diversity' or 'pluralism,'" wrote Shelby Steele in *Harper's*. Programs that divide by race, even well-intentioned ones like affirmative action, are too costly in *moral* terms. They send the wrong message—of racial division and aggrievement. A more profitable agenda is one that seeks to pull the poorest, regardless of race, into conformity with middle-class standards.

"Schools . . . have been dominated for far too long by the attitudes, the beliefs, and the value system of one race and class of people."

Schools Should Emphasize Ethnicity

Gerald J. Pine and Asa G. Hilliard III

In the following viewpoint, Gerald J. Pine and Asa G. Hilliard III argue that America's school curriculum fails to present enough multicultural material. The authors conclude that multicultural education can help students respond to racism, appreciate cultural diversity, and build pride in ethnic identities. Pine is professor of education and dean of the School of Human and Educational Services at Oakland University at Rochester, Michigan. Hilliard is a professor of education at Georgia State University in Atlanta.

As you read, consider the following questions:

1. How do Pine and Hilliard define racism?
2. According to the authors, how are minority students victimized by the school curriculum?
3. What does genuine multicultural education require, according to Pine and Hilliard?

From "Rx for Racism," by Gerald J. Pine and Asa G. Hilliard III, *Phi Delta Kappan*, April 1990, © 1990, Phi Delta Kappan, Inc. Reprinted with permission.

Every time we are almost convinced that the nation is rising above the muck of racism, there come reminders of how little headway we have made—even at eliminating the most vulgar and conspicuous manifestations of the disease. Blatant, crude, egregious, and overt racism has come out of the closet again and into our schools. Documented accounts of public slurs, threats, racist slogans, physical assaults, and racial conflicts now ring disturbingly from schools in every region of the country. Schools, which ought to be a civilizing influence in our society, seem instead to be incubators of racial intolerance. Racism, prejudice, and discrimination are shamefully sabotaging our nation's efforts to provide a high-quality education for all children.

The problem of racism demands the attention of all educators. As American society rapidly grows more diverse, we must give top priority to insuring that all students receive their birthright of educational equity. Unfortunately, although America is a multicultural society, [Louise Derman-Sparks writes] "it is not yet a pluralistic society—a place where all racial and cultural groups share equal access to opportunities for quality lives and power over their own lives." To achieve pluralism, racism must be abolished, and the mission of public education must be fully achieved. That mission is to provide all students with a high-quality education that will enable them to function successfully in an interdependent, multiethnic, multicultural, and rapidly changing world. The magnitude of the task is so great that it constitutes the most significant challenge to America's system of education.

Valuing Diversity

Octavio Paz reminds us that "life is plurality, death is uniformity. Every view that becomes extinct, every culture that disappears, diminishes a possibility of life." When education takes place, every individual—teacher, student, or administrator—brings his or her cultural background to that process. Unless we educators learn to prize and value differences and to view them as resources for learning, neither whites nor minority groups will experience the teaching and learning situations best suited to prepare them to live effectively in a world whose population is characterized by diversity.

Many American children are affected by institutional racism. Education is their best hope for breaking racism's chains. Yet, although such issues as equal opportunity, desegregation, and inequities in educational achievement have received considerable attention in recent years, very few schools have developed deliberate and systematic programs to reduce prejudice. The prevailing attitude seems to be that society has done away with the problem of racism through legislative action and special programs. But continuing instances of overt racism belie this notion, and institutionalized manifestations of racism—less blatant and thus more insidious—continue to stunt the aspirations and talents of minority children and to distort the views and psyches of white children.

Educational Inequity

Despite the grave importance of educational equity in our changing society, low-income minority groups have lost ground and are in imminent danger of losing a great deal more. As Asa Hilliard has pointed out elsewhere:

> It should not require proof here that the educational outcomes are vastly different for different racial, language, economic, and gender groups in this nation. Look at dropouts, suspensions, and expulsions; look at academic achievement indices of any kind. Look at the patterns of coursework completed by high school graduates. Look at the cultural retardation of all our high school graduates, minority or majority. . . . But most especially look at the ignorance of and alienation from their natal culture experienced by the millions of children who are on the bottom economically, socially, and politically.
>
> It should also require little proof here that the process of education is vastly different for different racial, language, economic, and gender groups in the nation. Look at the scandalously disproportionate placement of students in special education categories, where low-level demands cause them to miss exposure to higher levels of educational activity. Look at the meager attempts nationally to pluralize the standard European-centered curriculum so that it conforms to the truth of all human experience, rather than reflecting a glorification of the narrow, parochial cultural experience of dominant groups.

These inequities reflect the persistence of racism and bigotry in the general culture. If we have learned anything at all in the last few years, surely it is how difficult and grievous a struggle human beings have in dealing with racial differences. The effort to learn to treat one another as members of the same human family grinds on. Those who discriminate and those who tolerate discrimination are graduates of our schools. We have had our chance to teach lessons about equity and to make them a priority, but it appears that we have failed. Why? Thomas Arciniega's analysis seems to be as relevant today as it was in 1977:

> Public education has successfully shifted the blame for the failure of schools to meet the needs of minorities onto the shoulders of the clients they purport to serve. They have pulled off the perfect crime, for they can never be truly held accountable, since the reasons for failure in school are said to be the fault of poor homes, cultural handicaps, linguistic deficiencies, and deprived neighborhoods. The fact that schools are geared primarily to serve monolingual, white, middle-class, Anglo clients is never questioned.

How will we meet the challenge of providing a high-quality

education for all students in a culturally diverse society? Do we educators know how to deal with institutional racism? Do we know how to develop healthy, prejudice-free attitudes in all our students? Can we be sure that educational practice will reflect a commitment to educational equity so that all Americans can achieve what we now falsely believe only the elite can attain?

Understanding Racism

In order for Americans to embrace diversity, the conscious and unconscious expressions of racism within our society must be identified and done away with. The first step is to develop an understanding of the history and nature of racism and its relationship to prejudice and discrimination. *Prejudice* consists of unjustifiable negative feelings and beliefs about a racial or ethnic group and its members. It is characterized by preconceived opinions, judgments, or feelings that lack any foundation or substance. *Discrimination* consists of unjustifiable negative behavior toward a racial or ethnic group and its members. It expresses itself in distinctions and decisions made on the basis of prejudice. *Racism* describes the combination of individual prejudice and individual discrimination, on the one hand, and institutional policies and practices, on the other, that result in the unjustified negative treatment and subordination of members of a racial or ethnic group. By convention, the term *racism* has been reserved to describe the mistreatment of members of racial and ethnic groups that have experienced a history of discrimination. *Prejudice, discrimination, and racism do not require intention.*

Students Need to Know

Whether in elementary school or a university campus, students in this nation need to know about the heritage and contributions of people of African descent and of Asian descent and of Latin American descent as well as people of European descent. An education that views the European heritage as central, and, by assumption, superior, and that views non-European heritages as peripheral, and, by assumption, inferior, is a deficient education. For it fails to prepare our youth for the reality of a world that is increasingly interdependent and a nation that will increasingly be composed of non-white peoples or, the preferred term these days, "people of color."

Franklyn G. Jenifer, *The Washington Post National Weekly Edition*, November 26-December 2, 1990.

Racism can be thought of as a sick belief system. A "healthy" belief system reflects a good match between the real world and the ideal world. A sick belief system reflects a poor match.

Colonization, motivated by greed and a lust for power, depended on creating a sick belief system for both the colonizer and the colonized in order to support colonial expansion. Therefore, the concept of race was invented (conceptually separating Europeans from the people to be dominated), and racism emerged.

Racism is a mental illness characterized by perceptual distortion, a denial of reality, delusions of grandeur (belief in white supremacy), the projection of blame (on the victim), and phobic reactions to differences. A colonizer may be a racist, but a victim cannot be so. A victim may become pro-racist, however, which means that he or she identifies with the aggressor and initiates many racist behaviors. To make racism work it is necessary to destroy the victim's identity and to claim superiority for the oppressor. Colonizers accomplished this aim by destroying the history and the culture of their victims and rewriting history to assert their own claim to superiority. . . .

Historically, every academic discipline—psychology, biology, geography, religion, philosophy, anthropology, literature, history—has been used to justify colonialism and racism. Under colonialism, information is rigidly controlled in several ways: it can be destroyed, distorted, fabricated, suppressed, or selectively emphasized. Those in power can also limit the access of others to information or present it in a manner designed to confuse the recipients.

Monocultural Environments

Through the omission of information, America's schools have become monocultural environments. They dispense a curriculum centered on western civilization that encapsulates only narrowly the truth, reality, and breadth of human experience. This curriculum reinforces institutional racism by excluding from discourse and from the ethos of the school and the classroom the intellectual thought, scholarship, history, culture, contributions, and experience of minority groups. Schools have become sites for producing and making acceptable myths and ideologies that systematically disorganize and neutralize the cultural identities of minorities. Consequently, schools—where the hearts and minds of children are shaped and controlled—have been dominated for far too long by the attitudes, the beliefs, and the value system of one race and class of people. This is not a politically, socially, morally, or economically justifiable situation in a democratic, multicultural society.

Because the U.S. system of education is built so solidly on a monocultural, Euro-American world view, it tends to benefit white students, whose cultural patterns and styles are more attuned to this world view. As white students progress through the education system and move into the world of work, the development of their cognitive styles and their learning styles is

197

linear and self-reinforcing. Seldom, if ever, are they required to be bicultural, bilingual, or bicognitive.

For children of color, being bicultural is not a free choice but a prerequisite for success in the education system and for eventual success in the society at large. Nonwhite children are generally expected to be bicultural, bilingual, and bicognitive; to measure their performance against a Euro-American yardstick; and to maintain the psychic energy necessary to sustain this orientation. At the same time, they are castigated whenever they attempt to express and validate their indigenous cultural and cognitive styles.

The Consequences of Racism

The consequences of institutional racism and a monocultural education are pervasive and profound. White students tend glibly to accept the idea of equality and multiculturalism or of the superior position of their group in society without speculation or insightful analysis. They become oblivious to all but the most blatant acts of racism or ethnic discrimination and often re-label such acts as something else. They seldom give serious thought to cultural, ethnic, or racial differences or to their meaning for and influence on individuals and groups. They are subliminally socialized, enculturated, and oriented to believe that the western experience, culture, and world view are superior and dominant.

Students of color, by contrast, experience conceptual separation from their roots; they are compelled to examine their own experiences and history through the assumptions, paradigms, constructs, and language of other people; they lose their cultural identity; and they find it difficult to develop a sense of affiliation and connection to a school. They become "universal strangers"—disaffected and alienated—and all too many eventually drop out of school. . . .

If we are in the "business" of educating people, then we are in the business of communicating truth and reality—of telling the complete story of history and human experience. That means that we must learn how to tap the rich vein of cultural, ethnic, and racial diversity to improve education for all children. A multicultural, gender-fair, nonparochial curriculum is essential if students are to broaden their understanding of their own cultures and of cultural diversity.

We need to incorporate into the curriculum another story, a nonwestern story of the world. Education has long been used to create distorted perceptions and beliefs about minority groups. By leaving out nonwestern history, culture, and ideas, we have falsified education for everyone. Schools need to integrate into all curricular areas the ideas, the literature, the contributions, and the history of minority groups. A curriculum based on truth and reality can provide students with a sense of continuity, of self-esteem, and of identity. Portland, Oregon, has developed such a curriculum.

The Need for Multicultural Education

Considering the importance of addressing the inequalities in the curriculum and of preparing all children effectively for a multicultural society, restructuring classroom instruction to reflect the diversity of the society seems to be a viable alternative. From the perspective of educational policy and practice, public education must seek whatever information the social sciences can provide concerning the different sociocultural system from which its children come. Teacher education programs must expose students to the unique communication, human relational, learning, and motivational patterns that are produced in African-American and other culturally different children through the offering of courses on African-American and other minority experiences. Knowing what these unique patterns are, public education must adopt policies and instructional programs that are consistent with the diversity of the society and the unique socialization patterns. This has been referred to as multicultural education.

Felix Boateng, *Going to School*, 1990.

As Glenn Pate has pointed out, a genuinely multicultural approach that permeates the K-12 curriculum—horizontally and vertically, in all subject areas—and that is supported by high-quality instructional materials is far more effective than "add-on" programs designed to reduce prejudice, elevate self-esteem, and enhance learning. Programs that are added on to the regular curriculum are viewed as supplementary. They do not effectively attack students' prejudices, may be seen as patronizing, and may be implemented in such a way that they alienate both majority and minority students.

In his review of approaches to a multicultural curriculum, James Banks noted that, while add-on programs can be used as steppingstones to more intellectually challenging approaches, they do not involve a restructuring of the curriculum. Thus they often trivialize ethnic cultures; they tend to evade significant issues, such as racism, poverty, and oppression; and they view ethnic content from the perspective of mainstream historians, writers, artists, and scientists. An effective multicultural curriculum is achieved when we change the basic assumptions of the curriculum; enable students to view concepts, themes, issues, and problems from several ethnic perspectives; and infuse throughout the curriculum the frames of reference, history, culture, and perspectives of various ethnic groups. Such an approach extends students' understanding of the nature, development, complexity, and dynamics of a multicultural, pluralistic society and leads them to social action and decision making that reduce prejudice and discrimination in their schools.

Genuine multicultural education demands a major commitment of time, energy, and resources. Developing appropriate materials, collecting resources, conducting historical research, and integrating multicultural content into all parts of the curriculum require sustained effort. Such effort can be regarded as a measure of authentic commitment to educational equity. A curriculum that honors and values the rich contributions that culturally diverse groups have made to society and to civilization is the foundation on which to build interactive, multicultural, gender-fair communities of learning. . . .

Stop Racism

To become moral communities that are supportive and caring, schools need to model empathy, altruism, trust, cooperation, fairness, justice, compassion, democracy, and celebration of diversity. In schools, the quality of communal caring and the sense of community conscience are largely defined by the degree of harmony and mutual respect between white and minority groups. Harmony and mutual respect are measured by how well we live the values we teach and how fully we practice the ideals to which we are committed. Caring and just schools—characterized by intervention programs to counteract racism, by diverse teaching staffs, by truly multicultural curricula, by appropriate pedagogical practices, by high expectations, and by continuing emphasis on the development of character and self-esteem—are essential to the achievement of genuine educational equity and to the elimination of institutional racism.

"Almost any idea, carried to its extreme, can be made pernicious, and this is what is happening now to multiculturalism."

Emphasizing Ethnicity Encourages Racism

Diane Ravitch

Diane Ravitch is an adjunct professor of history and education at Teachers College at Columbia University in New York City, and has written several books including *The Troubled Crusade: American Education, 1945-1980*. In the following viewpoint, she argues that America's schools and textbooks already incorporate teaching about racial minority groups in their curriculum. She argues that placing too much emphasis on the ethnic and racial identity of minority students would worsen race relations and do little to improve education.

As you read, consider the following questions:

1. How does Ravitch differentiate between what she sees as two kinds of multiculturalism?
2. How can multicultural education distort history, according to the author?
3. What is the central purpose of public education, according to Ravitch?

Excerpted from "Multiculturalism: E Pluribus Plures," by Diane Ravitch. Reprinted, with permission, from *The American Scholar*, vol. 59, no. 3, Summer 1990. Copyright © 1990 by Diane Ravitch.

As a result of the political and social changes of recent decades, cultural pluralism is now generally recognized as an organizing principle of this society. In contrast to the idea of the melting pot, which promised to erase ethnic and group differences, children now learn that variety is the spice of life. They learn that America has provided a haven for many different groups and has allowed them to maintain their cultural heritage or to assimilate, or—as is often the case—to do both; the choice is theirs, not the state's. They learn that cultural pluralism is one of the norms of a free society; that differences among groups are a national resource rather than a problem to be solved. Indeed, the unique feature of the United States is that its common culture has been formed by the interaction of its subsidiary cultures. It is a culture that has been influenced over time by immigrants, American Indians, Africans (slave and free) and by their descendants. American music, art, literature, language, food, clothing, sports, holidays, and customs all show the effects of the commingling of diverse cultures in one nation. Paradoxical though it may seem, the United States has a common culture that is multicultural.

Our schools and our institutions of higher learning have in recent years begun to embrace what Catherine R. Stimpson of Rutgers University has called "cultural democracy," a recognition that we must listen to a "diversity of voices" in order to understand our culture, past and present. This understanding of the pluralistic nature of American culture has taken a long time to forge. It is based on sound scholarship and has led to major revisions in what children are taught and what they read in school. . . .

Two Types of Multiculturalism

Alas, these painstaking efforts to expand the understanding of American culture into a richer and more varied tapestry have taken a new turn, and not for the better. Almost any idea, carried to its extreme, can be made pernicious, and this is what is happening now to multiculturalism. Today, pluralistic multiculturalism must contend with a new, particularistic multiculturalism. The pluralists seek a richer common culture; the particularists insist that no common culture is possible or desirable. The new particularism is entering the curriculum in a number of school systems across the country. Advocates of particularism propose an ethnocentric curriculum to raise the self-esteem and academic achievement of children from racial and ethnic minority backgrounds. Without any evidence, they claim that children from minority backgrounds will do well in school *only* if they are immersed in a positive, prideful version of their ancestral culture. If children are of, for example, Fredonian ancestry, they must hear that Fredonians were important in mathematics, science, history, and literature. If they learn about great Fredonians and if their studies use Fredonian examples and Fredonian concepts, they will do well in school. If they do not, they will have low self-esteem and will do badly.

"They used to call them schools."

© Allen/Rothco. Reprinted with permission.

At first glance, this appears akin to the celebratory activities associated with Black History Month or Women's History Month, when schoolchildren learn about the achievements of blacks and women. But the point of those celebrations is to demonstrate that neither race nor gender is an obstacle to high achievement. They teach all children that everyone, regardless of their race, religion, gender, ethnicity, or family origin, can achieve self-fulfillment, honor, and dignity in society if they aim high and work hard.

By contrast, the particularistic version of multiculturalism is unabashedly filiopietistic and deterministic. It teaches children that their identity is determined by their "cultural genes." That something in their blood or their race memory or their cultural DNA defines who they are and what they may achieve. That the culture in which they live is not their own culture, even though they were born here. That American culture is "Eurocentric," and therefore hostile to anyone whose ancestors are not European. Perhaps the most invidious implication of particularism is that racial and ethnic minorities are not and should not try to be part of American culture; it implies that American culture belongs only to those who are white and European; it implies that those who are neither white nor European are alienated from American culture by virtue of their race or ethnicity; it implies that the only culture they do belong to or can ever belong to is the culture of their ancestors, even if their families have lived in this country for generations. . . .

Particularism has its intellectual roots in the ideology of ethnic separatism and in the black nationalist movement. In the particularist analysis, the nation has five cultures: African American, Asian American, European American, Latino/Hispanic, and Native American. The huge cultural, historical, religious, and linguistic differences within these categories are ignored, as is the considerable intermarriage among these groups, as are the linkages (like gender, class, sexual orientation, and religion) that cut across these five groups. No serious scholar would claim that all Europeans and white Americans are part of the same culture, or that all Asians are part of the same culture, or that all people of Latin-American descent are of the same culture, or that all people of African descent are of the same culture. Any categorization this broad is essentially meaningless and useless.

Afrocentricity

Several districts—including Detroit, Atlanta, and Washington, D.C.—are developing an Afrocentric curriculum. *Afrocentricity* has been described in a book of the same name by Molefi Kete Asante of Temple University. The Afrocentric curriculum puts Africa at the center of the student's universe. African Americans must "move away from an [sic] Eurocentric framework" because "it is difficult to create freely when you use someone else's motifs, styles, images, and perspectives." Because they are not Africans, "white teachers cannot inspire in our children the visions necessary for them to overcome limitations." Asante recommends that African Americans choose an African name (as he did), reject European dress, embrace African religion (not Islam or Christianity) and love "their own" culture. He scorns the idea of universality as a form of Eurocentric arrogance. The Eurocentrist, he says, thinks of Beethoven or Bach as classical, but the Afrocentrist thinks of Ellington or Coltrane as classical; the Eurocentrist lauds Shakespeare or Twain, while the Afrocentrist prefers Baraka, Shange, or Abiola. Asante is critical of black artists like Arthur Mitchell and Alvin Ailey who ignore Afrocentricity. Likewise, he speaks contemptuously of a group of black university students who spurned the Afrocentrism of the local Black Student Union and formed an organization called Interrace: "Such madness is the direct consequence of self-hatred, obligatory attitudes, false assumptions about society, and stupidity."

The Issue of Universalism

The conflict between pluralism and particularism turns on the issue of universalism. Professor Asante warns his readers against the lure of universalism: "Do not be captured by a sense of universality given to you by the Eurocentric viewpoint; such a viewpoint is contradictory to your own ultimate reality." He insists that there is no alternative to Eurocentrism, Afrocentrism, and other ethnocentrisms. In contrast, the pluralist says, with the Roman playwright Terence, "I am a man: nothing human is alien to me." A contemporary Terence would say "I am a person" or might be a woman, but the point remains the same: You don't have to be black to love Zora Neale Hurston's fiction or Langston Hughes's poetry or Duke Ellington's music. In a pluralist curriculum, we expect children to learn a broad and humane culture, to learn about the ideas and art and animating spirit of many cultures. We expect that children, whatever their color, will be inspired by the courage of people like Helen Keller, Vaclav Havel, Harriet Tubman, and Feng Lizhe. We expect that their response to literature will be determined by the ideas and images it evokes, not by the skin color of the writer. But particularists insist that children can learn only from the experiences of people from the same race.

Particularism is a bad idea whose time has come. It is also a fashion spreading like wildfire through the education system, actively promoted by organizations and individuals with a political and professional interest in strengthening ethnic power bases in the university, in the education profession, and in society itself. One can scarcely pick up an educational journal without learning about a school district that is converting to an ethnocentric curriculum in an attempt to give "self-esteem" to children from racial minorities. A state-funded project in a Sacramento high school is teaching young black males to think like Africans and to develop the "African Mind Model Technique," in order to free themselves of the racism of American culture. A popular black rap singer, KRS-One, complained in an op-ed article in the New York Times that the schools should be teaching blacks about their cultural heritage, instead of trying to make everyone Americans. "It's like trying to teach a dog to be a cat," he wrote. KRS-One railed about having to learn about Thomas Jefferson and the Civil War, which had nothing to do (he said) with black history. . . .

Cultural Predestination

Particularism is akin to cultural Lysenkoism, for it takes as its premise the spurious notion that cultural traits are inherited. It implies a dubious, dangerous form of cultural predestination. Children are taught that if their ancestors could do it, so could they. But what happens if a child is from a cultural group that made no significant contribution to science or mathematics? Does this mean that children from that background must find a culturally appropriate field in which to strive? How does a teacher find the right cultural buttons for children of mixed heritage? And how in the world will teachers use this technique when the children in their classes are drawn from many different cultures, as is usually the case? By the time that every culture gets its due, there may be no time left to teach the subject itself. This explosion of filiopietism (which, we should remember, comes from adults, not from students) is reminiscent of the period some years ago when the Russians claimed that they had invented everything first; as we now know, this nationalistic braggadocio did little for their self-esteem and nothing for their economic development.

Cultural Diversity

More courses on racial and cultural experiences cannot help women, blacks, Hispanics, Native Americans, or any other "minority," if students and citizens are unable to recognize and avoid flawed reasoning. Logical reasoning and a human identity may be necessary for the appreciation of the richness and diversity of human cultural expressions. Such an identity cannot emerge, given the incessant official and academic bombardment of the population with racial and ethnic labels. No amount of cultural immersion will prevent promiscuous generalizations. Indeed, an identification of a person as an Asian American, for example, is a stereotype in that it attaches an identity which is fraught with particular expectations to someone who "looks" Asian. Multicultural courses would heighten the very identities which underlie discrimination, self-isolation, and segregation.

Yehudi O. Webster, "The Multicultural Education Debate," 1990.

In school districts where most children are black and Hispanic, there has been a growing tendency to embrace particularism rather than pluralism. Many of the children in these districts perform poorly in academic classes and leave school without graduating. They would fare better in school if they had well-educated and well-paid teachers, small classes, good materials, encouragement at home and school, summer academic programs, protection from the drugs and crime that ravage their neighborhoods, and higher expectations of satisfying careers upon graduation. These are expensive and time-consuming remedies that must also engage the larger society beyond the school. The lure of particularism is that it offers a less complicated anodyne, one in which the children's academic deficiencies may be addressed—or set aside—by inflating their racial pride. The danger of this remedy is that it will detract attention from the real needs of schools and the real interests of children, while simultaneously arousing distorted race pride in children of all races, increasing racial antagonism and producing fresh recruits for white and black racist groups. . . .

American Public Education

The spread of particularism throws into question the very idea of American public education. Public schools exist to teach children the general skills and knowledge that they need to succeed in American society, and the specific skills and knowledge that they need in order to function as American citizens. They receive public support because they have a public function. Historically, the public schools were known as "common schools" because they were schools for all, even if the children of all the people did not attend them. Over the years, the courts have found that it was unconstitutional to teach religion in the common schools, or to separate children on the basis of their race in the common schools. In their curriculum, their hiring practices, and their general philosophy, the public schools must not discriminate against or give preference to any racial or ethnic group. Yet they are permitted to accommodate cultural diversity by, for example, serving food that is culturally appropriate or providing library collections that emphasize the interests of the local community. However, they should not be expected to teach children to view the world through an ethnocentric perspective that rejects or ignores the common culture. For generations, those groups that wanted to inculcate their religion or their ethnic heritage have instituted private schools—after school, on weekends, or on a full-time basis. There, children learn with others of the same group—Greeks, Poles, Germans, Japanese, Chinese, Jews, Lutherans, Catholics, and so on—and are taught by people from the same group. Valuable as this exclusive experience has been for those who choose it, this has not been the role of public education. One of the primary purposes of public education has been to create a national community, a definition of citizenship and culture that is both expansive and *inclusive*.

History should not be confused with filiopietism. History gives no grounds for race pride. No race has a monopoly on virtue. If anything, a study of history should inspire humility, rather than pride. People of every racial group have committed terrible crimes, often against others of the same group. Whether one looks at the history of Europe or Africa or Latin America or Asia, every continent offers examples of inhumanity. Slavery has existed in civilizations around the world for centuries. Examples of genocide can be found around the world, throughout history, from ancient times right through to our own day. Governments and cultures, sometimes by edict, sometimes simply following tradition, have practiced not only slavery, but human sacrifice, infanticide, cliterodectomy, and mass murder. If we teach children this, they might recognize how absurd both racial hatred and racial chauvinism are.

"To use transracial adoptions as a solution to the child-welfare crisis in the African American community weakens the cultural integrity of the community."

Allowing White Families to Adopt Black Children Harms Ethnic Identity

Timothy Johnson

One important issue concerning ethnic identity is the question of whether white parents should be allowed to adopt black or other minority children. In the following viewpoint, Timothy Johnson argues against this type of adoption because it destroys the children's sense of ethnic identity and weakens African-American culture. He calls instead for more aggressive policies to encourage minority families to adopt children. Johnson is associate professor of church social work at Southern Baptist Theological Seminary in Louisville, Kentucky.

As you read, consider the following questions:

1. What two conditions must exist before Johnson will accept transracial adoptions?
2. Why is preserving African-American culture so important to Johnson?
3. What is the greater challenge facing whites and blacks, according to the author?

Timothy Johnson, "Transracial Adoptions: No, Not One," *The Other Side*, March/April 1991. Reprinted with permission from *The Other Side*, 300 W. Apsley, Philadelphia, PA 19144. Copyright © 1991. $29.50 per year.

When will the matter of transracial adoption be put to rest? When will it be all right for European Americans to adopt African American children?

We in the African American community will not begin to view transracial adoptions as even cautiously acceptable until two conditions are true of the majority of European Americans. First, it must be generally acceptable among European Americans to permit their daughters to marry African American men (not because we *want* our men to marry European American women but because such an acceptance would be a reliable indicator of a fundamental change in racial attitudes). Second, a majority of European Americans must reach the point where they sincerely desire to live their lives as African Americans, wishing to experience the world as a "person of color."

It may strike you as odd to raise these issues in the context of transracial adoption. But these two issues point to the core of the matter—the generally held perception by European Americans that African American culture is negative and inferior to European culture.

Over ninety years ago, W.E.B. DuBois uttered these prophetic lines: "The problem of the twentieth century is the problem of the color line." Attitudes on these two issues serve as barometers measuring the degree to which the problem of the color line has been successfully solved. Only when the majority of European Americans accept interracial marriage and express desire to live as African Americans will they be ready and worthy of adopting an African American child. Until White values regarding African Americans are realigned in this way, transracial adoption is "cultural genocide."

The Importance of Culture

Why is culture so important to African Americans? Because a strong cultural base is the only protection African Americans have against the negative valuations regarding who and what they are in the United States.

I firmly believe reconstruction of the African American culture is the most pressing and compelling task African Americans face in the twenty-first century. Our history teaches us that a strong African American community increases the power of its people to withstand the social injustice, victimization, and scarce resources which have characterized the Black American experience at the hands of the White power structure.

If our task is to build community, we cannot afford to lose one child to the cultural marginality of transracial adoption. It is imperative that each African American understand both the dimensions of racial oppression in the United States and how to live creatively and victoriously within a society steeped in racial oppression. These lessons must be written in the heads and hearts of our young people. And these lessons can only be taught by the victims themselves.

History also teaches that controlling the socialization of a community's children is one of the final methods by which oppressors gain total control over that community. Such was the case with Native Americans and the mission schools in which their children were placed by the European settlers. After Whites had violated treaties, made war upon the Native American people, and forced them off their lands and into reservations, the final step of the decimation of the Native American community was requiring it to give up its children.

Cultural Genocide

We are opposed to transracial adoption as a solution to permanent placement for Black children. We have an ethnic, moral and professional obligation to oppose transracial adoption. We are therefore *legally* justified in our efforts to protect the rights of Black children, Black families, and the Black community. We view the placement of Black children in white homes as a hostile act against our community. It is a blatant form of race and cultural genocide.

William T. Merritt, National Association of Black Social Workers, testimony before Congress, June 25, 1985.

From enslavement to the present time, African Americans have had a similar experience. We have not been allowed to raise, control, and protect our children. Repeatedly, we have had only a limited say in what will or will not happen to our offspring. Yet the African American community has always been able to care creatively for its children, even when the child-welfare agencies which our taxes supported would not give services to our children because they were Black.

Given the creativity of African American communities, the answer to the child-welfare crisis (and there is a child-welfare crisis in the African American community) is *not* transracial adoption. Transracial adoption comes about not because African Americans need help with the increasing numbers of displaced children but because European Americans have nurturing needs which are not being met because of the shortage of White babies available for adoption. Many African Americans suspect an additional, even darker side of the transracial adoption business. They perceive the adoption of African American children by European Americans as a way of realigning the U.S. social structure to better maintain White hegemony.

211

There are, to be certain, some European Americans who have a sense of the social injustices which have been, and continue to be, committed upon African Americans. Some of these exceptional persons are motivated to adopt across racial lines as their piece in making a difference.

Yet, given the current crisis in African American culture, these altruistic motivations at best add more problems than they solve. There are ample testimonies of African Americans who grew up with White adoptive parents and can attest to the loneliness they experienced as they struggled to come to cultural self-knowledge. They are able to relate sad vignettes about racial abuse by relatives of their adoptive parents. They carry with them scars caused by feeling a misfit in both European American and African American cultures and the ravages of anger they experienced toward adoptive parents who tried to pretend there was no racial problem in the United States.

Christian Issues

Often Christians disagree with prohibitions against transracial adoption because they believe "God sees no racial differences." Yet to believe such about God is to impose upon the Almighty our own ambivalence about racial diversity. If Jehovah ordained that there should be racial diversity in creation, then Jehovah is certainly aware of its existence. For God to be true to God's self, God must relate positively and passionately to a world which is racially diverse. In this context, racial diversity and its expression through cultural diversity are to be celebrated and affirmed.

Clearly we are not speaking of a racial and cultural diversity which makes one human being superior to another. Rather, our distinctive racial and cultural orientations can humanize and enhance the experience of each individual, and can strengthen the entire community. The same truth can be understood in the Pauline teaching that the gifts of the Spirit are diversities which lead to unity. The biblical lessons on gifts of the Holy Spirit reveal the importance of this balance of diversity and unity.

A theology of a "racially oriented God" ought to lead sincere Christians to do those things which enhance the racial and cultural well-being of persons. To use transracial adoptions as a solution to the child-welfare crisis in the African American community weakens the cultural integrity of the community. Neither can the selfish nurturing needs of Whites be the motivation for the adoption of African American children, if such adoptions destroy the African American community.

All European Americans, and particularly Christians, must seek to understand how transracial adoptions affect the African American community as a whole. They must exercise true Christian liberty, forgoing what is lawful for them in favor of

212

that which is beneficial for all. Rather than "saving" African American children by adopting them into White homes, European Americans must creatively forge partnerships with African Americans, working to remove obstacles which negatively affect the quality of life for our children.

Find Alternatives

In the late sixties and early seventies, one-third of all adoptions of Black infants were by Whites. By the mid-eighties, most child-welfare agencies had explicit or implicit policies against transracial adoption. Unfortunately, the pendulum may be beginning to swing back. The National Committee for Adoption is working in thirty-five states to remove restrictions on transracial adoption.

A Sense of Rejection

Transracial adoptions in the long term often disrupt and the Black children are returned to the foster care program. Children suffer a further sense of rejection as they try to understand why their adoptive as well as their biological parents gave them up.

William T. Merritt, National Association of Black Social Workers, testimony before Congress, June 25, 1985.

Will the adoption of African American children by European American parents ever be OK? Decisions are never black and white. And I would certainly say that if an African American child is faced with being homeless or not being loved, then transracial placement is a better option.

But I hasten to add that there is *almost always* someone in the African American community who can provide the alternative placement. If it appears that none are available, agencies should *not* conclude that qualified African American adoptive or foster parents do not exist. Rather these agencies should first explore the ways in which their criteria have interfered with traditional child-welfare strategies within the African American culture, rendering potential adopting or foster parents invisible. These criteria tend to be biased in favor of White culture, thereby contributing to the very crisis they attempt to solve.

A Band-Aid Solution

The adoption of African American children by European American parents is, at best, a Band-Aid solution. It may remove some African American children from the child-welfare crisis, but it does not deal with the crisis. Until the United States fully and honestly confronts—and eliminates—the problem of the "color line," there will continue to be inequities which favor European Americans over African Americans in health, education, employment, political power, and other areas of social, physical, and spiritual well-being. These areas of inequality are tied directly to the reality of transracial adoption. The greater challenge, and the road less traveled, is for European Americans to deal directly with these social justice concerns, making transracial adoption a moot issue.

"Evidence accumulated by us and other researchers . . . investigating the effects of [transracial adoption] indicates positive results."

Allowing White Families to Adopt Black Children Does Not Harm Ethnic Identity

Rita J. Simon and Howard Altstein

Rita J. Simon is the dean of the School of Justice at The American University in Washington, D.C. Howard Altstein is a professor at the School of Social Work at the University of Maryland at College Park. Together they have written several books on transracial adoption. In the following viewpoint, excerpted from their book *Transracial Adoptees and Their Families*, they describe the results of a survey in which they questioned over two hundred white couples who had adopted black or Asian children. Families were questioned three times over a period of twelve years. Simon and Altstein concluded from this study that for most families, transracial adoption has been a success, and recommend it as an option for minority children placed in orphanages.

As you read, consider the following questions:

1. How do the authors criticize arguments against transracial adoption?
2. What kind of ethnic identity did adopted children develop, according to Simon and Altstein?

Excerpted from *Transracial Adoptees and Their Families*, by Rita J. Simon and Howard Altstein (Praeger Publishers, an imprint of Greenwood Publishing Group, Inc., New York, 1987), pages 1, 27, 108-111, 116-118, 140-142. Copyright © 1987 by Rita J. Simon and Howard Altstein. Reprinted with permission.

A belief that transracial adoption (TRA) is unnatural and therefore "bound to be unsuccessful" continues to be popular among many child welfare professionals. Many adoption officials claim that there are studies that indicate that TRA is too fragile an experience not to result in serious problems once the TRAs leave their families. But to this date no data have been presented that support the belief that in the long run TRA is detrimental to those involved: the transracial adoptees, the adoptive parents, or the siblings. On the contrary, evidence accumulated by us and other researchers over more than a decade of investigating the effects of TRA indicates positive results. . . .

Researching Families

The research described began in 1972 when we contacted 206 families living in five cities in the Midwest who were members of the Open Door Society and the Council on Adoptable Children, and asked them whether we could interview them about their decision to adopt a nonwhite child. All but 2 of the families agreed to participate in the study. The parents allowed a two-person team to interview them in their home for 60 to 90 minutes at the same time that each of their children who were between three and eight years old was being interviewed for about 30 minutes.

Seven years later we sought out these families again and were able to locate 71 percent of them. This time we interviewed only the parents by mail and telephone. In the fall of 1983 and the winter of 1984, the families were contacted a third time, when we returned to our original research design and conducted personal interviews in the respondents' homes, including the parents and the adolescent children who were still living with them. . . .

The collective portrait that we draw is . . . intended to depict the dominant themes, the life patterns, the emotions, and the interactions among . . . the families in the study. This picture was developed after reading all of the parents' and children's interviews and examining the tables derived from the descriptive statistics. . . .

We believe that the portrait that emerges is a positive, warm, integrated picture that shows parents and children who feel good about themselves and about their relationships with each other. On the issue of transracial adoption, almost all of the parents would do it again and would recommend it to other families. They believe that they and the children born to them have benefitted from their experiences. Their birth children have developed insight, sensitivity, and a tolerance that they could not have acquired in the ordinary course of life. Their transracial adoptees may have been spared years in foster homes or institutions. They have had the comfort and security of loving parents and siblings who have provided them with a good home, education and cultural opportunities, and the belief that they are wanted.

We found that almost all of the families made some changes in their lives as a result of their decision to adopt. Most of the time, however, the changes were not made because of their decision to adopt a child of a different race, but because they decided to add another child to the family. Thus, the parents talked about buying a bigger house, adding more bedroom space, having less money for vacations and entertainment, and allowing less time for themselves. In retrospect, most of the parents do not dwell on what they wished they had done but did not do; nor do they berate themselves for things they did and wished they had not done. Most of them feel that they did their best. They worked hard at being parents and at being parents of children of a different race.

Promoting Ethnic Culture

In the early years, many of them were enthusiastic about introducing the culture of the TRAs' backgrounds into the family's day-to-day life. This was especially true of the families who adopted American Indian and Korean children. They experimented with new recipes; sought out books, music, and artifacts; joined churches and social organizations; travelled to the Southwest for ceremonies; and participated in local ethnic events. The parents of black children primarily introduced books about black history and black heroes, joined a black church, sought out black playmates for their children, and celebrated Martin Luther King's birthday. In a few families, a black friend is the godparent to their TRA child. One mother told us: "Black parents regard us as black parents."

But as the years wore on, as the children became teenagers and pursued their own activities and social life, the parents' enthusiasm and interest for "ethnic variety" waned. An increasing number of families lived as their middle and upper middle class white neighbors did. Had the children shown more interest, more desire to maintain ethnic contacts and ties, most of the parents would have been willing to follow the same direction; but in the absence of signals that the activities were meaningful to their children, the parents decided that the one-culture family was an easier route. Almost all of the parents said that they were affected by the stance of the National Association of Black Social Workers and that of the Native American Councils in the 1970s vis-a-vis the adoption of blacks and Indian children by white families. Almost all of the parents thought that the position taken by those groups was contrary to the best interests of the child and smacked of racism. They were angered by the accusations of the Black Social Workers that white parents could not rear black children, and they felt betrayed by groups whose respect they expected they would have. "Race," they believed, was not and should not be an important criterion for deciding a child's placement. In their willingness to adopt, they were acting in the best interest of a homeless, neglected, unwanted child. One parent said: "Our children are the ones no one wanted. Now they are saying you are the wrong family."

Building Bridges

In spite of its problems, transracial adoption (like interracial marriage) may be a means of building bridges between widely separated cultures, bringing people together. But it cannot be overemphasized that any true coming together involves movement from both sides. There must be a commitment to making sure that neither identity is lost, that both cultures will be incorporated into a family's life together.

Letha Dawson Scanzoni, *The Other Side*, March/April 1991.

Some (a handful) parents felt guilty as a result of the attacks on them, and that guilt resulted in their decision not to adopt a second or, in some instances, a third nonwhite child. "Perhaps," some of them said, "the position of the Black Social Workers is right." They had ventured into a far more complicated social world than the one for which they were prepared. Good will and the desire to have and love a child (or another child) were not sufficient reasons for adopting someone for whom they could not provide the desired or necessary racial or ethnic heritage. Among this handful, some said that they could understand "their [the Black Social Workers] position because our kids have white values." Others among this small group said: "We are not and cannot be appropriate black role models. We've learned that is important." But, we emphasize, only a handful of parents made those observations.

While almost all of the parents felt that they had been affected one way or another by the Black Social Workers' position, practically none of them believed that it had any effect on their children, primarily because the children were too young to hear about and understand the issues. . . .

Responses of Children

The children answered the questions posed to them about their relationship to family members with the same frankness and honesty that was apparent among the parents. Somewhat to our surprise, in many families the children made more positive evaluations of the quality of their family relationships than did the parents. The parents, in some instances, seemed willing to step back and disengage themselves from the situation; the children—and here we have to take special note of the TRAs—continually said: "They are my parents. Yeah, we've had our differences, but I know I can count on them and I want to be close." That is not meant to indicate that many of the older ones (those in their late teens) were not anxious and ready to move out of the parental home; they were. But the TRAs unequivocally did not perceive their relationships with their parents as temporary or transitional. Practically none of them, even those who expressed anger and bitterness about their current relations, said that they were likely to cut off ties completely or walk out of the family. . . .

The Families' Experience

At the conclusion of both of our earlier books, we emphasized that it was still too soon to draw any conclusions on two matters. One concerned the parents' evaluations of how "good," how "meaningful," how "positive" an experience their decision to adopt transracially had been; and the other pertained to our evaluation of the families' experiences; that is, whether they had lived together in a positive, loving, committed relationship. The bases for our eventual conclusions on the latter issue would be a study of the families themselves over the 12-year period, including the parents' as well as the children's responses, and our observations of the family's interactions.

We would also take into account our comparison of these families with other studies of families who have adopted transracially, as well as with our knowledge of middle class families in the urban United States. For example, in the concluding chapter of their book, Ruth G. McRoy and Louis A. Zurcher wrote:

> The transracial and inracial adoptees in the authors' study were physically healthy and exhibited typical adolescent relationships with their parents, siblings, teachers, and peers. Similarly, regardless of the race of their adoptive parents, they reflected positive feelings of self-regard. Throughout the book, the authors have shown that the quality of parenting is more important than whether the black child has been inracially or transracially adopted. Most certainly, transracial adoptive parents experience some challenges different from inracial adoptive parents, but in this study, all of the parents successfully met the challenges.

Owen Gill and Barbara Jackson, in summarizing the results of their study, wrote:

> We found no general evidence of the children being isolated within their families. Close and intimate family relations had developed for the large majority of the children. The children saw themselves as "belonging to this family.". . .
> In spite of their often having very little contact with other

children of the same racial background, we found that the large majority of children were able to relate effectively to peers and adults outside the family. Also, there is no evidence of the children doing worse academically than their agemates; if anything, the study children seemed to be doing better.

We turn finally to the judgments made by the parents in our study about their experiences. . . .

They emphasized love and the desire for a child as the major reasons why anyone should want to adopt transracially. One family said, "It is the best thing that has happened to us." They warned that the families should be prepared for complications and problems—but is any child rearing free of anxiety and difficulties? Just as in 1972, the parents warned: Do not adopt for political motives; do not do it as part of a crusade, or to wave a banner, or out of white liberal guilt. They also cautioned prospective adoptive parents that the race issue could prove more complicated than they anticipated, and urged learning as much as possible about the child's racial heritage. The major and strongest messages were: "Be sure you are committed to adoption." "Adopt if you love and want children." "Pray about it, keep your motives straight; adopt because you need and love a child.". . .

Conclusions

Twelve years have gone by since our initial contact with the families. We met them in 1972, when they had only recently embarked on a largely untraveled and potentially difficult road of adopting children of different racial backgrounds than their own, some of whom had mental and physical disabilities, while at the same time parenting children to whom they had given birth. As ready as they might have been for hostility and rejection by their relatives, friends, and neighbors, they were least prepared for the attacks upon them by blacks, native American leaders, and professional social work groups, who charged them with everything from ignorance to participation in racial genocide. The results of the second and third surveys showed that, with a few exceptions, all of the parents believed that they had done well by the children whom they adopted and that, had they not adopted them, the children would have spent their childhood in an institution or in one or more foster homes. The parents repeatedly emphasized that they made their decision to adopt because they wanted a child and were prepared to love and care for it regardless of the child's racial or personal background. Again, with few exceptions, all of the parents are still committed to that view and are willing to urge other families to adopt transracially.

As we said many times, the children seem even more committed to their adoptive parents than the other way around. For the children, even during these sensitive, complicated years of adolescence, their adoptive parents are the only family they have and the only set of parents they want. Some of the family relationships have been rocky, accusative, and angry—and some remain so—yet they are a family and they are fully committed to one another.

At the end of both the 1972 and 1979 studies, we emphasized the tentativeness of our conclusions. While focusing on the positive experiences that we were able to report, we also stressed how young the children were and how many difficult periods lay ahead. This time, we believe that the families have reached a different stage. In many of them, some children are married and living on their own; in others, some are away at school. Practically all of the children, even the youngest, are adolescents. The quality of the relationships is established, and the ties are not likely to be severed by some future event. The families have weathered the most difficult years of child rearing, and the large majority have come through the experience committed to each other and intact.

Race Is Not Important

A 16-year-old black girl commented at the end of the interview: "I really don't see my family as a white family. Each of us is color blind. Each person has his or her own personality." In another family, a child born into the family said about his black brother, "I don't look on him as a person of a different race. I look at him as a brother." A 14-year-old black girl commented, "Race doesn't matter; love is what is important."

Rita J. Simon and Howard Altstein, *Transracial Adoptees and Their Families*, 1987.

It would be foolish to say that these families will have smooth sailing from here on. Who can say that with authority or certainty about any set of family relationships? But we can and do emphasize that more than 12 years have elapsed; and the large majority are still convinced of the rightness of their decision to adopt, still optimistic about their relationships with each other. . . .

An examination of available figures from a variety of sources shows conclusively that transracial adoption no longer occurs in any appreciable numbers. As we stated at the conclusion of our second study, TRA was not halted because data indicated that it was a failure, that adoptees and/or their adoptive families suffered any damaging social or psychological effects. It was not stopped because transracial adoptees were experiencing racial confusion or negative self-images. It did not end because there were no longer any nonwhite children in foster care or in institutions requiring permanent placements. It was not eradicated because the supply of families willing and able to adopt a child of another race was exhausted. Transracial adoption died because child welfare agencies no longer saw it as politically expedient, even though none of the 50 states recognizes race as a sufficient factor in denying an adoption.

Recommendations

What practical recommendations are suggested by the data in this work to agencies charged with locating permanent placements for nonwhite children? Clearly, agency efforts should be initially directed at locating permanent inracial placements for their children. There are data that support the efficacy of recruiting inracial adoptive placements. But, successful as these programs have been, they have not significantly reduced the great numbers of nonwhite children requiring permanent placements.

We believe that there should be exploration of all permanent and viable inracial opportunities. But where no suitable placement is located, applications from white families seeking to adopt transracially should be examined in as objective and unbiased a manner as possible. We do not believe that inracial foster care placement is preferable to transracial adoption, because by definition foster care is temporary placement. It is a testimonial to the failure of our child welfare system that in many instances it has become permanent. . . .

The message offered by our work is that transracial adoption should not be automatically excluded as one of several permanent placement options. Adoption, in almost all cases, is a "forever" placement, whereas the best foster care placement is by definition temporary. Where no appropriate permanent inracial placement can be found for a nonwhite child, the results of this study demonstrate that TRA should be seriously considered.

Understanding Words in Context

Readers occasionally come across words they do not recognize. And frequently, because they do not know a word or words, they will not fully understand the passage being read. Obviously, the reader can look up an unfamiliar word in a dictionary. By carefully examining the word in the context in which it is used, however, the word's meaning can often be determined. A careful reader may find clues to the meaning of the word in surrounding words, ideas, and attitudes.

Below are excerpts from the viewpoints in this chapter. In each excerpt, one of the words is printed in italicized capital letters. Try to determine the meaning of each word by reading the excerpt. Under each excerpt you will find four definitions for the italicized word. Choose the one that is closest to your understanding of the word.

Finally, use a dictionary to see how well you have understood the words in context. It will be helpful to discuss with others the clues that helped you decide on each word's meaning.

1. White America's cultural *VACUITY* has resulted in millions of white Americans adopting elements of African-American music, dance, literature, and language.

   VACUITY means:

   a) richness   c) racism
   b) emptiness   d) intolerance

2. Despite the *DEBILITATING* effects of racism and segregation, blacks have been able to instill a sense of self and community.

   DEBILITATING means:

   a) neutral   c) weakening
   b) total   d) caring

3. Race is an issue that has been deemed unfit for politicians to discuss openly in all but the most *PLATITUDINOUS* manner.

PLATITUDINOUS means:

a) simplistic
b) offensive
c) courageous
d) expensive

4. Minority children are expected to learn about European-dominated culture, and are *CASTIGATED* whenever they attempt to express their own cultural styles.

CASTIGATED means:

a) praised
b) punished
c) interviewed
d) happy

5. Ethnic groups in the U.S. who wish to *INCULCATE* their religion or ethnic heritage into their children have traditionally used private schools in which the children's classmates and teachers are all from the same group.

INCULCATE means:

a) abandon
b) instill
c) change
d) forget

6. There are, to be certain, some European Americans who are motivated to adopt minority children because of their desire to help end the social injustices committed upon African Americans. Yet such *ALTRUISTIC* motivations cause these children to grow up as misfits in both cultures.

ALTRUISTIC means:

a) racist
b) greedy
c) unknown
d) unselfish

7. Looking back, most of the adoptive parents we surveyed felt that they did their best. They did not *BERATE* themselves for things they did and wished they had not done.

BERATE means:

a) criticize
b) tickle
c) reward
d) compliment

8. The minority adopted children *UNEQUIVOCALLY* did not perceive their relationships with their white parents as temporary. Practically none of them, even those who expressed anger, said that they were likely to cut off ties completely.

UNEQUIVOCALLY means:

a) angrily
b) half-heartedly
c) sadly
d) clearly

Periodical Bibliography

The following articles have been selected to supplement the diverse views presented in this chapter.

Edward K. Braxton	"Loaded Terms," *Commonweal,* June 23, 1989.
James S. Coleman	"A Quiet Threat to Academic Freedom," *National Review,* March 18, 1991.
Lynne Duke	"White Man's Burden: Staying Afloat in a Sea of Diversity," *The Washington Post National Weekly Edition,* January 14-21, 1991.
June Jordan	"Diversity or Death," *The Progressive,* June 1990.
Barbara Kantrowitz	"Can the Boys Be Saved?" *Newsweek,* October 15, 1990.
John Leo	"Teaching History the Way It Happened," *U.S. News & World Report,* November 27, 1989.
Manning Marable	"A New Black Politics," *The Progressive,* August 1990.
Harold Orlans	"The Politics of Minority Statistics," *Commentary,* March/April 1989.
Adolph Reed Jr.	"The Rise of Louis Farrakhan," *The Nation,* January 21, 1991.
Letha Dawson Scanzoni	"Transracial Adoptions: Bridge or Stumbling Block?" *The Other Side,* March/April 1991. Available from The Other Side, 300 W. Apsley St., Philadelphia, PA 19144.
Fred Siegel	"The Cult of Multiculturalism," *The New Republic,* February 18, 1991.
Jim Sleeper	"Moving Beyond Race to a Common Agenda," *The Washington Post National Weekly Edition,* March 25-31, 1991.
Shelby Steele	"Ghettoized by Black Unity," *Harper's Magazine,* May 1990.
Andrew Sullivan	"Racism 101," *The New Republic,* November 26, 1990.
Charles Whitaker	"Do Black Males Need Special Schools?" *Ebony,* March 1991.

How Can Racism Be Stopped?

Chapter Preface

In a 1990 article in *Time* magazine, journalist William A. Henry III examined the changing population in the United States and concluded that by the middle of the twenty-first century, blacks, Hispanics, and other minority racial groups will outnumber whites in the U.S. Henry believes this changing demographic picture means that controversies over race and racism are likely to remain with the U.S. for some time. "White Americans are accustomed to thinking themselves as the very picture of their nation," he writes. "Becoming a conspicuously multiracial society is bound to be a somewhat bumpy experience for many ordinary citizens."

The articles in the following chapter examine how the U.S. can best overcome racism and become a successful multiracial society. While differing in their approaches and solutions, the authors all attempt to point the way for America to live up to its ideals of freedom and equality for members of all races.

"Few, if any, whites can hold fast to their veneer of racism once it is exposed to an inescapable black anger and truth."

Aggressive Confrontational Techniques Can Stop Racism

Vern E. Smith

Many businesses, colleges, and other organizations have resorted to special classes and seminars to combat racism. In the following viewpoint, *Newsweek* reporter Vern E. Smith describes one such seminar run by Charles King, the head of the Urban Crisis Center in Atlanta, Georgia. The seminars King runs use highly controversial techniques that include aggressively confronting whites about their hidden racist assumptions about minorities.

As you read, consider the following questions:

1. What kind of atmosphere does the seminar try to create, according to Smith?
2. Why is racism invisible to most people, according to the author?
3. How is racial oppression redirected toward whites, according to Smith?

Vern E. Smith, "Seeing Through Black Eyes," *Newsweek,* March 7, 1988, © Newsweek, Inc. All rights reserved. Reprinted by permission.

Don Mitchell crosses his legs and tries to come up with an honest answer to the question raised by the imposing black man standing before the semicircle of 33 whites and blacks in a Memphis conference room.

"What is the basic cause of the race problem in America?" thunders Charles King.

Mitchell, 27, squirms uncomfortably as the stock answers begin to come from around the room.

"Fear."

"Ignorance."

"Misunderstanding."

Mitchell wants to talk about his work as an equal-employment officer at Federal Express. Back home in Kentucky, he wants to say, he had been a member of a predominantly black high-school basketball team, had once proudly sipped from a can of Coke after black players, proving his solidarity—and, he'd always assumed, his freedom from racial prejudice.

"Don?" King fires the question like a prosecutor.

"Ignorance," Mitchell blurts out.

Across the room, Gay Johnston feels the same disquiet as she struggles to compose her own answer. She doesn't even like to think about the words that punctuate King's conversation— "racism, prejudice, oppressor." That any of those words could somehow apply to her is unthinkable. Gay wants to talk about her work as the executive director of the Memphis Literacy Council, where many of the clients are poor blacks. She could mention Rita, the black nanny on the Tennessee farm where she grew up, a woman she loved like her own mother, her "black mother," she used to tell her friends; Gay's son had been a pallbearer at Rita's funeral.

Invisible Racism

But King has forbidden the use of any personal experiences in his two-day "awareness" seminar, the nation's only traveling laboratory in race relations. The participants, mostly employees of local corporations, would have to confront this alarmingly angry black man without the comforting defense of a belief in their own goodness. They are here, King says, to discuss the relationship between majority and minority. "There are many minorities in this country," he adds, "but this country is fraught with the tensions and problems of race based upon the dynamics of black people and white people."

White institutions are inherently racist, King argues, but it is invisible to all except the victims. "Whites cannot perceive their racism because racism is by definition the normal practices, customs and habits of a majority group that tend to disadvantage a minority group," he says calmly from the front of the room, his opening question still unanswered. "Please do not inform me, or tell me who you are, or what your experiences are. Gay, what's the cause of the problem?"

"I don't know!" says Gay.

"Racism," says the man next to her.

"Slavery," says another man.

The leader glowers behind his horn rims. "No one wants to give the cause as white people and their attitudes," he says. "Everybody knows it's true but nobody'll say it, blacks or whites. Nobody in this room wants to deal with the problem."

King eschews an intellectual approach to the race problem in favor of a no-holds-barred, frontal assault. His goal is to achieve a hothouse atmosphere of "oppression" that will give whites a sense of "what it is like to be black." By which he means: persecuted, abused, forced to conform to someone else's expectations and demands. Very much, in fact, the way one of the black participants, Robert Finney, felt a few weeks earlier when he had been stopped by a white cop for a traffic violation. Although he was sure he was innocent, he suppressed the anger within him and cautiously, slowly, carefully handed over his driver's license, got out from behind the wheel with his arms out from his sides, got into the officer's car and patiently waited for the cop to ascertain that Finney hadn't stolen his own vehicle. Watching the whites wilt under King's remorseless barrage of questions and arguments, Finney feels both satisfaction and empathy; now, he thinks, they know how I feel most of the time.

King, the head of the Atlanta-based Urban Crisis Center, has conducted these starkly emotional workshops on American racism for nearly 20 years. Among the clients that have sent employees to the two-day sessions, which average $275 a person, are Bell Laboratories, AT&T, Mead Corp. and government agencies ranging from the CIA [Central Intelligence Agency] to the Census Bureau. Despite the revolutions in American society over that time, he says he has seen few changes in the attitudes and reactions of the white people who come to his seminars. A former minister and college professor, he evolved into a kind of "Pied Piper" on white racism almost by accident. As a history teacher at Ohio's Wittenberg College in the 1960s, he became so frustrated at his white students' inability to deal honestly with the question of race in America that he exploded in an emotional tirade one afternoon, coining the phrase that has become a theme of his seminars: "Shut up and listen to black people for a change."

The Vulnerability of Racism

After his outburst, he stalked from the room, fully expecting to be fired on the spot. Instead, a white colleague who had observed the scene asked King to return to the room. When he did, the students responded with a standing ovation. King was stunned. "I realized then," he says, "that I had discovered the vulnerability of individual white racism. It was the discovery that few, if any, whites can hold fast to their veneer of racism once it is exposed to an inescapable black anger and truth."

And there is no escaping from his anger now, as this heavyset, dark-skinned man moves around the room, putting names to faces in the semicircle. He pauses to size up a young, clean-cut fellow named Tracy. "And Tracy doesn't like me, right, Tracy?"

"Wrong." But Tracy seems taken aback.

"You see," King says to the group, "I can tell expressions. All black people can. You are going to learn that black people can discover negative whites just by the way they look at them." He turns to Bhalander Boyd, a 28-year-old Federal Express human-resources-development assistant, one of the black women in the group, for confirmation. She nods in agreement.

"We're accustomed to looking for negatives," King says. "When you're black you anticipate a negative."

Admitting the Truth

Racism—white-black relations—is the greatest threat to this republic, as it has been since the turn of the century, the 19th Century. Black-Korean disputes, Anglo-Latino tensions, anti-Semitism, scholarship discrimination against Asian-Americans are all real, but they are comparatively small problems. Black and white is the American problem—not all blacks or all whites by any means, but blacks and whites almost everywhere in America.

No one wants to talk about some of this because it is painful to be misunderstood. We might do better to begin by admitting there is some racism in all Americans.

Richard Reeves, *Los Angeles Times*, June 15, 1990.

King looks around the room. Here and there, a white and a black sit side by side, but more often whites cluster together in the semicircle and the handful of blacks sit in groups of two or three.

"You notice how the white people are sitting?" King says. "Why do y'all always sit together?"

Nervous coughs punctuate the silence. "Didn't that sound funny when I said, 'Why do white people sit together?' That's what white people say to us, never acknowledging *they* stay away."

King plays a recording of free verse titled "Just Like You," then asks each participant to describe what he or she heard. He had predicted earlier that only a few people in the room would acknowledge that the speaker was a black man, and he is right. One of the white males suggests that the voice on the tape is "a composite of all people." Another says, "I think he could've been a white man."

"Why?" King asks.

"Because I believe everybody has the same interests, same desires."

King's face takes on a pained look. "Listen to you," he says. "You think that black men, white men have the same desires?"

The man shifts in his seat, feeling all eyes in the room turn to him.

King points out that some participants heard the black man on the tape crying out in anguish. "Why would a white man cry out in anguish in urban America?" King's baritone rises in mock indignation. "For what reasons would he cry out, the white man?"

"For . . . the same reasons that we're here, to improve relations. . . ."

Unrelenting Anger

King is unrelenting. "Would a white man cry out to improve relations? Look how foolish you sound, my friend! White people aren't in anguish to improve relations. The person who's affected by bad relations is the one in anguish, right?"

The man, chastened, quickly agrees. "But you make it sound like there's no sensitivity at all to the problem."

"There isn't enough," King snaps. "If there was we wouldn't have a problem.". . .

Gay Johnston thinks she never had felt anything as oppressive as the tension in the brightly lit conference room. She is determined, though, to stand her ground.

"I'm not convinced absolutely," she says when her turn comes again to address the cause of the problem. "I . . ."

"Give me the answer!" King shouts. "You must have some other ideas of the cause?"

"I-I don't know," Gay stammers.

"She doesn't know," King says derisively. "I'm telling her, yet she's not convinced."

"I hear *you* saying what you think is the cause," Gay tries again.

"No one knows better the cause of the problem than a black person," King shoots back. "Ask one and he'll tell you."

Gay turns, smiling at the black man on her right, a United Way official and a friend. Could she ask him the question?

"He's probably as white as you are at this moment," King says. Nervous, scattered laughter greets this remark; the man says nothing.

King offers another demonstration of the effects of racism. He orders one of the white women to stand with a cup balanced on her head and sing "The Star Spangled Banner." The entire room grows silent, sensing the woman's discomfort and embarrassment, but not daring to interfere. When King asks for responses, everybody blames the woman for not being able to carry out what King admitted was an impossible task. Nobody blames him for creating her predicament.

"Now you can understand racism," King says. "Nobody blamed me, with all the power. You didn't want to deal with the problem. The victim doesn't cry out. If the victim doesn't cry out, white people assume that everything is OK."

White vs. Black Perceptions

One structural feature of human experience separates people of color from our white friends, accounting in large part for our differing perceptions in matters of race. This structural feature, which dwarfs almost everything else, is simply stated: white people rarely see acts of blatant or subtle racism, while minority people experience them all the time.

Few acts of clear-cut racism come into the field of vision of most white people; when they do, they cause a deep impression. Minorities, by contrast, live in a world dominated by race. We experience racial treatment every day of our lives. We are bathed in it. A high percentage of our social interaction is tinged by it. And, when we meet with others of color, we trade stories of racial treatment and how our friends are dealing with it. Race is a recurring reality of our lives.

Richard Delgado, *Harvard Civil Rights-Civil Liberties Law Review*, Summer 1988.

King abruptly asks the blacks to leave the room "and let the whites deal with what I leave you with. Come to grips with the problem. Be honest for once in your lives," he urges them. Confused—but relieved—the whites left behind begin to talk among themselves.

"One guy mentioned slavery [as the cause of race problems] and I never thought of that . . ." Gay says thoughtfully.

When King returns he explains the dynamics of racial discussions in America. "Whites are fearful of discussing race in the presence of blacks," he says. "They know what the problem is and they go through all kinds of maneuvers to keep from facing it.

"Gay, what's the cause of the problem?"

"The attitudes of white people," Gay says.

King lets out a heavy sigh. "You've come a long way," he says. He means: she has capitulated to his power. She knows how it feels to be oppressed.

A New Perspective

"What King's seminars do is give a basic perspective on race in America," says David Gunn, president of the New York City Transit Authority, where hundreds of managers have undergone

King's seminars. "It's a very powerful technique that he uses. It gives a perspective that in normal, day-to-day conversation you won't get." Kate Gooch, a former director of Leadership Memphis, which sponsors several King seminars a year, has detected a lasting effect. "I will be in a group of people I know have participated in the seminars and I see that their sensitivity to racial issues is just keener than those who haven't done it," says Gooch. Adds John G. Keane, director of the Census Bureau: "You may not be comfortable with the tactics at the time, but you come to know why he's doing it and why it's justified."

King himself, toward the end of the day, admits that he has been "duplicating society as blacks see it." Only then, as he dropped the mask of hostility and reached for a sense of reconciliation and common purpose, did some of the whites in the room get the point. "At first you resent what I do," King explains, "then after a while you conform to it. I know I'm being a bastard but that's how black people live their lives in America, and for whites to change you must *feel* what we feel." "He made you conform," says one, a transplanted Midwesterner who works for a Memphis paper-products firm. "And you shifted your role to accommodate." "I came away with a new sense of confidence in terms of discussing the issue openly," says Don Taddia, a Massachusetts native and senior manager for Federal Express. "It would be nice if everybody could get the same message, if it could be given to high-school students."

"Prior to coming in here, I didn't feel like I had a lot of prejudices," says Gary Dillon, a 36-year-old father of two. "I feel like I do now. I guess I never put myself in the position he put me in." And Gay Johnston, driving home, thinks about how she has been sensitizing her daughters to sexism without ever considering racism: "I'd been telling my girls, I don't care what they tell you in school, it's still a man's world. I'd been saying it for years, it's a man's world. So why in the hell didn't I ever realize it was a *white's* world?"

And for Boyd, the young black woman in the group, a revelation as well, for what it may be worth: "For two days we were really in charge of this class. I almost felt sorry for the whites."

"Certain approaches and programs, though well-intentioned, can hinder the goal of reducing bigotry by developing an atmosphere of hostility, defensiveness, hopelessness, and resistance."

Fostering Mutual Understanding Can Stop Racism

Erin A. Oliver and Dvora Slavin

Erin A. Oliver is associate director of personnel at the University of Maryland at College Park, and an associate with the National Coalition Building Institute (NCBI), an organization which conducts workshops and seminars on conflict resolution and reducing prejudice. Dvora Slavin is training director for NCBI. In the following viewpoint, Oliver and Slavin describe the principles underlying NCBI seminars. Among these principles are the assumption that everyone has experienced some kind of mistreatment, and that emphasizing guilt or creating hostility are counterproductive in reducing racial tension.

As you read, consider the following questions:

1. What three basic assumptions underlie the seminars run by NCBI?
2. Why do the authors argue that guilt and anger are not the best approaches for stopping racism and prejudice?
3. How are the seminars described by Oliver and Slavin organized?

From "The NCBI Prejudice Reduction Model," by Erin A. Oliver and Dvora Slavin. Reprinted, with permission, from the Fall 1989 *Journal of the College and University Personnel Association*, Washington, D.C. All rights reserved.

The National Coalition Building Institute (NCBI) Prejudice Reduction Model . . . can be a powerful tool . . . to use in bringing about a change in attitude and to enable people of diverse backgrounds to work together toward shared goals. It teaches concrete skills in interrupting prejudice and in conflict resolution that are applicable to a variety of groups. . . .

Theory and Assumptions

The Prejudice Reduction Workshop Model is based on a teaching methodology which trains participants to: combat discrimination of all forms, facilitate resolution of polarized intergroup conflicts, and build intergroup coalitions. It presents a consistent theoretical basis for understanding the sources of discrimination and an easily replicable workshop which can be used by participants in their own . . . settings. In this way a broader institutional approach to ending intergroup prejudice . . . can be developed. . . .

There is a set of basic assumptions which influence the workshop leaders' facilitation and guides the content and sequence of the workshop exercise. The assumptions are:

1. *Everyone has experienced some kind of mistreatment through bigotry and discrimination.* There are certain forms of institutionalized discrimination (racism, sexism, anti-Semitism, and homophobia) which are particularly important to look at on campus. In assisting participants from outside these groups to look at these issues, it has been found that what most enables people to become advocates of these particular groups is to be given an opportunity to first look at how their own group has been mistreated.

2. *Emotional stories of personal experiences of mistreatment are the single most effective means to achieve attitudinal change.* Individual experiences with bigotry, whether they involve us as direct targets or as actors or onlookers to another's experiences, are deep hurts. They affect our ability to think and act effectively. Undoing the effects of these experiences must involve giving people the opportunity to share the emotional details in an environment of respectful attention. For the speaker, it becomes a chance to sort through the confusion and move through the isolation that is part of the original experience. For the listener, it is oftentimes an opportunity to hear for the first time the real emotional impact of discrimination, to develop new understandings about intergroup prejudice by connecting their own hurts with the hurts being shared, and to arrive at insights that often shift prejudicial attitudes.

3. *Certain approaches and programs, though well-intentioned, can hinder the goal of reducing bigotry by developing an atmosphere of hostility, defensiveness, hopelessness, and resistance.* These are:

• Usual Approach: "People need to be told how serious racism and other forms of bigotry are."

• NCBI Approach: All forms of bigotry are serious but getting rid of them does not have to be. In fact, the more upbeat and hopeful the program is, the more effective it will be.

• Usual Approach: "People can be so apathetic. All these programs are just for the converted. How do we reach those who really need it most?"

• NCBI Approach: People are not always apathetic; they often just feel powerless. Few have a sense of daily control over their lives. If participants are to reduce bigotry, they need to be given practical, day-to-day skills that give them a sense of empowerment.

• Usual Approach: "We must help people face their guilt and individual responsibility for prejudice."

• NCBI Approach: Guilt is the glue that holds prejudice in place. Feelings of guilt can prevent people from looking at their own prejudices. Guilt increases defensiveness, which leaves people frozen in their original way of thinking and acting.

• Usual Approach: "The way to get people to stop acting in bigoted ways is to make them recognize how bigoted they are."

• NCBI Approach: Shame or lack of pride fuels prejudicial attitudes and behaviors. Every place that one feels ashamed of oneself or one's group is a place where misinformation and stereotypes about others can seep in. Individuals are hurt first in their own sense of themselves before they take on invalidating and prejudicial thoughts or actions toward others. Assisting people to claim pride in themselves and their own groups is a step in the direction of reducing intergroup prejudice.

• Usual Approach: "Prejudicial attitudes are not polite, and decent people don't express these thoughts."

• NCBI Approach: Silence, especially under the guise of politeness, leaves prejudicial attitudes intact. The reality is that all people have "those thoughts" because we all grew up in a prejudicial society. The goal is to teach participants how to talk about their prejudices and how to listen to and elicit the details in a healing way.

Each exercise of the workshop model is based on the preceding assumptions, in both content and sequence. The following is a brief description of the model.

Workshop Summary

1. *Group Identities.* Participants are given many opportunities to identify and look at strengths and difficulties of the different groups to which they belong, including ethnic, race, religion, class background, gender, nationality, and sexual orientation. These introductions begin a process that allows a concise sharing of information regarding the possible basis for future intergroup coalitions and to identify and raise vital multicultural issues.

2. *Healing and Bridge Building.* Through the sharing of specific

incidents of discrimination and the facilitated opportunities to convey the real emotional details of prejudice, the unraveling of anger, lack of awareness, and humiliation begin to occur. Participants start to make connections between their own painful experiences of prejudice and those felt by other groups. As one participant said, "The terror I see in my father who is a Holocaust survivor and the terror I see in your face as a result of racism is the same terror."

Signe Wilkinson. Reprinted with permission.

3. *Effective Intervention Strategies.* The last part of the model addresses the notion that prejudice makes us feel powerless and that truly assisting people to reduce prejudice must include opportunities to learn and practice skills for effectively shifting attitudes and making changes.

Principles for decreasing polarization and defensiveness and increasing communication and unity are explored. Through role plays, participants are coached in strategies which effectively interrupt bigoted comments, slurs, jokes, or behaviors.

A conflict process for dealing with emotional, polarized issues (e.g., abortion and mandatory drug testing) also is taught. Participants learn to identify the common concerns underlying rigid positions and to reformulate the issue in such a way as to include both sides.

Lastly, individual goal setting and prejudice reduction projects are developed. . . .

Conclusion

The Prejudice Reduction Model can be an effective approach for dealing with prejudice and intergroup tensions. . . . The model, particularly when it is institutionalized with a team of trainers and on-going support meetings, provides a workable framework for developing the skills that are needed in a workforce which is growing in diversity.

"Without economic inequality to sustain it, racism as we know it today will wither away."

Reducing Economic Inequality Can Stop Racism

Len M. Nichols

Len M. Nichols is an associate professor of economics at Wellesley College in Massachusetts. In the following viewpoint, Nichols argues that economic inequality is the main cause of racism. He argues that because blacks and other minorities are more likely to be poor, they are also more likely to become involved in crime. One result of this development, he writes, is that minorities have become associated with violent crime in the minds of many Americans and that this fear of minority crime leads to racist beliefs and behaviors. Nichols calls for government programs that reduce poverty and inequality, which he argues would reduce crime and, in turn, reduce racism.

As you read, consider the following questions:

1. What motivated opponents to school busing and housing desegregation, according to Nichols?
2. How are crime and economic inequality related, according to the author?
3. What kinds of social programs does Nichols recommend?

Len M. Nichols, "The New Racism: A Product of Economic Inequality." Reprinted from *USA Today* magazine, November 1990, © 1990 by the Society for the Advancement of Education.

I was born in rural Arkansas, one year prior to *Brown v. Board of Education*, four years before Federal troops forced Little Rock Central High School to admit black students. American race relations have come a long way in my lifetime, and there is a much larger black middle class today than there was almost four decades ago. Nevertheless, the Willie Horton ads in the 1988 presidential election, the emotional reactions to a gang rape in New York's Central Park in April, 1989, and an elaborate hoax to frame a black man for the brutal murder of a pregnant white woman in Boston in January, 1990, indicate that racial animosity lurks very near the surfaces of our urban veneers.

No one, not even the wisest sociologist, completely understands the evolution of racial attitudes in post-World War II America. It is a long and complicated path from waving the Confederate flag outside Central High to the stop-and-search-young-black-men policy implemented by Boston police in certain neighborhoods during the winter of 1989-90 in a desperate, but futile, attempt to stop random urban brutality. I do not claim a complete understanding, but since I grew up 70 miles from Central High and have lived 15 miles outside Boston for the last 9 years, I do have a perspective that may have some validity, or at least interest. Accordingly, I make two claims: the racism of today differs from the racism of my youth in a fundamental way; and economic reasoning can help clarify some implications of the differences.

Past and Present Racism

The "Confederate flag" racism of the 1950's and 1960's was based on a rather old belief that people of color are intellectually—and therefore morally—inferior to white people. My grandparents' generation held this belief as naturally as they believed in God, and it took exposure and experience with the outcomes of equal educational opportunity to more or less stamp it out in my generation of adults. Remnants of this attitude persist, of course, but the new Ku Klux Klan members and Skinhead converts among the young hardly constitute a major force.

Today's racism is based primarily on a fear that poor people of color are more violent and more likely to commit major crimes than are white people. The opposition to housing desegregation and busing in the late 1960's and 1970's, especially in Chicago and Boston, galvanized around this fear, though the symbols and language of Confederate flag racism were appropriated and exploited in the name of preserving neighborhood "purity." There simply was neither enough time nor imagination to invent new symbols.

J. Anthony Lukas' Pulitzer Prize-winning *Common Ground* makes it clear that white opponents to busing mostly were fearful for their children's safety and the expected decline in educational quality inevitable in a contentious and violent atmosphere. Similarly, homeowners in all-white sections of Chicago who violently resisted attempts to desegregate housing primarily were afraid that their property values, still the most valuable asset in most Americans' portfolios, would decline as blacks brought crime with them into formerly all-white (i.e., safe) neighborhoods.

Take on the Ghettos

[We must] take on, as a society, the project of addressing comprehensively the problems of the ghettos, which . . . constitute the great obvious failure in our domestic life and the most pressing piece of unfinished business in our long-running quest to solve the American dilemma.

Yes, I'm talking about government programs—programs to make the streets safe again, to improve inner-city education, to train people for jobs and then find them the jobs for which they've been trained. These would have a multiplicity of advantages: if they were run well enough to produce real results in terms of improving life for the black poor, they could help heal the severest grievance between the races, which is a deep tangle of feelings about crime and poverty.

Nicholas Lemann, *The Washington Post National Weekly Edition*, August 27/ September 2, 1990.

Opponents of busing and housing desegregation shared three beliefs: everyone else in society was gaining economic and political power relative to their groups; the only bulwark against these forces was their neighborhoods' uniqueness and closeness; and these neighborhoods were threatened mortally by the racial mixing imposed by Federal law and police power.

Class Differences

The very successes of the civil rights movement served to expose class differences in both races that had remained submerged in the days of Jim Crow and Confederate flag racism. When *all* blacks were denied economic and housing opportunity, black neighborhoods had much lower crime rates than today, since the vast majority of residents shared and enforced many values along with the dominant white culture. Perhaps most important among these shared values was a belief that hard work within the existing political and economic systems was the best way to accomplish change, both for one's individual life and the community.

When doors finally were opened for those talented and trained enough to walk through them in undeniably meritorious ways, class differences among blacks became apparent to most whites for the first time. As blacks acquired middle-class status, just like whites before them, they moved out of the central cities, and the sustaining buffers between lower-class blacks and the surrounding white economic mainstream—neighborhood groups, churches, role models, etc.—largely were removed. Today, middle-class blacks usually are accepted by middle-class whites, at least by most measures, for whites have learned that they are no threat to—and, indeed, share—their most precious values. The people who remain in the inner cities today, however, largely are members of an economic underclass, cut off from much hope of ever earning a sufficient piece of the American pie, even by working hard within the system.

People cut off from the economic mainstream always have been more violent and crime-prone than those within it. The histories of London, New York, Boston, and Chicago are full of examples of different groups of immigrants, regardless of race, successively taking up residence as the newest, poorest, and least law-abiding on the block. The profound difference between our largely black underclass today and the Italians, Russian Jews, and Irish before them who "made it" to middle-class status seems to be the absence of hope. The prevalence of drugs and the willingness to use handguns seemingly at random are symptoms, not causes, of the lack of hope.

Crime and Race

It's a fact that a disproportionate share of violent crime *is* committed by young black men. Statistics reported by the Sentencing Project, a governmental task force, showed that almost 25% of all black men between the ages of 20 and 28 are involved somehow in the criminal justice system. The public was shocked by the magnitude, not the relative ranking, of the higher probabilities that blacks commit criminal acts (almost four times the rate for white men and eight times for violent crimes). These probabilities of criminal behavior feed a new racism that has come to be accepted as naturally as the cruder racism of my grandparents. It is not anti-black or anti-people of color in general, however, but specifically anti-poor-people of color. Our prejudices have been refined to a "scientifically" defensible level, for they now are based on objectively observed probabilities.

With unshakable (if somewhat contradictory) faith in the philosophy of individualism, Americans always have balked at the idea that any person is not ultimately responsible for his or her own actions, good or bad. Failure to acknowledge this principle, I believe, is the reason that liberals have lost so much political clout. Left-wing sociology notwithstanding, most people refuse to believe that "society" made Willie Horton kidnap and rape while on a weekend furlough for murder.

I agree about Horton, but my training as an economist will not let me stop there. Most individuals respond to the incentive structures that are relevant for them. It is much more "costly" for a young, inner-city, black boy to take school seriously and avoid the lure of street crimes than it is for a suburban, middle-class boy of any race. The costs to the urban black include ridicule by his peers and those who wield money, power, respect, and influence in his community, as well as the physical danger of rejecting the criminal path dictated as "normal" by ever-growing gangs. Peer pressure is strongest at exactly the time when a boy's manhood is emerging. Detest them though we might, gangs serve a vital social function for the young people who belong to them. The relative absence of positive adult male role models at this time of life makes gangs more attractive as mechanisms for earning respect and a sense of belonging.

What would be the gain to the urban black boy of studying hard in mediocre-to-poor schools and working at, say, McDonald's, eventually achieving the rank of assistant manager? When he can make five to 10 times that weekly salary in merely one hour's worth of drug deliveries, why should he take the long route of self-denial to working-class status? All youth believe in their immortality, so fear of eventual punishment easily is dismissed. It is still a long way from delivering and dealing drugs to killing and raping. Yet, from dealing to fighting over the right to deal in certain locations is a short step. Once fighting and killing become commonplace, all life and human dignity become debased.

Contrast this path with the incentives available to the average middle-class youth—good public schools, virtually guaranteed admission to a high-quality college, and even post-graduate training paid for by concerned and largely supportive parents. Unlike in the inner-city case, peer pressure here *lowers* the cost of the "hard-working" choice. The simple fact is that the environment one is born into affects the costs and benefits and thereby the probabilities of an individual choosing a particular path. The best analogy may be that emigration from the Soviet Union always increases when the social and personal costs of applying for visas are reduced. The decision to take the lawful, hard-working path within the inner city is a choice for attempting to emigrate slowly from an oppressive and dangerous land. I and most economists would predict that, if faced with the same objective conditions, a large percentage of white males would make the same choices so many young, urban, black men are making today.

Whites React to Probabilities

This is not to say it is impossible to make the "right" choices, even in the face of terrible conditions (high costs). The majority of urban residents are law-abiding citizens virtually terrorized by the mayhem around them, and many dedicated teachers and social service workers are trying to be and find other role models. What is apparently impossible is for white suburbanites to imagine taking a path of violent crime. It is natural to convince our-selves that we would act differently than what we observe, for we can not conceive being without our *existing* values, attitudes, and skills. We might behave quite differently if we had been shaped by the environment we now shrink from in horror. Since we can not imagine doing so ourselves, those who do use vio-lence are defined to be outside the mainstream of society, or "sub-human." Given the correlation between race and violent crime that every day's news brings us, it is a short step from this defini-tion to the new racism. It is really class-racism, but it is based on just enough facts to be much easier to defend than the Con-federate flag racism of yesterday. Racism always has been the act of attributing stereotypical characteristics to all members of a par-ticular group without regard to an individual's uniqueness. We simply may be better than my grandparents at statistical infer-ence. We are hardly morally superior, for we still largely refuse to engage individuals on their own.

Racial Fears

My fear is that the separation of the late 1980s will lead to full-fledged polarization in the 1990s. The policies of the Reagan years and the passing of the 1960s from historical memory have had re-gressive effects on Black-white relations. If the economic problems that underlie racial tensions are not addressed, the dangers will be even greater than they were in the sixties when prosperity at least provided some cushion for reforms.

We therefore need a national policy that reverses the eighties trend of income transfer from the poor and working classes to the rich. We need a jobs policy for inner-city ghetto youth, and full employ-ment for working-class and middle-class men and women.

Bob Blauner, *Tikkun*, January/February 1990.

Another way of saying this is, if a white person gets on a sub-way car with a group of young black males, the current probabili-ties of crime and life apparently justify being wary and avoiding contact if at all possible. This is hardly an environment in which tolerance and racial harmony can develop and flourish. Innocent black males justifiably are incensed at being treated stereotypi-cally without having a chance to "prove" or assert their funda-mental human dignity, but white people simply are too afraid to give them that chance. Blacks also resent that they have to prove their decency, whereas, for whites, it is assumed. Meanwhile, whites have a hard time understanding why blacks so often are angry when these matters are discussed or ignored. The gulf con-tinues to expand.

Is there a solution to the new racism? Stop the crime, one might say, but that can not happen until the incentive structures for urban blacks are fundamentally different than they are today. Not only must we strengthen the criminal justice system's ability to remove and keep the already hopelessly violent from our midst (raise the costs of the criminal choice), but the economic opportunities available to blacks have to be comparable to those open to whites if we reasonably are to expect similar aggregate behaviors (raise the benefits of the lawful choice).

Economic Inequality

Both of these are going to take a lot more tax money than we heretofore have manifested a willingness to spend. However, not spending it now may be more expensive for our society in the long run. Consider the statistics which show that 20% of all children in the U.S. currently are growing up in poverty; over 40% of all black households are single-parent (primarily female-headed) ones; and 43% of all inmates in Massachusetts state prisons are functionally illiterate. These figures are related. Devoting resources to education and economic opportunity in the inner city no longer should be thought of as charity necessitated by a moral imperative. A social survival imperative compels us to redirect resources or lose whole sections of our cities and society entirely— or at least for a very long time.

The new racism based on differential probabilities of criminal behavior ultimately is a symptom of inequality of economic opportunity. There is a profound self-interest in generosity now that will help alleviate this condition. Without economic inequality to sustain it, racism as we know it today will wither away. With economic inequality, it will continue to haunt us.

"The proper way to deal with hatred is not with more hatred, but with a neutral attitude of patient strength and forbearance."

Changing Individuals' Attitudes Can Stop Racism

Roy Masters

Roy Masters is a stress management counselor who hosts a syndicated radio program and has written several books, including *How to Control Your Negative Emotions*. In the following viewpoint, he argues that racists have a psychological need to feel superior to others. Masters asserts that the best way to combat these racists is for victims of racism to avoid succumbing to anger and racism themselves.

As you read, consider the following questions:

1. What phenomenon does Masters say resembles racism, but actually is not?
2. How do children become racists, according to the author?
3. Why does Masters believe it is important not to return the hatred of racists?

From "The Psychology of Racism," by Roy Masters, *New Dimensions*, December 1990. Reprinted with permission of *New Dimensions* magazine, PO Box 811, Grants Pass, OR 97526.

Today we are witnessing the renewal of a hate-based ideology, one based on identifying and persecuting scapegoats for personal and national problems. After the promise of the Civil Rights movement of the 1960s, people of good will the world over had hoped widespread racism would be a thing of the past. And although it has mushroomed in the last decade, this attitude of contempt for one group by another has unfortunately always been present, not only in this country, but throughout the world.

The Need to Feel Superior

What exactly is this insidious need some people have to feel superior to other races? The answer to the riddle of racism becomes self-evident for anyone willing to probe just beneath the surface of this most inhuman of human characteristics. There are several important dynamics involved, but one of the most important is this simple but unpleasant truth: Those who have been subjected to humiliation and degradation in their own lives come under a powerful compulsion to "take it out" on someone else. Losers can feel like winners only when they look down their noses at others, and make others feel the same humiliation they have experienced.

This process is readily observed between siblings. The older brother cruelly humiliates his younger brother, who then turns around and picks a fight with his younger sister. By upsetting and degrading her, the middle child experiences what feels like a restoration of the power he lost to his older brother. Each participant in this process is unaware that his identity has been altered—each has inadvertently joined a human pecking order.

Racism often manifests a similar process. A sense of loss or violation results from failing to deal properly with the cruelty and injustice of others. Like the siblings in the story, the victim is tricked into stealing happiness from others to replace what he has lost. Although the newly created racist "power monger" may feel a rush of accomplishment, he has not really retrieved what he lost. What he gains is an *illusion* of strength and value. Those who are "weak before the strong" become—in their own eyes—strong before the weak. Let's call this principle "living by comparison." All those who have been psychologically and emotionally damaged, who refuse or do not know how to face their own sense of shame, are then forced to live by degrading others to minimize by comparison their own sense of loss.

The Influence of Negative Experiences

To better understand this unconscious need to degrade, we must first distinguish it from a phenomenon that masquerades as racism, but is actually not. Negative impressions about one group or another are formed through personal experiences. Let's say a person of a particular race does great harm to you—rape, fraud, mugging, whatever. Obviously, this one experience does not prove that all persons of the same race, whether Asians, blacks, whites, Jews, or Hispanics are bad. Yet negative experiences with individuals of a certain racial group have the effect of stigmatizing the whole group in the mind of the victim.

The victim, realizing his prejudice is based on a single experience, may be embarrassed by his hostility. He may unconsciously cover up this angry emotion by bending over backwards to be nice to the very people he secretly judges. This behavior can have the curious but observable effect of subtly enticing the same type of person (whatever his race, color, or creed) as the one who did the original harm to perpetrate a similar offense. . . .

It is relatively easy to overcome this type of conditioning (i.e., the reflexive reaction resulting from a negative experience with a person which taints our relationship with people of similar characteristics). The victim must essentially become mature enough to accept the fact that although an injustice was inflicted upon him, it is neither right nor productive to hold on to his anger for the rest of his life. He must drop the resentment toward the perpetrator. Interestingly, when he does so, the event ceases to be so traumatic, and often stops being a negative focal point in his life. . . .

Redefining Right and Wrong

But for those people who have built their lives on comparing themselves with others, racism may be largely independent of negative experience. For these self-righteous bigots, hatred is not necessarily sparked by injustice, but by a personal need to look down on others. All it requires is some identifiable difference in one's fellow man. And as many differences as exist between people, so are the number of grounds for self-righteous comparisons. . . .

For racists, the focus of comparison is skin color:

• *White against black*: White supremacist groups have a sick need to feel "righteous" by identifying white as good and blacks (and all other races) as bad. With exhortations to "save the white race" these people eulogize "racial hygiene" and white unity against the "mud people" (minorities of color). From the KKK [Ku Klux Klan] to the latest racist incarnations—the neo-Nazi Skinheads; The Order, whose members believe in an inevitable white revolution; and the Aryan Nations, whose followers advocate a migration of all white people to the Northwest—the all-consuming emotion is hatred, aroused by identifying and attacking a scapegoat.

• *Black against white*: Some black intellectuals, such as psychologist Dr. Naim Akbar and James Small, professor of black studies at the City College of New York, consider all whites to be racists, even those who were active participants in the '60s civil rights movement. Louis Farrakhan of the Nation of Islam claims that AIDS is a "manufactured virus" designed by white America to exterminate other races by spreading viruses and drugs.

• *Black against black*: In the inner cities, youth gangs attack one another over territorial rights. In Los Angeles, between 70,000 and 100,000 youths are involved with street gangs who differentiate themselves from other gangs through their colors ("Bloods" wear red, "Crips" wear blue) and hand signals. Black on black crime is a major concern in the inner cities where murder and mugging for drug money are all too common.

• *Black against Asian*: Many Asian-Americans have found their way into predominantly black neighborhoods and have built successful businesses; black violence against these newcomers has been on the upswing.

New Understanding

I feel that there is hope for great progress in the youth of today. We take both new and old approaches to learn about the causes and effects of racism. We try to understand each other, as well as those who came before us.

This understanding could very well be the key to abolishing racism. The protest marches and lobbyists will still be needed to achieve key goals from figureheads. However, attempts by individuals of one race to understand the thoughts and actions of people of another race are still the most personal and direct method we have.

James Wiemken, *Christan Social Action*, May 1989.

There are thousands of variations of racism based on this pattern of one person or group uniting with another in their common hatred of differences and experiencing a rush of superiority over the condemned difference. This is the "hate wrong to feel right" principle. Hating an imaginary wrong or physical difference to elevate oneself into a sense of superiority over another is a very common (in)human practice. This form of self-righteous superiority is both wrong and counter-productive. It is as dehumanizing to the perpetrator as it is to the victim, so it causes more inferiority, shame, and guilt than it cures. And so the need for hatred—which supports the ego's illusion of righteousness—grows and becomes addictive.

We come now to the reason for finding and judging a particular "distinguishing marker"—that which differentiates one man from another, whether it be color, race, size, or intelligence. The person who is addicted to hating can work himself into a sense of being omnipotently right as judge, jury, and executioner, without fear of ever being wrong, as long as he hates a permanent characteristic. To a twisted, racist mind, a condemned feature like skin color cannot "repent" of its "sin"—can't "reform" and embarrass the "judge." No, to ensure a ready "fix" of judgment, the hateful person must condemn a feature that is unchangeable.

It is risky to feel superior to someone who is fat compared to your thinness. The fat person may diet, and you may put on a few pounds. This changes the delicate balance of "superiority"—a depressing and threatening prospect that can be avoided only by condemning a permanent characteristic such as color, gender, or height. The color of one's skin or slope of one's eyes, which cannot be altered, is a safe focus of condemnation for the person playing supreme judge.

Of course, this process of hating is tremendously addictive. Instead of becoming more right in the process, one is becoming more wrong, less human, and therefore in ever greater need of identifying more and more wrong in the world to hate, so as to distract oneself from the guilt that always follows close on the heels of hate. . . .

Initiating the Next Generation

This ingrained need to feel superior to others is the hallmark of racial bigotry in which there is one prime focus for self-righteous judgment—racial differences. Each new generation of bigots goes through an initiation process before entering wholeheartedly into this life built on hatred.

Consider what happens to a child born into a racist family, one that views minority groups as inferior beings. If the child shows even a hint of possessing an independent, mature point of view, this budding betrayal of the family philosophy will be detected at an early age, and the child will be degraded until he acquiesces and conforms to the clan. The family's "head bigot" knows full well the awesome power of degrading—after all, it is the process that has made him what he is. The child must be degraded so that he or she will learn to appreciate the "joys" of degrading others, and discover that, compared to his victim's helplessness, he is strong; compared to the uncontrolled emotion he has provoked, he is in control; compared to the humiliation he has dished out, he is superior. Through reducing another to a wretched state lower than his own, the racist feels restored to what he believes to be his former glory. Thus a military chain of command of compulsive hatemongers is formed—dominated and justified by a merciless instigating leader (such as the Ku Klux Klan's Imperial Wizard).

To reiterate, those who have been degraded by any form of authority tend *automatically* to live by comparison. In principle, a person who feels miserable because he has no shoes feels fortunate when he meets someone who has no feet. Therefore, a dehumanized white man who has not made it in life may feel better when he looks down and compares himself to someone he fantasizes to be less than himself—a member of a minority group. He has to look down because if he looks up he will realize his own failure.

Whether or not a racist can stop being a racist depends, basically, on the hardness of his heart. Some people can be Nazis for years, continuing to affirm the rightness of their battle against the "evil" Jews. But after experiencing the pain involved in this state of mind for a long time they may realize their error—that they have obtained a false sense of rightness through hating someone they judge as evil and/or inferior. The truth may finally catch up with them. Unfortunately, others who are more stubborn in holding on to their illusions never want to be wrong; that is where the problem lies. Such persons experience no gradual tempering of views over the years, only a further hardening of the heart and a steady progression of error.

Anyone caught on the receiving end of this blind, unjust, unwarranted hostility is in danger of conforming to the judgments against him. That is to say, accuse an innocent man of being a thief and he may unwittingly become a thief. Let me explain: If a man is judged unfairly, accused of stealing, and actually sent to jail, he may become so bitter that he begins to think, "I've paid the price for something I never did; I may as well commit the crime."

Mistreatment and false accusations have a strange way of seeping into the very fabric of our thinking and can lead us to become a reflection of someone else's opinion. So a black youth who is continually made the brunt of scorn, hostility, and distrust may find himself fulfilling the negative expectations projected onto him by others.

For the racist, that is icing on the cake—actual confirmation of his original judgment. Again, the racist mentality never wants to admit to being wrong. Of course, it is human nature to want to feel good about ourselves—never to be wrong in our own eyes. Yet there are two ways of doing that: One of them is simply to develop the maturity and wisdom to deal graciously with people who are cruel to us. A person who lives this way evolves real character and does not need to degrade others, nor does he allow others to degrade him. He retains his own original integrity.

Finding Lost Dignity

But until victims of cruelty find their way back to their lost dignity, which is to say, as long as they continue to hate the abuse they have received, the alternative kicks in quite unconsciously—and I do mean unconsciously. Relief comes only by losing consciousness of humiliation and pain by becoming "conscious" of a superior position in relation to another's humiliation. So, as the saying goes, we do unto others what was done unto us. And for any ego caught in this mechanism, abusing others does not seem cruel, because it *feels* so right. Feeling justified, good, and superior becomes the only standard of right and wrong.

Ed Gamble. Reprinted with permission.

Hating wrong has a strange way of making a person feel right about himself. People may actually feel they have a *duty* to hate what they consider to be wrong. The danger of this is that hatred, like a whirlpool, can suck consciousness into it so profoundly that a person loses sight of his true condition. Hatred can generate an alternate "reality" that tells a person he is superior—right by comparison. For this reason alone, hatred is difficult to drop. It creates a peculiar vision. It converts true enemies into "friends" and what might have been true friends into enemies.

Delusions of Righteousness

Those with real strength and integrity tend to threaten the racist's delusions of righteousness. The contrast between true virtue and the hate-based variety is just too painful. Therefore, for the racist, true dignity in others has to be destroyed. Remember, in this process what *feels* good *is* good, and evil is anything that makes a person feel uncomfortable. This myopic standard of discretion is all the racist sees—perhaps that's all he wants to see. Hate produces an altered state of consciousness, and no civil rights law in the world can govern that unruly passion. It is an addiction worse than any drug. . . .

In a previous era, white racist organizations and individuals perpetrated terrorism against blacks. Blacks were intimidated, hunted down like wild animals, brutally beaten, castrated, lynched. Today, Skinheads use steel-toed boots, knives, and baseball bats on minorities of all races. The predator is still very much alive and with us today. . . .

Controlling Resentment

So, how can we defend ourselves against becoming casualties of hatred and psychological abuse? The answer is to learn to stand up to personal put downs with dignity and courage, *without returning the same hate as the racist's*. Feel the hurt (the pain of the cruelty or humiliation) without hating back. Granted, we are only human, with many feelings we cannot control. But when we are subjected to cruelty, there is one response we *can* control, and that is resentment.

Without the extra dimension of resentment, cruelty has only a temporary sway over us. We may feel its impact, but it will not have the power to convert us into one of the haters. By dealing with racism in this way, the character of the targeted victim grows, and holds up a mirror to the racist. If this "psychic self-defense" principle could be taught to the victims of persecution in sufficient numbers, they would grow in strength and grace and bring the age of racism to a screeching halt. The philosopher Nietzsche said, "What does not kill a man makes him grow stronger."

Adversity is overcome by meeting the challenge with dignity and character. The proper way to deal with hatred is not with more hatred, but with a neutral attitude of patient strength and forbearance. Traditional Christian faith calls it "longsuffering." Responding in that way, you will never descend into the realm of your adversary. Even if someone treats you in a degrading way, you will not *feel* degraded. Instead, you evolve your humanness. . . .

As a Jew living in England during World War II, I personally experienced persecution at the hands of vicious anti-Semites. Most of my family was lost in the Nazi holocaust. And I was constantly confronted with degrading remarks and violence for being Jewish. Through the school of hard knocks, I learned not to return hate for hate. This discipline set me free from being a victim of racism. Moreover, the benefit this understanding bestowed on me throughout my life, which I never could have imagined at the time, has been nothing short of miraculous. For my part, forgiving those who had been cruel to me saved my sanity. But it also converted many enemies into friends. It's amazing what a little bit of good will can do.

"A true and appropriate answer to our race problem . . . would be a restoration of our communities."

Restoring America's Communities Can Stop Racism

Wendell Berry

Wendell Berry is an author and environmentalist whose books include *The Hidden Wound,* from which this viewpoint is taken. He argues that the root of America's race problem is that minorities and whites live in separate, isolated worlds. This lack of contact between minorities and whites results in racist attitudes. Berry calls for a true integration of communities in which all ethnic and economic groups would share responsibilities and privileges to end racism.

As you read, consider the following questions:

1. Why is racial prejudice and prejudice toward poor whites similar, according to Berry?
2. In what ways are America's communities disintegrating, according to the author?
3. What should the role of government be, according to Berry?

Adapted from the Afterword of *The Hidden Wound,* copyright © 1989 Wendell Berry. Published by North Point Press and reprinted by permission.

Recently I attended the commencement exercises of a California university at which the graduates of the school of business wore FOR SALE signs around their necks. It was done as a joke, of course, a display of youthful high spirits, and yet it was inescapably a cynical joke, of the sort by which an embarrassing truth is flaunted. For, in fact, these graduates were for sale, they knew that they were, and they intended to be. They had just spent four years at a university to increase their "marketability." That some of the young women in the group undoubtedly were feminists only made the joke more cynical. But what most astonished and alarmed me was that a number of these graduates for sale were black. Had their forebears served and suffered and struggled in America for 368 years in order for these now certified and privileged few to sell themselves?

How, remembering their history, could those black graduates have worn those signs? Only, I think, by assuming, in very dangerous innocence, that their graduation into privilege exempted them from history. The danger is that there is no safety, no *dependable* safety, in privilege that is founded on greed, ignorance, and waste. And these people, after all, will remain black. What sign will they wear besides their expensive suits by which the police can tell them from their unemployed and unemployable brothers and sisters of the inner city?

The Root of America's Racial Problem

The root of our racial problem in America is not racism. The root is in our inordinate desire to be superior—not to some inferior or subject people, though this desire leads to the subjection of people—but to our condition. We wish to rise above the sweat and bother of taking care of anything—of ourselves, of each other, or of our country. We did not enslave African blacks because they were black, but because their labor promised to free us of the obligations of stewardship, and because they were unable to prevent us from enslaving them. They were economically valuable and militarily weak.

It seems likely, then, that what we now call racism came about as a justification of slavery after the fact, not as its cause. We decided that blacks were inferior in order to persuade ourselves that it was all right to enslave them. That this is true is suggested by our present treatment of other social groups to whom we assign the laborious jobs of caretaking. For it is not only the racial minorities who receive our indifference or contempt, but economic or geographic minorities as well. Anyone who has been called "redneck" or "hillbilly" or "hick" or sometimes even "country person" or "farmer" shares with racial minorities the experience of a stigmatizing social prejudice. And such terms as "redneck" and "hillbilly" and "hick" have remained acceptable in public use long after the repudiation of such racial epithets as "nigger" and "greaser." "Rednecks" and "hillbillies" and "hicks" are scorned because they do what used to be known as "nigger work"—work that is fundamental and inescapable. And it should not be necessary to point out the connection between the oppression of women and the general contempt for household work. It is well established among us that you may hold up your head in polite society with a public lie in your mouth or other people's money in your pocket or innocent blood on your hands, but not with dishwater on your hands or mud on your shoes.

What we did not understand at the time of slavery, and understand poorly still, is that this presumption of the inferiority of economic groups is a contagion that we cannot control, for the presumed inferiority of workers inevitably infects the quality of their work, which inevitably infects the quality of the workplace, which is to say the quality of the country itself. When a nation determines that the work of providing and caretaking is "nigger work" or work for "hillbillies" or "rednecks"—that is, fundamental, necessary, inescapable, *and inferior*—then it has implanted in its own soul the infection of its ruin.

Limited Solutions

The problem of race, nevertheless, is generally treated as if it could be solved merely by recruiting more blacks and other racial minorities into colleges and then into high-paying jobs. This is to assume, simply, that we can solve the problems of racial minorities by elevating them to full partnership in the problems of the racial majority. We assume that when a young black person acquires a degree and achieves a sit-down job with a corporation, the problem is to that extent solved.

The larger, graver, more dangerous problem, however, is that we have thought of no better way of solving the race problem. The "success" of the black corporate executive, in fact, only reveals the shallowness, the jeopardy, and the falseness of the "success" of the white corporate executive. This "success" is a private and highly questionable settlement that does not solve, indeed does not refer to, the issues associated with American racism. It only assumes that American blacks will be made better or more useful or more secure by becoming as greedy, selfish, wasteful, and thoughtless as affluent American whites. The aims and standards of the oppressors become the aims and standards of the oppressed, and so our ills and evils survive our successive "liberations."

There is no safety in belonging to the select few, for minority people or anybody else. If we are looking for insurance against want and oppression, we will find it only in our neighbors' prosperity and goodwill and, beyond that, in the good health of our worldly places, our homelands. If we were sincerely looking for a place of safety, for real security and success, then we would begin to turn to our communities—and not the communities simply of our human neighbors, but also of the water, earth, and air, the plants and animals, all the creatures with whom our local life is shared. We would be looking too for another kind of freedom. Our present idea of freedom is only the freedom to do as we please: to sell ourselves for a high salary, a home in the suburbs, and idle weekends. But that is a freedom dependent upon affluence, which is in turn dependent upon the rapid consumption of exhaustible supplies. The other kind of freedom is the freedom to take care of ourselves and of each other. The freedom of affluence opposes and contradicts the freedom of community life. Our place of safety can only be the community, and not just one community, but many of them everywhere. All that we still claim to value depends on that: freedom, dignity, health, mutual help and affection, undestructive pleasure, and the rest. Human life, as most of us still would like to define it, is community life.

Disintegrating Communities

How, then, can "integration" be achieved—and what can it mean—in communities that are conspicuously disintegrating?

Mostly, we do not speak of our society as disintegrating. We would prefer not to call what we are experiencing social disintegration. But we are endlessly preoccupied with the symptoms: divorce, venereal disease, murder, rape, debt, bankruptcy, pornography, soil loss, teenage pregnancy, fatherless children, motherless children, child suicide, public child care, retirement homes, nursing homes, toxic waste, soil and water and air pollution, government secrecy, government lying, government crime, civil violence, drug abuse, sexual promiscuity, abortion as "birth control," the explosion of garbage, hopeless poverty, unemployment, unearned wealth. All the plagues of our time are symptoms of a general disintegration.

We are capable, really, only of the forcible integration of centralization—economic, political, military, and educational—and always at the cost of social and cultural disintegration. Our aim, it would appear, is to "integrate" ourselves into a limitless military-industrial city in which we all will be lost, and so may do as we please in the freedom either to run wild until we are caught or killed, or to do "all the things that other people do."

People don't work or shop or amuse themselves or go to church or school in their own neighborhoods anymore, and are therefore free to separate themselves from their workplaces and economic sources, and to sort themselves into economic categories in which, having no need for each other, they remain strangers. I assume that this is bad because I assume that it is good for people to know each other. I assume, especially that it is good for people to know each other across the lines of economy and vocation.

Professional people should know their clients outside their offices. Teachers should know the families of their students. University professors and intellectuals should know the communities and the households that will be affected by their ideas. Rich people and poor people should know each other. If this familiar knowledge does not exist, then these various groups will think of each other and deal with each other on the basis of stereotypes as vicious and ultimately as dangerous as the stereotypes of race.

Restoring the Community

A true and appropriate answer to our race problem, as to many others, would be a restoration of our communities—it being understood that a community, properly speaking, cannot exclude or mistreat any of its members. This is what we forgot during slavery and the industrialization that followed, and have never remembered.

A proper community, we should remember also, is a commonwealth: a place, a resource, and an economy. It answers the needs, practical as well as social and spiritual, of its members—among them the need to need one another. The answer to the present alignment of political power with wealth is the restoration of the identity of community and economy.

Overcoming Fear

Prejudices can be overcome through peaceful means. Diverse groups of people can overcome their diversity by focusing on those issues and values that they share in common. Fear of the unknown is replaced by the affirming sense of accomplishment. Fear of individual loss is replaced by a newly gained knowledge that cultural diversity, racial differences and variety in religious creeds indeed enrich, rather than rob, the vitality of the community.

Joseph A. Fiorenza, *America*, May 13, 1989.

Is this something the government could help with? Of course it is. Community cannot be made by government prescription and mandate, but the government, in its proper role as promoter of the general welfare, preserver of the public peace, and forbidder of injustice, could do much to promote the improvement of communities. If it wanted to, it could end its collusion with the wealthy and the corporations and the "special interests." It could stand, as it is supposed to, between wealth and power. It could assure the possibility that a poor person might hold office. It could protect, by strict forbiddings, the disruption of the integrity of a community or a local economy or an ecosystem by any sort of commercial or industrial enterprise, that is, it could enforce

259

proprieties of scale. It could understand that economic justice does not consist in giving the most power to the most money.

The government *could* do such things. But we know well that it is not going to do them; it is not even going to consider doing them, because community integrity, and the decentralization of power and economy that it implies, is antithetical to the ambitions of the corporations. The government's aim, therefore, is racial indifference, not integrated communities. Does this mean that our predicament is hopeless? No. It only means that our predicament is extremely unfavorable, as the human predicament has often been.

Spiritual Issues

What the government will or will not do is finally beside the point. If people do not have the government they want, then they will have a government that they must either change or endure. Finally, all the issues that I have discussed here are neither political nor economic, but moral and spiritual. What is at issue is our character as a people. It is necessary to look beyond the government to the possibility—one that seems to be growing—that people will reject what have been the prevailing assumptions, and begin to strengthen and defend their communities on their own.

We must be aware too of the certainty that the present way of things will eventually fail. If it fails quickly, by any of several predicted causes, then we will have no need, being absent, to worry about what to do next. If it fails slowly, and if we have been careful to preserve the most necessary and valuable things, then it may fail into a restoration of community life—that is, into understanding of our need to help and comfort each other.

"Universities may . . . restrict harassment expressions without resorting to censorship. . . . Such policies are needed to promote understanding."

Rules Restricting Racist Speech Can Stop Racism

John T. Shapiro

Many colleges and universities have responded to racist incidents by making rules proscribing racist speech and conduct. In the following viewpoint, John T. Shapiro argues that such rules can reduce racism and foster a healthier learning environment. Shapiro is a law student at the University of Minnesota in Minneapolis.

As you read, consider the following questions:

1. What events does Shapiro cite to demonstrate the problem of racism on campus?
2. According to the author, how does the 1964 Civil Rights Act provide justification for rules banning racist speech?
3. Why is curbing racism in colleges and universities so important, according to Shapiro?

Adapted from John T. Shapiro, "The Call for Campus Conduct Policies: Censorship or Constitutionally Permissible Limitations on Speech," *Minnesota Law Review*, vol. 75, October 1990. Reprinted with permission.

In recent years, universities have witnessed an increasing number of harassment incidents on their campuses. These incidents have ranged from hate-filled graffiti and distribution of hate-filled fliers to destruction of anti-apartheid shanties, displaying of Ku Klux Klan robes at anti-apartheid rallies, and shouting anti-Semitic insults at students. For example, a fraternity at the University of Wisconsin threw a "Fiji Island Party," painted themselves in blackface, and set up a large caricature cutout of a black man with a bone through his nose on the lawn outside their fraternity house. A black student at Vassar College hurled anti-Semitic insults such as "dirty Jew," "stupid Jews," and "fucking Jew" at a Jewish student. University of Delaware campus sidewalks were defaced with anti-gay slogans such as "Step Here, Kill a Queer" and "Stay in the Closet Fag." Students driving by a black student walking home from a campus bar yelled "Niggers, go home" and "Niggers, we ought to lynch you."

Hate or bias incidents—those motivated by an animus against the victim's race, religion, sexual orientation, ethnicity or national origin—can have a unique emotional and psychological impact on the victim and the university community. These incidents can [according to the Anti-Defamation League of B'nai B'rith] "exacerbate racial . . . tensions, and lead to reprisals by others in the community, thereby . . . escalating violence and turmoil." The problem worsens when particularly isolated and vulnerable individuals lose faith in the institution's willingness or ability to ameliorate the situation.

Regulating Harassment

Administrators at numerous universities and colleges are searching for appropriate constitutional methods for regulating harassment on campus. Drafting regulations that comport with the Constitution, however, is a difficult task. Many institutions have adopted varying anti-harassment conduct codes. Some conduct codes impose an outright ban on offensive expression in certain contexts. For example, the University of Connecticut expels students from classes if students use disparaging names, inappropriately directed laughter, insensitive jokes, or conspicuously exclude another student from conversation. The University of Pennsylvania penalizes students for "any behavior, verbal or physical, that stigmatizes or victimizes individuals" and "creates an intimidating or offensive environment." At Tufts University, students are penalized for using slurs in classrooms or residence halls, but students may use the same insults in student newspaper articles, on the campus radio station, or in a public lecture.

Other universities attempt to mediate when a group on campus finds certain speech or actions offensive. In these instances, the conduct codes focus on restricting the place and manner of expression, rather than on restricting the right of expression per se. For example, a Confederate flag flying outside a white fraternity house disturbed black students at Clemson University. The fraternities met with school administrators and reached a compromise: the flag would be hung inside the house.

The Supreme Court is cautious when resolving freedom of expression cases arising in an academic community context. The Court's deliberations involve two competing interests. First, students, faculty, and administrators have a mutual interest in having an environment free from disruption of the educational process. In addition, the academic community has an innate interest in the greatest liberty for "free expression and debate consonant with the maintenance of order" [*Healy* v. *James*]. . . .

A Proposed Solution

How does a university balance first amendment rights with academic interests to promulgate a policy adequately encompassing these interests? Courts have already addressed similar questions in another area of law—workplace hostile environment harassment. Workplace hostile environments pit the victim's right to freedom from harassing expression against an alleged harasser's free speech right. To deal with this situation, the Supreme Court has sanctioned a type of time, place, and manner restriction. Universities may adapt the same analysis from hostile environment cases to control egregious harassment on campus.

Protecting the Community

Criminalizing racist speech has the advantage of shifting the focus from the relations between a particular victim and perpetrator to the question of the wilful violation of basic norms from which the community derives not only stability but also its legitimacy as a community respectful of the elemental dignity of its constituent members. The use of racist epithets, in particular, is ordinarily a knowing, wilful breach of minimal community solidarity, and it is appropriate that the judicial response take the form of an authoritative expression of repudiation in the name of the community itself.

R. George Wright, *Mississippi College Law Review*, Fall 1988.

Title VII of the Civil Rights Act of 1964, and Title IX of the Educational Amendments of 1972, are federal statutes designed to attack or prevent discrimination. Courts interpret both Title VII and Title IX to preclude harassment as a form of discrimination. Title VII prohibits workplace discrimination based on race, sex, religion, or national origin. Title IX prohibits discrimination in educational institutions on the basis of sex. To determine whether an action violates Title VII or Title IX, courts may look for a hostile environment. Courts find hostile environments when a person is subjected to demeaning and offensive slurs, epithets, suggestions, or similar statements or acts that alter the conditions of the work environment. The legal analyses used in Title VII and Title IX hostile environment harassment cases provide guidance for constructing constitutional campus harassment policies.

Title VII

The courts first applied hostile environment analysis to harassment allegations in race, religion, and national origin cases. For example, in *Rogers v. EEOC*, an Hispanic employee brought a Title VII suit against her former employer, an optical company that had segregated patients by national origin. The Fifth Circuit concluded that Title VII protected the employee's psychological, as well as economic, fringe benefits. Similarly, a federal district court held that Title VII may be applied to protect an employee who is subject to religious intimidation in the workplace in *Weiss v. United States.*

The Supreme Court more clearly outlined the factors that must be proven to establish a hostile environment in a workplace sexual harassment case in *Meritor Savings Bank v. Vinson*. The *Meritor* Court specified that Title VII applies to a hostile or offensive work environment, and it is not limited to "economic" or "tangible" discrimination. Title VII grants employees the right to work in an environment free from discrimination, intimidation, derision, and insult. Sexual misconduct creates prohibited sexual harassment when such conduct unreasonably hinders an individual's work performance or creates an intimidating, hostile, or offensive working environment.

The Supreme Court found that not all "harassment" affects a term, condition, or privilege of employment within the meaning of Title VII. Harassment is not actionable under hostile environment analysis unless its severity or pervasiveness alters the conditions of the victim's employment and creates an abusive working environment. The atmosphere must be so degrading or tainted with harassment that the psychological well-being of a reasonable employee would be affected adversely.

Title IX was intended to prohibit institutions of higher learning from discriminating on the basis of gender. Only a few plaintiffs, however, have presented claims of sexual harassment under Title IX making hostile environment analysis under Title IX unclear. It is uncertain whether Title IX requires a showing of tangible harm to establish a valid claim of sexual harassment, or whether the creation of a hostile environment is sufficient. . . .

Hostile environment analysis under Title VII and Title IX demonstrates that speakers are free to utter words and phrases of their choice, no matter how abhorrent to listeners, until those utterances go beyond mere verbalization and create a hostile environment. Universities should borrow this hostile environment concept to draft constitutional campus conduct codes.

The Campus Environment

Critics may argue that the workplace is not analogous to the academic environment. They may argue that the workplace is more routinized, and that it is more difficult to avoid harassment in the workplace because of its limited physical area. On a university campus, however, there are greater opportunities to avoid harassment. More importantly, critics may argue that first amendment concerns are greater in the academic community than in the workplace because the workplace is concerned mostly with productivity, while the academic environment is concerned with the robust debate of ideas.

Intransigent Racism

The ideal is that everybody should have a chance to speak and everybody should be listened to. But racism . . . has proved intransigent and we live in a real world, not an idealized marketplace of ideas.

Mary Ellen Gale, *Human Events*, October 13, 1990.

Such criticisms are not necessarily valid. The physical layout of campuses and academic facilities often provide only one path, one lab, or one library, necessarily limiting the areas that students traverse and frequent. Students are assigned to particular classrooms and dorm rooms, and are limited to specific libraries and buildings by the nature of their research, effectively eliminating choice of locale. In this fashion, a student's day on campus may be more routinized than a day in the workplace. Further, unlike a workplace, students often live on or near campus, thus making the environment even harder to escape.

Because first amendment concerns may be greater on a university campus due to the institutional interest in promoting vigorous debate, the hostile environment concept employed in this [viewpoint] is designed to protect that interest. By limiting only sufficiently egregious or pervasive harassment speech, the hostile environment concept distinguishes the expression of ideas—no matter how abhorrent to the listener—from harassment. Hostile environment jurisprudence protects workplace productivity by maximizing workers' freedom of expression. It creates a productive work atmosphere by balancing workers' freedom of expression against the violation of other workers' work environments. The hostile environment concept similarly would ensure an academic environment conducive to learning. Applying hostile environment analysis in a university context would balance all students' rights to debate and to express ideas against all students' rights to be free from hostile learning environments.

One commentator suggests that recognition of environmental harassment claims in the academic setting is even more important than in the workplace. If a university cannot regulate harassment on campus, it may not be able to fulfill its mission—the creation and fostering of an environment conducive to intellectual growth. An abusive environment may inhibit harassed students from fully developing their intellectual potential and from receiving the complete benefit of the academic program. Any pollution of that academic environment because of racial or sexual harassment is a reduction in the educational benefit that the student receives.

Even if Title VII and Title IX hostile environment harassment and campus harassment are not completely analogous, the Supreme Court has held that universities may still issue campus conduct codes imposing reasonable time, place, and manner restrictions on expression when that expression interferes with a substantial academic interest. Combining time, place, and manner restrictions with hostile environment analysis permits universities to determine the proper balance between a university's duty to promote the free exchange of ideas and the university's goal of providing all students with a nondiscriminatory learning environment. . . .

Conclusion

A university may proscribe harassment speech through a campus policy that restricts the manner in which expression is made but does not attempt to regulate the advocacy of a particular idea. Universities have the obligation to promulgate campus conduct policies that protect the educational environment. To withstand constitutional challenge, the policies must not prohibit the communication of a constitutionally protected idea. This viewpoint suggests affording university students the same protection from all forms of discriminatory harassment that employees receive. Title VII and Title IX provide a framework universities use to satisfy first amendment concerns.

By carefully balancing the first amendment's principle of freedom of expression, especially in the academic context, against the importance of providing a non-discriminatory academic environment, universities may draft constitutional regulations that will restrict harassment expressions without resorting to censorship. . . . Such policies are needed to promote understanding and educate people about hatred, facilitate the exchange of ideas, and to provide equal access to education.

"The underlying problem is racism, not racist speech."

Rules Restricting Racist Speech Will Not Stop Racism

Ira Glasser

Ira Glasser is executive director of the American Civil Liberties Union (ACLU), a national organization that works to defend the constitutional rights of Americans, including the freedom of speech. In the following viewpoint, he argues against rules forbidding racial insults and epithets, arguing that such rules violate the First Amendment of the U.S. Constitution and do nothing to solve the problem of racism. Glasser argues that colleges and universities should take other steps, such as revising their curriculum, to stop racism on their campuses.

As you read, consider the following questions:

1. Why do minorities have a special interest in the First Amendment, according to Glasser?
2. Why does the author assert that there is no clash between freedom of speech and racial equality?
3. What belief does Glasser affirm at the end of the viewpoint?

Ira Glasser, "Fighting Bigotry, Preserving Freedom." Reprinted, with permission, from the Fall 1990 *Civil Liberties*, the membership newsletter of the ACLU.

I grew up at a time when people believed in the power of integration to solve the problem of racial prejudice. During those years, it seemed that if the legal structures supporting racism in this country were dismantled, the playing field would become level, and in our lifetimes we would see racial bias wither, if not entirely disappear. Integration in all areas, but especially in education, was the great hope. Integrated education, we believed, would cause all those attitudes the young had inherited from a culture of racism to fade away.

Do I still believe? I'll come back to that question.

Racist Incidents

The epidemic of racist incidents that has raged in recent years on college campuses has severely tested my faith. Twenty-five years after the civil rights movement culminated in the passage of landmark legislation prohibiting racial discrimination in voting, housing, employment and public accommodations, the Supreme Court has eroded some of that legislation, President George Bush has vetoed a Congressional effort to restore it, and too many young people feel it's legitimate to be openly racist.

How alarming, puzzling and frustrating it is for those of my generation to observe that even though all the laws we wanted were passed, we confront a racial climate in 1990 that seems in some ways worse instead of better. It is as if racism was a layered structure from which only the hard outer shell has been removed: Gone are the Bull Connors with their cattle prods, the George Wallaces standing in the schoolhouse door, the Selma sheriffs, the folks who killed people for trying to vote. Gone are some of the patterns of employment discrimination. Yet, increasingly, Americans are living in two separate societies, and separation among the young is especially hard to swallow.

The incidents that trigger campus racial flare-ups vary. It could be one student hurling a racial epithet at another or a fraternity holding a mock slave auction; a speech somebody makes or the choice of a guest speaker; an article written, or a statement made, by a professor; disagreements about curricula or about affirmative action. Whatever the catalyst, it provokes the sometimes brutal expression of racial animus. Of course, the racial animus was always there. But the problem has moved to a new level now that white kids seem, suddenly, to feel *comfortable* yelling nigger or harassing people on the basis of race.

Many universities have responded to this development in a distressing way. The solution to the problem, they've decided, is to pass rules outlawing racist speech. Those of us who believe that freedom of speech and academic freedom are just as important as equal opportunity and racial justice, and who believe that universities must protect free speech *and* promote equal opportunity, have naturally opposed the speech restrictions. So in Michigan, New York, California, Connecticut and Wisconsin, the ACLU [American Civil Liberties Union] vigorously opposed college regulations that restricted free speech.

A Trap

Campus bans on racist speech should also be opposed because, strategically, they are a trap for minority students. Although such bans are intended to protect minorities against racial slurs, that is not the only way they can be used. The decision as to how and against whom to enforce speech restrictions rests, not with the minorities themselves, but with authorities who have far more power than minorities have. Minorities do not have an interest in ceding enforcement decisions to any of those authorities. If a rule is passed that allows the banning of offensive speech, then inevitably minority speakers will be frequent targets of that rule. In the 1960s, Malcolm X would have been a target. In short, such rules are like poison gas: It can be blown back in your face with powerful fans by your enemies in high places. Hurtful as racist name-calling is, minorities never have an interest in supporting bans on speech.

To the contrary, the First Amendment is often an important strategic weapon for minorities, who, having serious grievances and lacking the power possessed by the government and other authorities, require free speech more than anybody else as a means of spotlighting their grievances. The people who were on the front lines with Martin Luther King, Jr. in the early '60s instruct us that the First Amendment was the best friend civil rights activists had. Why? Because every time they marched, picketed, demonstrated and protested to dramatize to the nation what was going on down South, the sheriffs would arrest them under ordinances (every Southern town had one) that prohibited activities the white majority found offensive or emotionally distressing. And what offended and distressed the white Southern majority was black and white people—particularly black men and white women—marching hand in hand. When King and his colleagues landed in jail, as they frequently did, it was the First Amendment that got them out.

Of course, colleges are not precluded from punishing harassment or intimidation, which is criminal conduct in many instances. And words used to accompany such conduct do not immunize it against sanction. For example, a threatening phone call made to a black woman in her dorm room in the middle of the night is not protected by the First Amendment. But if all we're talking about is unpleasant public expression that insults whole classes of people, such speech has to be protected. First Amendment principles either protect everyone or we are all vulnerable to the discretion of public authorities.

269

When universities react to campus racism by simply curbing speech, they're often tap dancing to divert attention away from the underlying problem. *The underlying problem is racism, not racist speech.* That is why the ACLU has not only opposed speech restrictions but has also criticized the failure of many universities to deal with student bigotry seriously.

Universities must address the problem of racism in a variety of ways: through more vigorous recruitment of minority faculty and students; by changing Eurocentric curricula that marginalize and/or ignore the contributions of minorities to American culture; and by investigating why it is that minority students feel isolated and unwelcome on most supposedly "integrated" campuses.

Driving Racism Underground

Racism is a problem which must be addressed with more than misguided measures like limiting offensive speech. Not only are such measures open to abuse, they also drive racism underground where it thrives.

Jonathan D. Karl, *The Christian Science Monitor*, August 23, 1990.

Here's one example of how minorities can be made to feel marginalized. At one state university, where minorities comprise 20 percent of the student body, the reality of campus life is one of almost total segregation. Whites and minorities rarely mingle. Few whites and minorities are friends. They eat separately. They party separately. Segregation today has become something deeper than denying people access to an education based on skin color: It is now a matter of language and music and style.

Biased Education

There was a music course at that university called "Beethoven For Non-Music Majors." The course was offered because Beethoven is an icon of Western culture and, presumably, every educated person, even if he or she doesn't aspire to become a professional musician, needs to know something about Beethoven. Yet at this same "integrated" university, there was no course called "Duke Ellington For Non-Music Majors"—which said to the black kids that European music is important, but indigenous American music, created by an American of African descent, is not. That sort of "integration" feels to many black students as if they are being subordinated and marginalized. It tells them that all "integration" means is that you blacks should learn about "us" and what we've generated, but we whites don't need to learn about you and what you've generated because you blacks aren't important.

Most of the black students didn't take the Beethoven course as a kind of protest and were perceived by many white students and some faculty as anti-intellectual. Some whites said they expected blacks not to take the course because most of them "were probably here because of affirmative action anyway."

Such broadly held attitudes only get spoken out loud every now and then, in a moment of tension, or when somebody loses his temper or drinks too much. And when something gets said, the university is embarrassed, so their goal is to get past the incident as quickly as possible. So they outlaw the expression. The universities never seem to ask, what is the underlying problem that produced the expression?

Limited Background

Most white students come to college campuses today from highly segregated communities, where they attended de facto segregated schools. They've had no substantial multiracial contacts, and they've grown up hearing our major political leaders state that the civil rights movement has achieved all of its goals, equality is here, and affirmative action is reverse discrimination. If blacks can't make it, it's no longer due to racism; it's due to their own inadequacy—that's the message many white kids cut their teeth on in this country. Then we throw them together with minorities in college dorms and call it "integration." And we're surprised when seemingly mundane conflicts erupt into racial confrontations.

Example: There's a black and white party going on in the dorm on Saturday night. The white kids are playing Elvis and the black kids are playing Public Enemy—one of whose songs trashes Elvis. The music is so loud on both sides that it's intrusive. So they keep turning it up until everybody's irritated. Then they have an argument and, in the course of which somebody spews out a racial epithet. And then the university pretends that the epithet is the problem, as if you could make the children play nicely, and make the problem go away, just by suppressing that epithet.

The truth is that many universities aren't anxious to do the hard work of revamping their educational programs to correct the marginalization of minority cultural achievements, or to teach 18-year-olds how to live together in a multiracial society. They would rather take the low road of restricting racist speech because the minority students were up in arms and "we had to make a gesture." That gesture is meaningless, destructive and counterproductive.

There is no clash between the constitutional right of free speech and racial equality. Both are crucial to society. Moreover, the persistent problem of racial prejudice and bigotry cannot be swept under a rug of rules that violate freedom of speech and academic freedom, which are the lifeblood of universities.

The Heart of the Matter

Universities should go to the heart of the matter: Let them consider, for example, having a required course on the history of racism in this society. Let them embrace as part of their role the task of educating people about the meaning of life in a pluralistic democracy. What about counseling programs on race relations for new students? We have orientation programs for students on nearly everything—on sexism and date rape, on what to do if you're homesick, on how to acquire good study habits, on word-processing, on speed-reading. Where are the programs to teach people how to respect differences, how to appreciate each other's contributions?

Universities (and the rest of us, too) ought to think about what integration means beyond the numbers. They should stop restricting speech and start *teaching*. *Brown v. Board of Education* gave us integration in form. Now it's time for the substance.

By the way . . . I still believe.

a critical thinking activity

Distinguishing Between Fact and Opinion

This activity is designed to help develop the basic reading and thinking skill of distinguishing between fact and opinion. Consider the following statement: "More than two hundred colleges have enacted rules that ban racist speech and insults." This is a fact which can be checked by looking up reports in the *Chronicle of Higher Education* and other news sources. But the statement "Rules against racist speech are an effective way to reduce racial tension in our nation's colleges" is an opinion. Many people would argue that such rules only treat a symptom of racism and leave more fundamental problems unaddressed.

When investigating controversial issues it is important that one be able to distinguish between statements of fact and statements of opinion. It is also important to recognize that not all statements of fact are true. They may appear to be true, but some are based on inaccurate or false information. For this activity, however, we are concerned with understanding the difference between those statements which appear to be factual and those which appear to be based primarily on opinion.

Most of the following statements are taken from the viewpoints in this chapter. Consider each statement carefully. *Mark O for any statement you believe is an opinion or interpretation of facts. Mark F for any statement you believe is a fact. Mark I for any statement you believe is impossible to judge.*

If you are doing this activity as a member of a class or group, compare your answers with those of other class or group members. Be able to defend your answers. You may discover that others come to different conclusions than you do. Listening to the reasons others present for their answers may give you valuable insights into distinguishing between fact and opinion.

> O = *opinion*
> F = *fact*
> I = *impossible to judge*

273

1. A National Opinion Research Center report showed that a majority of whites believed blacks to be lazy and less intelligent than whites.
2. Racism remains a cancer on American society that must be purged.
3. The government should not be in the business of dictating beliefs and attitudes. Eliminating racism is the job of individuals.
4. The attitudes of white people are the cause of America's race problem.
5. The unemployment rate for blacks is about twice as high as the rate for whites.
6. Most people tend to say nothing or respond with anger to bigoted comments.
7. Blacks commit a disproportionate share of violent crime.
8. The majority of residents in ghetto neighborhoods are law-abiding citizens.
9. Employing a few minorities in high corporate executive positions will not solve America's race problem.
10. Whites cannot perceive their racism because it is ingrained in their normal habits and customs.
11. Charles King charges $275 a day per person for his race-awareness seminars.
12. Racism should be dealt with in conjunction with the problems of sexism and homophobia.
13. Many blacks still live in segregated neighborhoods.
14. The key to combating racism is to respond to it with dignity, but not hatred.
15. The Ku Klux Klan and the White Aryan Resistance are examples of white-racist hate groups.
16. The number of reported racial incidents on America's college campuses has increased in recent years.
17. The U.S. passed significant civil rights legislation in 1964.
18. Passing rules against racist speech does not violate the Constitution if it is done correctly.
19. Criminalizing racist speech only drives racism underground, where it thrives.
20. Many white students entering college have grown up with minimal multiracial contacts.
21. At many state universities, white and minority students rarely associate with each other in the dormitories and cafeterias.

Periodical Bibliography

The following articles have been selected to supplement the diverse views presented in this chapter.

David Bernstein — "Racial Tensions: The Market Is the Solution," *The Freeman*, July 1989. Available from The Foundation for Economic Education, Irvington-on-Hudson, NY 10533.

Bob Blauner — "Black-White Relations: From Bensonhurst to Ballot Box," *Tikkun*, January/February 1990.

Walter Block — "Racism, Public and Private," *The Freeman*, January 1989.

Rosemary L. Bray — "A Dialogue on Race," *Glamour*, August 1990.

Ossie Davis — "Challenge for the Year 2000," *The Nation*, July 24-31, 1989.

Robert R. Detlefsen — "White Like Me," *The New Republic*, April 10, 1989.

Joseph A. Fiorenza — "Racism, Fear and Reconciliation," *America*, May 13, 1989.

Vanessa Gallman — "How to Hurt the Klan: Ignore It," *New Dimensions*, December 1990.

Barbara Grizzuti Harrison — "Can TV Switch Off Bigotry?" *Mademoiselle*, November 1990.

Nicholas Lemann — "Healing the Ghettos," *The Atlantic*, March 1991.

Nicolaus Mills — "Doing the Right Thing(s)," *Commonweal*, September 22, 1989.

Yashica Olden — "When We Think of Racism," *Christian Social Action*, May 1989. Available from 100 Maryland Ave. NE, Washington, DC 20002.

David Rieff — "The Case Against Sensitivity," *Esquire*, November 1990.

Jim Sleeper — "In the Mix," *The New Republic*, February 18, 1991.

Shelby Steele — "I'm Black, You're White, Who's Innocent?" *Harper's Magazine*, June 1988.

Charles J. Sykes and Brad Miner — "Sense and Sensitivity," *National Review*, March 18, 1991.

Organizations to Contact

The editors have compiled the following list of organizations that are concerned with the issues debated in this book. All of them have publications or information available for interested readers. The descriptions are derived from materials provided by the organizations. This list was compiled upon the date of publication. Names and phone numbers of organizations are subject to change.

American-Arab Anti-Discrimination Committee (ADC)
4201 Connecticut Ave. NW, Suite 500
Washington, DC 20008
(202) 244-2990

The ADC is an advocacy organization working to protect the rights of people of Arab descent and to promote their ethnic heritage. It combats discrimination against Arab-Americans and protests defamation of Arab-Americans in the U.S. media. The committee publishes the magazines *ADC Times* and *ADC Issues*.

American Civil Liberties Union (ACLU)
132 W. 43rd St.
New York, NY 10036
(212) 944-9800

The ACLU champions the human rights set forth in the U.S. Declaration of Independence and the Constitution. It works for minority rights and publishes a variety of newsletters, including *Civil Liberties Report* and research papers, including *Racial Justice*.

American Enterprise Institute (AEI)
1150 17th St. NW
Washington, DC 20036
(202) 862-5800

AEI is a conservative think tank that analyzes national and international economic, political, and social issues. It has published articles on U.S. race relations in its bimonthly journal *American Enterprise*.

Anti-Defamation League of the B'nai B'rith (ADL)
823 United Nations Plaza
New York, NY 10017
(212) 490-2525

The ADL works to stop the defamation of Jewish people and to ensure fair treatment for all citizens. Its education project, A World of Difference, publishes books and teaching materials designed to help Americans understand and counteract racism and prejudice.

Asian American Legal Defense and Education Fund (AALDEF)
99 Hudson St.
New York, NY 10013
(212) 966-5932

AALDEF includes attorneys, legal workers, and community members who employ legal and educational methods to help Asian-Americans. The organization monitors and reports incidents of racial discrimination against Asian-Americans. It publishes the newsletter *Outlook* and pamphlets in Chinese, Japanese, Korean, and English.

The Brookings Institution
1775 Massachusetts Ave. NW
Washington, DC 20036
(202) 797-6000

The institution, founded in 1927, is a think tank that conducts research and education on economics and government issues. It has published research on racism and civil rights in its quarterly *Brookings Review* and various books and reports.

Center for Democratic Renewal (CDR)
PO Box 50469
Atlanta, GA 30302-0469
(404) 221-6614

The center works to build public opposition to racist groups and their activities and assist victims of bigoted violence. It researches activity by the Ku Klux Klan and other racist organizations and provides training and assistance in developing nonviolent resistance to such groups. CDR publishes a newsletter, *The Monitor*, as well as monographs, reports, and resource manuals. Titles of its available publications include *When Hate Groups Come to Town* and *Ballot Box Bigotry*.

Congress of Racial Equality (CORE)
1457 Flatbush Ave.
Brooklyn, NY 11210
(718) 434-3580

The Congress of Racial Equality works to promote civil liberties and social justice. CORE is a human rights organization that seeks to establish true equality and self-determination for all people regardless of race, creed, or ethnic background. The organization publishes *CORE Magazine* yearly and pamphlets.

Council for a Black Economic Agenda (CBEA)
1367 Connecticut Ave. NW
Washington, DC 20036
(202) 331-1103

CBEA attempts to advance the economic self-sufficiency of black Americans. It works to reverse the dependence of many blacks on government programs and advocates strategies based on a spirit of free enterprise and individual initiative. Publications include *On the Road to Economic Freedom* and *Entrepreneur Enclaves*.

The Heritage Foundation
214 Massachusetts Ave. NE
Washington, DC 20002
(202) 546-4400

The foundation is a conservative public policy research organization that opposes affirmative action and government regulation. It publishes papers on these and other social issues both separately and in the quarterly journal *Policy Review*. It has also published the book *A Conservative Agenda for Black Americans*.

Hispanic Policy Development Project (HPDP)
1001 Connecticut Ave. NW, Suite 310
Washington, DC 20036
(202) 822-8414

HPDP is a think tank focusing on public and private policy issues, such as education and employment, that affect Hispanics in the United States. It publishes *The Hispanic Almanac* as well as reports, monographs, and books.

Indian Law Resource Center
601 E St. SE
Washington, DC 20003
(202) 547-2800

The center is a legal, educational, and research service for American Indians. It seeks to combat discrimination in the law and U.S. public policy. The organization works within U.S. courts and the United Nations to advocate Native American rights. It publishes a handbook *Indian Rights-Human Rights,* articles, and reports.

The Lincoln Institute for Research and Education
2027 Massachusetts Ave. NE
Washington, DC 20036
(202) 223-5110

The Lincoln Institute is an organization that studies public policy issues that affect the lives of black Americans. It maintains that a free-market economy and minimal government interference will improve the lives of blacks most effectively. The institute sponsors conferences and publishes the *Lincoln Review.*

National Association for the Advancement of Colored People (NAACP)
4805 Mt. Hope Drive
Baltimore, MD 21215
(301) 358-8900

NAACP's purpose is to achieve equal rights for all and to end racial prejudice by removing discrimination in housing, employment, voting, schools, and the courts. The association publishes a variety of newsletters, books, and pamphlets, and the monthly magazine *Crisis.*

National Association for the Advancement of White People (NAAWP)
Box 10655
New Orleans, LA 70181
(504) 831-6986

The NAAWP strives to promote equal rights for all, including white people, and special favor for none. The association aims to end affirmative action programs, busing and forced integration, and anti-white racism. It works to limit immigration, reform welfare programs, and preserve the heritage of whites. It frequently publishes the newsletters *NAAWP News* and *NAAWP Program.*

National Association of Scholars (NAS)
20 Nassau St., Suite 250E
Princeton, NJ 08542
(609) 683-7878

NAS is an organization of college professors, administrators, and students who believe that college academic standards have been compromised by too much emphasis on racism and other political issues. They work to protect the expression of diverse opinion on campus and oppose affirmative action programs for admitting students and hiring faculty. The association publishes the quarterly *Academic Questions.*

National Coalition Building Institute (NCBI)
172 Brattle St.
Arlington, MA 02714
(617) 646-5802

NCBI runs training programs to reduce prejudice in schools and workplaces. It works to train leaders in communication and conflict resolution skills. The institute publishes the newsletter *Working It Out* and several manuals, including *The Art of Coalition Building* and *Face to Face: Black-Jewish Campus Dialogues.*

National Coalition to End Racism in America's Child Care System
22075 Koths
Taylor, MI 48180
(313) 295-0257

The coalition works to ensure that children requiring foster care or adoption should not be denied services on the basis of race, and supports transracial adoptions as a viable alternative for some children. It publishes the quarterly newsletter *The Children's Voice* and information on state laws concerning transracial adoption.

National Institute Against Prejudice and Violence (NIAPV)
31 S. Greene St.
Baltimore, MD 21201
(301) 328-5170

The institute is a national research center that focuses on the study of and response to violence and intimidation motivated by prejudice. It conducts research, provides information on model programs and legislation, and provides education and training to combat prejudicial violence. NIAPV publishes *Forum,* a monthly newsletter, and also publishes research reports and bibliographies.

National Urban League (NUL)
1111 14th St. NW, 6th Floor
Washington, DC 20005
(202) 898-1604

The league is a community service agency composed of civic, business, and religious leaders who aim to eliminate institutional racism in the United States and to provide services for minorities in employment, housing, welfare, and other areas. Its research department puts out a wide selection of reports and papers on topics such as racial violence and the economics of discrimination. It also publishes *The State of Black America,* an annual report.

Sojourners Resource Center
Box 29272
Washington, DC 20017
(202) 636-3637

Sojourners is a religious community based in Washington, D.C. It publishes the monthly magazine *Sojourners* as well as article reprints and books. Among the publications available from its resource center is *A Study Guide on White Racism.*

United States Commission on Civil Rights
1121 Vermont Ave. NW
Washington, DC 20425
(202) 376-8177

The commission is a fact-finding body that makes recommendations directly to Congress and the President of the United States. It evaluates federal laws and the effectiveness of equal opportunity programs. It also serves as a national clearinghouse for civil rights information. A catalog of its publications is available from the Publications Management Division at the above address.

Bibliography of Books

Richard D. Alba — *Ethnic Identity: The Transformation of White America.* New Haven, CT: Yale University Press, 1990.

Richard F. America, ed. — *The Wealth of Races.* Westport, CT: Greenwood Press, 1990.

Alan B. Anderson and George W. Pickering — *Confronting the Color Line.* Athens, GA: University of Georgia Press, 1986.

Molefi K. Asante — *Afrocentricity.* Trenton, NJ: Africa World Press, 1988.

Derrick Bell — *And We Are Not Saved: The Elusive Quest for Racial Justice.* New York: Basic Books, 1987.

Fletcher A. Blanchard and Faye J. Crosby, eds. — *Affirmative Action in Perspective.* New York: Springer-Verlag, 1989.

Bob Blauner — *Black Lives, White Lives.* Berkeley: University of California Press, 1989.

Clint Bolick — *Unfinished Business: A Civil Rights Strategy for America's Third Century.* San Francisco: Pacific Research Institute, 1990.

Thomas D. Boston — *Race, Class, and Conservatism.* Winchester, MA: Unwin Hyman, 1988.

Norman E. Bowie, ed. — *Equal Opportunity,* Boulder, CO: Westview Press, 1988.

Roy L. Brooks — *Rethinking the American Race Problem.* Berkeley: University of California Press, 1990.

Robert Cherry — *Discrimination.* Lexington, MA: Lexington Books, 1989.

Ward Churchill and Jim Vander Wall — *Agents of Repression.* Boston: South End Press, 1988.

Laura Coltelli — *Winged Words: American Indian Writers Speak.* Lincoln, NE: University of Nebraska Press, 1990.

Stanley Crouch — *Notes of a Hanging Judge.* New York: Oxford University Press, 1990.

Harold W. Cruse — *Plural but Equal: Blacks and Minorities in America's Plural Society.* New York: William Morrow, 1987.

Dinesh D'Souza — *Illiberal Education: The Politics of Race and Sex on Campus.* New York: Free Press/Macmillan, 1991.

John E. Farley — *Majority-Minority Relations.* 2nd ed. Englewood Cliffs, NJ: Prentice Hall, 1988.

Kevin Flynn and Gary Gerhardt — *The Silent Brotherhood: Inside America's Racist Underground.* New York: The Free Press, 1989.

George M. Fredrickson — *The Arrogance of Race: Historical Perspectives on Slavery, Racism, and Social Inequality.* Middleton, CT: Wesleyan University Press, 1988.

Lawrence H. Fuchs — *The American Kaleidoscope: Race, Ethnicity, and Civic Culture.* Hanover, NH: University Press of New England, 1990.

Lenora Fulani — *The Psychopathology of Everyday Racism and Sexism.* New York: Harrington Park Press, 1988.

Jewelle Taylor Gibbs, ed.	*Young, Black, and Male in America*. Dover, MA: Auburn House Publishing Co., 1988.
David Theo Goldberg, ed.	*Anatomy of Racism*. Minneapolis: University of Minnesota Press, 1990.
David R. Goldfield	*Black, White, and Southern*. Baton Rouge: Louisiana State University Press, 1990.
Robert A. Goldwin and Art Kaufman, eds.	*Slavery and Its Consequences: The Constitution, Equality, and Race*. Washington, DC: American Enterprise Institute, 1988.
Juan Gomez-Quinonez	*Chicano Politics*. Albuquerque: University of New Mexico Press, 1990.
Kathanne W. Greene	*Affirmative Action and the Principles of Justice*. Westport, CT: Greenwood Press, 1989.
Fred R. Harris and Roger W. Wilkins	*Quiet Riots: Race and Poverty in the United States*. New York: Pantheon Books, 1988.
Ethelbert Haskins	*The Crisis in Afro-American Leadership*. Buffalo, NY: Prometheus Books, 1988.
Janet E. Helms, ed.	*Black and White Racial Identity: Theory, Research, and Practice*. Westport, CT: Greenwood Press, 1990.
Bell Hooks	*Yearning: Race, Gender, and Cultural Politics*. Boston: South End Press, 1990.
Jayjia Hsia	*Asian Americans in Higher Education and Work*. Hillsdale, NJ: Lawrence Erlbaum Associates, 1988.
Gerald David Jaynes and Robin M. Williams Jr., eds.	*A Common Destiny: Blacks and American Society*. Washington, DC: National Academy Press, 1989.
Phyllis A. Katz and Dalmus A. Taylor, eds.	*Eliminating Racism: Profiles in Controversy*. New York: Plenum Press, 1988.
Harry H.L. Kitano and Roger Daniels	*Asian Americans: Emerging Minorities*. Englewood Cliffs, NJ: Prentice Hall, 1988.
Bart Landry	*The New Black Middle Class*. Berkeley: University of California Press, 1987.
Julius Lester	*Falling Pieces of the Broken Sky*. New York: Arcade Publishing, 1990.
Bernard Lewis	*Semites and Anti-Semites*. New York: W.W. Norton & Co., 1986.
Kofi Lomotey, ed.	*Going to School: The African-American Experience*. Albany: State University of New York Press, 1990.
Clarence Lusane	*Pipe Dream Blues: Racism and the War on Drugs*. Boston: South End Press, 1991.
Frederick R. Lynch	*Invisible Victims*. Westport, CT: Greenwood Press, 1989.
Samuel Myers Jr. and Margaret C. Simms, eds.	*The Economics of Race and Crime*. New Brunswick, NJ: Transaction Books, 1988.
Marcus D. Pohlmann	*Black Politics in Conservative America*. New York: Longman, 1990.
Dan Quayle	*Human Rights and Racism*. Washington, DC: U.S. Department of State, Bureau of Public Affairs, 1989.

Benjamin B. Ringer and Elinor R. Lawless	*Race-Ethnicity and Society*. New York: Routledge, 1989.
Clara E. Rodriguez	*Puerto Ricans*. Boston: Unwin Hyman, 1989.
Paula S. Rothenberg	*Racism and Sexism: An Integrated Study*. New York: St. Martin's Press, 1988.
Gary D. Sandefur and Martin Tienda, eds.	*Divided Opportunities: Minorities, Poverty, and Social Policy*. New York: Plenum Press, 1988.
Steven Shulman and William Darity Jr., eds.	*The Question of Discrimination: Racial Inequality in the U.S. Labor Market*. Middleton, CT: Wesleyan University Press, 1989.
Catherine Silk and John Silk	*Racism and Anti-Racism in American Popular Culture*. New York: St. Martin's Press, 1990.
Christine E. Sleeter, ed.	*Empowerment Through Multicultural Education*. Albany: State University Press of New York, 1991.
Shelby Steele	*The Content of Our Character: A New Vision of Race in America*. New York: St. Martin's Press, 1990.
Ronald Takaki	*From Different Shores: Perspectives on Race and Ethnicity in America*. New York: Oxford University Press, 1987.
Bob Teague	*The Flip Side of Soul*. New York: William Morrow and Co., 1989.
Gail E. Thomas	*U.S. Race Relations in the 1980s and 1990s: Challenges and Alternatives*. New York: Hemisphere Publishing Corporation, 1990.
Demsey Travis	*Racism—American Style: Corporate Gift*. Chicago: Urban Research Press, 1991.
Melvin I. Urofsky	*A Conflict of Rights: The Supreme Court and Affirmative Action*. New York: Charles Scribner's Sons, 1990.
Valora Washington and William Harvey	*Affirmative Rhetoric, Negative Action*. Washington, DC: School of Education and Human Development, George Washington University, 1989.
Thomas Wehr	*Hispanic U.S.A.* New York: Harper & Row, 1988.
Meyer Weinberg	*Racism in the United States: A Comprehensive Classified Bibliography*. Westport, CT: Greenwood Press, 1990.
William Wilbanks	*The Myth of a Racist Criminal Justice System*. Monterey, CA: Brooks/Cole Publishing Company, 1987.
Patricia J. Williams	*The Alchemy of Race and Rights*. Cambridge, MA: Harvard University Press, 1991.
Walter Williams	*All It Takes Is Guts: A Minority View*. Washington, DC: Regnery Gateway, 1987.
William Julius Wilson	*The Truly Disadvantaged*. Chicago: University of Chicago Press, 1987.
Bruce Wright	*Black Robes, White Justice*. Secaucus, NJ: Lyle Stuart Inc., 1987.
Samuel Kennedy Yeboah	*The Ideology of Racism*. London, UK: Hansib Publishing Limited, 1988.

Index

287